Sovereign Justice

Sovereign Justice

Global Justice in a World of Nations

Edited by
Diogo P. Aurélio, Gabriele De Angelis
and Regina Queiroz

De Gruyter

ISBN 978-3-11-024573-8
e-ISBN 978-3-11-024574-5

Library of Congress Cataloging-in-Publication Data:

Sovereign justice : global justice in a world of nations / edited by Diogo P. Aurélio, Gabriele De Angelis, and Regina Queiroz.
p. cm.
Proceedings of a conference held in Nov. 2008 in Lisbon, Portugal.
Includes bibliographical references and index.
ISBN 978-3-11-024573-8 (hardcover : alk. paper)
1. Justice--Congresses. 2. Cosmopolitanism--Congresses. 3. Nation-state--Congresses. I. Aurélio, Diogo Pires. II. De Angelis, Gabriele. III. Queiroz, Regina.
JC578.S68 2011
320.01'1--dc22
2010041720

Bibliographic information published by the Deutsche Nationalbibliothek

The Deutsche Nationalbibliothek lists this publication in the Deutsche Nationalbibliografie; detailed bibliographic data are available in the Internet at http://dnb.d-nb.de.

Typesetting: Michael Peschke, Berlin

Printing: Hubert & Co. GmbH & Co. KG, Göttingen

∞ Printed on acid-free paper

Printed in Germany

www.degruyter.com

Contents

IV. Economic Justice

Introduction

This volume collects papers presented at the conference on *Global Justice and the Nation State*, held in Lisbon in November 2008 with the support of the Portuguese Foundation for Science and Technology. The conference was part of a larger research project, still in progress, which tries to consider the idea of global justice against the background of the recent rise of transnational terrorism. It aimed chiefly at pondering on the challenge that thinking about "justice beyond borders", as Simon Caney calls it, represents to the existing international order.

Bibliography about this matter has been increasing over the last 20 years. Until the end of the 1980s politicians, theorists and scholars thought of global justice as if it were an exclusively moral issue. For instance, *A Theory of Justice* (1971), the most famous work of John Rawls, does not discuss the question of a fair international distribution of the world's wealth, assuming instead that the principles of justice are developed just for a more or less closed space, in which social cooperation is feasible and can be implemented. Between states the author endorsed, at best, a respectful relationship, regardless of their regimes. So, when the Cold War ended and the countries living under the communist political influence became once again independent nations, Rawls' book, linking nationalism and justice, seemed to present a very suitable theory.

However, by that time, globalization was already increasing, not only because of the new technologies, which made possible a free and fast communication among the people of all countries, but also because of a deeper awareness of several global problems whose solution was impossible to achieve only at a national level. In a word, we were facing global challenges and owning new means to face them. So, the idea of a cosmopolitan government might seem, at least to some people, as feasible as the international trade of agricultural goods, technology and knowledge. Despite the rebirth of the old nationalist feelings in Eastern Europe after the end of proletarian internationalism, the cosmopolitan idea was reborn as well, both in Political Theory and in common political discourse. When the upsurge of nationalisms started sparking new conflicts – such as the wars in the Balkans after the disintegration of Yugoslavia – people looked at the United Nations, for the first time in their history, not only as an international forum with moral authority, but also as a kind of legal and political power, which should claim the right to rule the world and to punish the «rogue states», if necessary militarily. That was the time after the fall of the wall, when the European Union was growing quickly, and the world seemed to become just one single globalised space. No wonder so many articles and books have been published contending that the sovereign state, at least as we have known it over the last three centuries, had already become useless, even if we do not know yet which political form could fulfil the functions that the state has been fulfilling until now. How far is this really true? This is the axis around which some of the most interesting debates in contemporary Political Theory are being developed, as well as the main question dealt with in this book.

In fact, if we agree that some kind of universal or global realm will be possible, we have, from an either moral or political point of view, to face two kinds of problems. The first one, and certainly the hardest, is transferring sovereignty from national states to a so-called international community: does it mean the end of the state, both national and multinational, as some people claim, or simply a change in its functions, or to make it subject to some kind of super power which will provide the back-up for the enforcement of global justice?

The second kind of problems deals with the principles according to which that allegedly universal realm should be governed: are there any moral principles overcoming the local cultures supporting national values, rights and duties? Can we infer any universal political rules from those hypothetical moral principles? Besides, who could indeed decide about the goodness of each one of such principles: the states, if they will still exist, or the citizens? In short, are we thinking of a democratic order whose foundation would lie in the will of the individuals or in the will of political units like nations, federations, etc.?

In a way, we are dealing here with some well known issues in the classic debate about law and justice, moral and politics. Who does not remember Antigone, Sophocles's tragic heroine, transgressing the law of the city to obey the law of her conscience? Or, more recently, the controversy about natural and positive law? Whenever we try to define a positive juridical order, we are facing a lot of diverging opinions and interests. But there is an important difference. In the past, the necessity of state powers, both national and sovereign, was more or less evident, regardless of the regime they adopted. Nowadays, on the contrary, economic and social globalization suggests the idea, or the belief, that a global power and a global government are not only possible, but also more suitable than the existing political forms. According to this idea, a universal power would be the only way of fostering justice, even distributive justice, regardless of the interests at governments would like to preserve.

If we consider this problem conceptually, we have to recognize that national law should always be just a local expression of global justice. From this point of view, it would be unavoidable to recognize that national rulers must respect, or are submitted to, human rights, which means, in a radical way, that they are not totally sovereign. Any government or political body has the right to decide against the universal humanitarian principles, which are above their own will and even above the interest or the culture of the nation they are supposed to represent. And if some of them do not respect those principles, the international community should have the right either to prevent this or to punish them.

But the idea of global justice goes beyond that. Besides condemning governments and states that act against individual rights, it disapproves of all kinds of unfairness as well, and demands the end of extreme poverty still existing in many countries all over the world. Unfortunately, the recent global progress of democracy did not stop the deepening of the gap between rich and poor countries. On the contrary, it has been accompanied by increasing economic inequality. How should the wealthiest people act in order to eliminate these situations? Shall they simply send humanitarian aid, as Rawls defends in his book *The Law of People* (1999), or, much more than that, are they obliged to narrow the above-mentioned gap, until a reasonable and just order is created at a universal level?

Apparently, it should be clear: there is no justice without a fair distribution of the existing economic and social goods, either within each country or across countries; and there is no justice when the authorities of a state act, make decisions, or give orders that are against human rights. Nevertheless, if we move from the theoretical to the practical level, justice demands more than a diffuse feeling of sympathy for humanity, even if the latter seems to be universal. In order to become a practice, global justice requires a concrete and particular expression, a political order, i.e., a system of social and juridical institutions. Can that order become a universal one, translating global justice into a set of laws which every country and every individual would accept? Or is it impossible to go beyond the national level, where each people remains sovereign and applies its own idea of justice?

Political consequences of each one of these approaches are, needless to say, very different. While the first demands the existence of an International Criminal Court, for instance, as a necessary instrument of justice, the latter will refuse any institution which undermines the state's power to judge, inside its boundaries, according to its own law. And while an international order, considered as a political embodiment of global justice, would demand institutions guided by universal principles, a juridical order based on a national level demands institutions supporting, first of all, the interest and values of a particular community, even if its supporters claim it is the best and perhaps the only possible way of promoting global justice. It is true that the pivotal point can be the same on both approaches, namely the moral duty to attend to the interest of all human beings. Kok-Chor Tan underlines the essentials on this matter, when he claims that «nothing in [his] interpretation of cosmopolitanism necessitates the idea of a world state», because, so he argues, «a moral cosmopolitan can as well defend national self-determination if he believes that the ideal of equal and impartial concern for individuals is best realized by respecting their claims to national sovereignty». In short, «there is no necessary conflict between moral cosmopolitanism and the idea of national self-determination».[1] However another, inevitable, question arises if we defend the necessity to pay attention to the weakest states and people, wherever the latter live: how is such a necessity to be met? How should governments deal, for instance, with immigrants, who claim the right to stay and have a job, when the country does not have enough jobs for the native people? What are exactly the reasons, if there are any, for the latter to be considered first? In a more radical way, is the state a political form still useful and suitable enough to answer fairly to the challenges the human groups are facing nowadays? What are, in short, the most efficient rules to reach global justice?

There are no easy answers to these questions, either in Political Theory or in the current activity of rulers. Nevertheless, over the last years some new theoretical and practical approaches have been emerging and stressing how much even the most realistic policy depends on ethical considerations. Even if a government wanted to rule only attending to its national interests without caring about what other countries think and wish, it would fail. The economic, financial and technical globalization, as well as the climatic changes or the scarcity of several essential goods, like petrol and water, brought along problems that are impossible to solve without leaving the national level and looking for sustainable international agreements. Maybe this is not exactly the same as what cosmopolitanism calls global justice. But it demands pacts, which require at least some shared values. Were it impossible to reach a universal law, or any kind of global government, then the rational solution to the above mentioned problems would still require more and more partnerships, both sustainable and lasting, among countries, despite their diversity. Nobody can say how far, in the next decades, even the strongest and most powerful states will have to give up several features of their sovereignty. However, it is already clear

1 Tan, Kok-Chor (2004). *Justice without Borders, Cosmopolitanism, Nationalism and Patriotism.* Cambridge. Cambridge University Press. P. 94.

that they shall do so if they really want to preserve the life and the interest of their own citizens.

This volume deals with some of the most relevant of these questions, trying to put them within the theoretical frame in which they have been debated over the last 20 years. Kant and Rawls, as everybody knows, are the obligatory background in this debate, and they are present in this volume, even when they are not explicitly mentioned. The contributors to the conference, far from remaining at the historical level, cover the core questions of current debate and focus chiefly on the most contemporary and controversial issues. On behalf of the Institute of Philosophy of Language I would like to thank all of them for their engagement and their active participation.

Finally, I would like to thank Gabriele De Angelis and Regina Queiroz for their work and extreme care in the organization of the conference and in the co-editing of this volume.

Diogo Pires Aurélio

I. On Cosmopolitanism

Nationalism and Global Justice: A Survey of Some Challenges

Kok-Chor Tan

As first presenter in a volume on global justice and the nation-state, I see my role to be that of highlighting some of the main philosophical questions and challenges the ideal of the nation-state presents for global justice, and to identify how these challenges could be addressed. No doubt some of the questions I will discuss and the distinctions that I will make will be transcended by the more sophisticated and detailed analysis to come in this volume. But I hope that in attempting to offer a *tour de'horizon* of the nationalism versus global justice debate, we will have one way of framing the discussions and debates to follow.

The aspect of global justice I will focus on here is that of global distributive justice or global economic justice. By global distributive justice, I mean the commitment to regulate economic inequalities between persons in the world as a whole. I leave aside other aspects of global justice, such as those having to do with individual liberty and state sovereignty and intervention, and so on. And I assume that global justice at minimum requires some kind of duty to alleviate severe poverty. The issue of global distributive justice is whether justice also requires some kind of equality with respect to the distribution of economic goods, apart from the question of poverty alleviation. In what follows, I will use the terms global justice, global egalitarianism and like terms to capture this ideal. I will also use the term nation-state quite broadly and generally without presupposing any particular theory of nationalism (though I will assume that to be defensible a nation-state must be at least decent.)

I will discuss the challenges the nation-state poses for global justice by examining the different stages in the evolution of the contemporary debate on global justice. I identify three stages, each presenting its distinctive challenge for global egalitarians. To be sure, any classification of the development of an idea into stages can only be schematic – rather than neatly and tidily sequential, the different stages of course overlapped and cut across each other in the development of an idea or discourse. But still a representation of the debate in terms of three developmental stages will help us better appreciate the distinctiveness of the challenges the nation-state presents in each.

We might say that in the very first stage of the discourse, the nation-state presented a *methodological challenge* for global justice (we can call this methodological nationalism). The task was to extend arguments for global justice conceived originally for the confines of the nation-state to the global arena, and the particular challenge was to overcome the methodological assumptions found in the influential constructions of theories of domestic justice, assumptions such as the state being a closed system and relatively self-sufficient (e.g., Rawls, 1971, p. 8).

As I will note briefly later, early defenders of global justice argue that these assumptions ought to be lifted and that arguments for justice apply as effectively (with slight modification) to the global arena. This is where the second stage of the debate enters. We may roughly call this the *patriotic challenge*. Critics of global justice point out that even if an independent case could be made for global distributive obligations, such obligations would run counter to various patriotic commitments and concerns that ordinary individuals have. Given the moral significance of such local commitments and obligations, and given, as some nationalists argue, the primacy of nation commitments of justice, global distributive commitments in general ought to be limited if not overridden (Miller, 1995, 1999). The task of global egalitarians here is to show how the primacy of global justice is sustained in spite of patriotic concerns.

It is here where we enter the present and third stage of the debate. The form of the criticism now is that demands of global justice aren't even valid in the first place – there isn't any case for such commitments to begin with. The charge, essentially, is that the extension in the first stage was not valid – the extension project failed to see that arguments for distributive justice apply only under circumstances that obtain nationally but not globally. This argument holds that the scope of distributive justice is limited to the borders of nation-states, and the real challenge for global justice is not simply a methodological one that can be assumed away. Therefore, the argument is not that there are competing demands that global justice has to be prioritized against, but that there is simply no basis for global justice at all. We can call this the challenge of the limited *national scope of justice*.

In this brief overview, I will comment on each of these challenges in turn. I don't claim that I will fully respond to these challenges on the global egalitarian's behalf, especially not in the third and current stage where debate is still ongoing. But I hope to at least indicate what acceptable responses should look like.

I. The Methodological Challenge

The methodological challenge presented in the first stage of the debate is largely familiar and I will recap only some key points. When Rawls presented his *A Theory of Justice* (1971) – it was of course a theory of justice conceived for the state – he reasonably made some simplifying assumptions to get started: that the state is imagined to be a closed system of social cooperation and self-sufficient.[1] In reaction to Rawls, globalists like Charles Beitz ([1979] 1999) and later Thomas Pogge (1989) argue that if we lift Rawls's methodological assumptions, as we should if we were to change the subject from that of confined domestic justice to that of *global* justice, then we would effectively arrive at a "globalized" version of Rawls's theory of justice. That is, Rawls's two principles of justice, including his distributive principle, would simply take on global scope. The argument is that once we reject the assumption of the state as a self-sufficient and closed system of social cooperation, but recognize states to be in fact interacting and even engaging in forms of social cooperation with other states, the Rawlsian method of reasoning must necessarily take on a global scope. Thus Rawls's well-known original position, the initial situation in which representatives of persons decide on the first principles of justice, ought also to be globalized, and consequently factors such as persons' national membership are also to be seen as arbitrary from the moral point of view. Once nationality is considered an arbitrary factor and to be discounted in a global original position, representatives of persons behind the veil of ignorance would opt for some global distributive commitments, analogous to the commitments Rawls says that persons within a *single* state would agree on. These arguments have been adopted and developed more recently by cosmopolitans such as Simon Caney (2005) and Darrel Moellendorf (2001).

Rawls himself lifts the methodological assumptions when he extends his own theory of justice to the international realm nearly three decades later (1999). It is important to note, however, that he does this via a two-tier process, first working out the requirements of domestic justice with the original methodological assumptions in place, and then only after, at the second stage, lifting the assumptions for the purpose of determining just relations between states. Rawls's theory of international justice has been criticized by globalists on various points, one being that it lacks a

---

1 There were some remarks on international justice in A Theory of Justice (pp. 377-79), but these were reflections appended to Rawls's discussion on civil disobedience and conscientious objection. For recent introductions to Rawls, see Freeman (2007) and Pogge (2007).

distributive egalitarian commitment. Some critics take this failure to be symptomatic of Rawls's method. They argue that Rawls's two-step procedure for developing an account of justice, one that begins by taking the state for granted in the first stage, necessarily commits the fatal error from the very start of granting citizenship and borders fundamental moral significance when it is part of the role of global justice to evaluate the justness of these status and boundaries. Hence Rawls's two-tiered approach, with the methodological assumptions built into the first stage, distorts our understanding of what global justice should really demand (O'Neill, 2000; Nussbaum, 2006).

So the first task in the global justice debate was to show how and why some of the nationalist assumptions can and ought to be dropped, and how if we transcend these assumptions that we can more or less extend arguments for distributive justice to the global arena. There appeared to be a powerful consensus at the early stage of the debate that this extension of arguments of justice to the global arena was entirely legitimate and required. Philosophers largely sympathetic to Rawls's basic project such as Scanlon (1975) and Barry (1974) took the globalists' side in this early part of the global justice debate.

II. Patriotic Concern

The next wave of challenge facing the globalists consists not of criticisms directed at their extension project as such but of arguments that global distributive demands are in tension with more local and special commitments that persons ordinarily have. In particular, the most poignant of these partial commitments and obligations are demands associated with persons' respective national memberships. As a member of a nation-state, one has special concerns and commitments to fellow members that one need not have towards strangers, and global egalitarianism runs the risk of running roughshod over these national or patriotic commitments, the objection goes.

One might say that the challenge of patriotism here replicates an issue familiar in moral philosophy: how can morality conceived as impartial and universalistic accommodate and philosophically account for the range of partial and personal pursuits that are valuable for an ordinary individual life? This challenge is especially poignant for utilitarianism given that it takes the ultimate moral end to be that of maximizing utility for the greatest number. But Kantians too, given the idea of universalizability central to the Kantian moral doctrine, have to explain how morality can allow space for partial and personal pursuits.[2]

Thus philosophers like Samuel Scheffler who find aspects of global justice appealing urge a more modest or moderate understanding of cosmopolitanism in order to accommodate these partial commitments (2001). But the more extreme form of the challenge comes from nationalist theorists like David Miller and Margaret Moore go further to hold that national justice has priority over global or cosmopolitan justice (Miller 1995, 1999; Moore, 2001).

The nationalists argue that when there is conflict between different domains or spheres of justice, it is not so straightforward to say which domain should be supreme. Thus when the demands of global justice compete with the demands of national justice, one cannot assume that the default is to grant primacy to global demands. To the contrary, there are good special reasons, reasons having to do with the ideal of the nation-state, for giving preference to national demands (Miller, 1999).

Now it is important to note the form of the challenge here. The patriotic challenge does not directly deny that there are valid global distributive principles. That is, it does not take issue with the extension project of the first stage. What it puts forward is what we may call a limitation argument (Jones), in the sense that while there could be good reasons for global distributive principles, there are also good (if not more important) reasons for other kinds of principles that are in competition with the global principles. The challenge aims to show that at the very least global distributive commitments have to be limited if not overridden altogether by patriotic commitments.

Understanding the form of the challenge is important because it shows what would count as an appropriate response. Faced with this particular limitation argument, the globalist need not provide another independent argument for global egalitarianism – that such commitments are valid is not challenged. The challenge denies the priority of global justice over national justice, and what the globalist has to do in light of this challenge is to show that where there is a conflict between global and patriotic commitments of justice, global commitments have priority.

In reply, thus, globalists have argued that national commitments cannot be *justly* discharged unless obligations of global justice have been met. For example, within domestic society, special cooperative groups within a society that have their own local distributive principles will not know what their respective fair shares are with which to distribute among their mem-

---

2 See Scheffler 1988 and Herman for two discussions of this problem for utilitarianism and Kantian morality respectively.

bers without reference to what domestic distributive justice as a whole requires of them. In short, it seems that by default, the claims of justice regulating relations in the dominant sphere has priority over claims of justice with any sub-spheres. Members of the sub-sphere would not know otherwise whether they are acting justly or not (unless they assume away the existence and the justice-demands of members in the dominant sphere). The priority of justice in the dominant set simply stems from the basic idea that individual members of a sub-sphere cannot distributive among themselves resources or goods that are *not* rightly theirs; and they can't know what is rightly theirs unless they first acknowledge and discharge their obligations to other groups within the dominant set.

Some commentators argue that the analogy invoked above between individual pursuits versus domestic justice on the one side, and domestic justice versus global justice on the other is flawed. They say that while "justice features only on one side of the balance" in the domestic case, "it features on both sides" in the second case (Miller, 2000, p. 167). Thus while it is plausible that justice takes precedence over personal pursuits, it is less clear when two sets of claims of justice compete, as in the case of domestic versus global justice, which should dominate. In reply, the globalist points out that even in the domestic context, there exist competing claims of justice, between justice of the state (domestic justice) and justice within private associations and groups (local justice). Yet, we accept that domestic justice takes priority in the sense that how private associations regulate their internal justice in distribution cannot be at the expense of the requirements of domestic justice that bind them. So too, it is not implausible that demands of global justice take precedence over the demands of domestic justice even if both are claims of justice (Tan, 2004).

Now, the priority of global justice does not mean implausibly that no nations may look after its own until it has meet all global needs (Miller, 2000, p. 45). The priority claim I am defending presupposes Hume's external circumstance of justice, that is, the presumption of moderate scarcity as opposed to abject scarcity. That is, it assumes that we are not in typical text-book desert island scenarios where we are faced with the task of deciding between the very basic needs of compatriots versus that of strangers. If we are in such a dire situation, the circumstance of justice does not obtain, and consequently the priority of global justice thesis simply doesn't kick in. In such a case, it is plausible that nations are free to save the lives of their own over those of strangers if indeed such a trade-off needs to be made.

What the priority of justice means is that nation-states under conditions of moderate global scarcity may engage in a variety of nationalistic projects and commitments *but only* so long as they do their fair share with respect to the demands of global egalitarianism, and in context of the present world this does leave ample space for meaningful national pursuits.

So if there are indeed valid demands of global egalitarian justice, then these demands determine the range of permissible patriotic concerns and nationalistic pursuits, not the other way around. To say that global justice ought to be limited by demands and commitments of nation-states is somewhat analogous to saying that demands of justice for the domestic state ought to be limited by commitments and concerns that various subgroups within the state have, which quite clearly gets the relationship between justice and personal commitments reversed.

III. The National-Scope Challenge

Defenders of global justice however now face a distinct challenge. The challenge in the third and current stage of the discourse on global justice holds that distributive justice applies only in the special context of the nation-state and does not extend to the global domain. In effect, it says that the extension attempt in the first stage was a serious and fundamental misstep – it wrongly applies reasoning for justice under a special context to an inappropriate context. Arguments for distributive justice take hold only when certain conditions obtain, and that while these conditions do obtain in the context of the nation-state, they are absent in the global context. Thus with regard to distributive justice, patriotic and national commitments are all the commitments there are. So the problem, unlike in the second stage is not merely a problem of priority, but a problem of establishing the validity of global justice in the first place.

This challenge demands that egalitarians revisit the reasons why distributive equality matters at all, and to examine whether these reasons are unique to the state or whether they obtain in some form globally as well. It is not surprising that the discussion on global justice has become more abstract recently because of the nature of the investigation. Some prominent recent papers nominally on global justice in fact devote more pages to fundamental questions of equality rather than to global justice per se. But this is not a bad thing – it clarifies for both sides the underlying basis of the value of distributive equality and the scope of this concern.

What are some of the reasons why equality matters and do these reasons limit the scope of equality to the nation-state? Since this is the most current nationalist challenge, I will devote the rest of this chapter to it. I will recount some of the recent prominent arguments that defend the limited (national) scope of equality, and outline possible responses to these arguments on the globalist's behalf.

A. Reciprocity

One argument is that equality matters because of the ideal of reciprocity – that under a common social system, members are required to justify to each other the shared arrangement that they are imposing on each other. The argument for equality based on reciprocity is that any common arrangement that allows for arbitrary inequalities would violate the ideal of reciprocity – that is such an arrangement could be reasonably rejected – unless such inequalities could be justified.

It is worth recalling that Rawls himself (when he presented his own account of international justice) pointed to the argument from reciprocity in his objection to those who had sought to globalize his theory to the global arena. The ideal of reciprocity in the domestic arena requires that the gap between rich and poor cannot be too wide; but in the global arena, Rawls argues, reciprocity can be satisfied without this egalitarian commitment. That is, while reciprocity generates distributive commitments among citizens of a liberal state, it does not generate distributive commitments among persons globally.

But one can ask here: what is the argument that the *criterion of reciprocity* takes different forms when we move from the domestic to the global arena? Why does reciprocity generate egalitarian commitments domestically but not globally? It seems to me that reciprocity by itself doesn't present a reason for equality that limits its scope to the nation state. We need to at least say something more about the special quality of the state such that reciprocity among citizens imposes demands significantly different from demands among persons globally (Tan, 2007).

B. Coercion

In this regard, some commentators have stressed that an important difference between the state and the global arenas is that the former is a legally ongoing coercive order. It is this fact of lawful coercion that generates egalitarian commitments among members of a nation-state; and because there isn't a lawful global coercive authority, there is no similar reason for caring about global equality (Blake, 2002; Miller, 1998).

One prominent argument, that of Michael Blake's, draws on the idea of autonomy, in that since lawful coercion is in the first instance autonomy restricting, it must be justifiable to those being coerced if the lawful coercion is to be legitimate. Such an arrangement would be justifiable on this account if no arbitrary inequalities are admitted. That is, such a coercive order is acceptable in spite of its restrictions on autonomy if it is tempered by some institutional distributive egalitarian commitments.

Blake's argument has received much attention recently, and hopefully without doing too much injustice to Blake's own complex arguments and the discussion it has elicited, I will point out two possible lines of response. One is to challenge the belief that coercion is the *sine qua non* of egalitarian justice. It might be the case that where there is lawful coercion, some distributive commitments need to be acknowledged to make that arrangement legitimate in the eyes of all subjects. But it does not follow that coercion must be a necessary condition for distributive justice – it is open to the argument that there are other reasons for caring about distributive inequalities besides that of needing to legitimize coercion.

The second response addresses the empirical claim of the coercion argument: that there isn't a global coercive order. Many observers point out that this premise is questionable. There is, they will say, an ongoing coercive global legal order that is both profound and pervasive and hence autonomy restricting. Just to take one example, the fact of border regulation and immigration restrictions. These are lawful institutional arrangements, enacted domestically, no doubt, but sanctioned by the international legal order that have profound impact on persons' autonomy.

Thus, if the need to legitimate domestic lawful coercion is that which generates the egalitarian commitment in the domestic setting, then global law coercion should similarly generate global egalitarian commitments.

One might say that there is something distinct about those who are coerced qua members of a state and those who are coerced as nonmembers. But a reason for this distinction has to be given and not just be assumed that membership enjoys *a priori* special moral standing.

C. Shared-governance

Thomas Nagel's already influential paper, "The Problem of Global Justice" (2005), introduces a second element in addition to coercion to draw out the difference between coercion among members and coercion against outsiders. If successful, Nagel's account will not be vulnerable to the objection offered above that there is ongoing coercion of persons at the global level.

The additional element Nagel introduces is the notion of shared authorship in the laws of one's society, or the implication of one's will in the system that one is a participating subject of. Unlike the coerced outsiders wanting to get inside, insiders aren't just under coercion; they are coerced under a system in which they also see themselves to be joint authors of a system whose establishment and maintenance engages their will (ie. their acceptance of this arrangement). It is only among joint-authors of a coercive arrangement, Nagel argues, that justifications for the legitimacy of that coercive arrangement can be demanded. One necessary condition for gaining legitimacy is that no arbitrary inequalities be admissible. Thus, the case for distributive justice is triggered. But since there is no global coercive order that all persons are seen to be the joint authors of, there is no basis for global distributive demands. Objections to global inequalities do not gain any foothold, as Nagel puts it.

Nagel's is a challenging thesis and will continue to be discussed. Let me here offer some observations. I think that both core premises of the argument, the normative and empirical, can be questioned. (i) The empirical premise that there isn't a global order that implicates wills of individuals globally situated seems questionable. The fact that we do challenge some decisions of global institutions on the grounds that they have ignored the view-points of persons affected suggests that we ideally conceive of these institutions as objects of joint authorship and expressions of the will of persons affected (e.g., Cohen and Sabel, 2006). So even if we accept that distributive demands can be made not just among persons affected by a common social arrangement but only by those who have the special status as joint authors of the system, it does not follow immediately that distributive justice has limited scope.

But the normative premise itself can also be questioned. As some commentators have pointed out (Julius, 2006; Abizadeh, 2007; Caney 2008; Tan 2007) the normative seems a little perverse. It suggests that my coercion of you requires no justification when you have no say at all about what I can do to you, whereas if you are regarded as someone having some say, I will need to justify the coercion. This removes protection from those who are the most vulnerable to our actions and policies – people, *outsiders in particular*, who have no say in our policies that impact them are most in need of protection and most entitled to demand that we justify the things that we do where these impact them. Joint-authors are by comparison less vulnerable by virtue of their role as collaborators in the design and sustenance of the system. So the normative premise does seem implausible – it protects members, but removes protection from non-members who are also often the ones most vulnerable with respect to us.

D. Social Cooperation

Recently, some philosophers have returned to the reciprocity ideal in defense of the limited scope thesis, but this time they stress the role of particular forms of social institutions that in turn ground the reciprocity ideal. The ideal of reciprocity that generates distributive commitments derives ultimately from institutions of social cooperation. That is, part of what it means to be participants in a scheme of social cooperation is to endorse the ideal of reciprocity – that is, the terms of social engagement be those that all participats can reasonably accept. But because there aren't global schemes of social cooperation, these commentators argue, there is no global reciprocity of the relevant sort that could generate distributive commitments (Sangiovanni, 2007; Freeman, 2006; 2007).

Again, the argument has both a normative and an empirical premise: that distributive justice arises only in the context of institutions of social cooperation and that there aren't institutions of social cooperation to be found globally. To respond to this argument one has to refute either (or both) of these premises. To refute the empirical premise, the globalist has to show that there are in fact global institutions based on social cooperation. The premise denies what several globalists have argued for a while now: that there is a basic global structure that reflects the ideal of social cooperation (Beitz, [1979] 1999; Buchanan, 2000).

The normative premise takes it that justice kicks in when there is social cooperation; but it leaves open the question as to whether justice itself could demand the establishment of institutions of social cooperation where none existed. So the globalist may attempt to refute this premise by presenting an argument that whereas distributive justice demands social cooperation in the sense that social cooperation is part of what is meant by the ideal of distributive justice, distributive justice commitments don't presuppose existing social cooperation. That is, demands of justice could be made among persons prior to any cooperative arrangements existing among themselves.

For example, one could argue that in a state of affairs where there is sufficient interdependence and interaction among agents, these agents have a duty of justice to ensure that their interaction and independency are on fair terms. That is, why not hold that these agents have the duty to ensure that they in fact cooperate with each other when interaction among them is unavoidable? Where social cooperation requires certain institutional arrangements, why not say that these agents have the duty of justice to create such institutions? Rawls's own remarks that there is the natural duty to establish just institutions where they don't exist supports this idea that justice need not rely on existing institutions as a condition of its applicability (Rawls, 1971). Rather, the demands of justice can in fact demand that institutions of appropriate kinds be put into place.

In other words, the response to the argument from social cooperation is to reject the idea that social cooperation provides the necessary (rather than just the sufficient) basis for any commitment to distributive equality. If it can be established that distributive egalitarian concerns are generated when there is adequate and sustained interaction between parties even in the absence of social cooperation among them, then even if the global arena does not resemble a socially cooperative arrangement it does not imply that global justice has no place there. The fact of sustained global interaction, a fact sustained by globalization, could be sufficient for generating global distributive commitments.

The nationalist challenge of this third stage is perhaps the most challenging for it involves the fundamental question of the conditions or circumstances of distributive justice. The debate here is ongoing, and I don't claim that my brief remarks above have fully addressed the challenge in its different forms. Indeed, the arguments presented by Blake, Nagel, Sangiovanni and Freeman are receiving much attention (e.g., by several papers in this volume), and my discussion above has only touched on some of the more general points in each of these arguments. These arguments demand greater attention and deeper analysis. My goal here is merely to indicate what some possible responses could look like.

IV. Concluding Remarks

As we can see, the current state of the debate on global justice has returned to the basic question as to whether distributive equality is even a value conceivable at the global level. In a sense then, the global justice discourse is back to where it started: global egalitarians are back in the business of trying to show how arguments for equality do apply to the global domain. Yet there has been progress along the way. The philosophical debate and arguments have become a lot more sophisticated and informed and complex; indeed, as we have seen, the current state of the debate has ignited a series of new discussions on why equality matters, and both sides of the debate have benefited and contributed to this question. Our understanding of why equality matters has been enriched due to the global justice debate, and this surely can be seen as a progress.

I believe that the defense of global justice will (i) require continuing engagement with the philosophical question as to why distributive equality matters. In addition to attempts to show how dominant accounts of why equality matters (as discussed just above – reciprocity, coercion, shared governance, etc.) generate global justice obligations, global egalitarians have the potential of moving the debate on equality forward by introducing or reviving alternative arguments for distributive equality. For instance, global egalitarians can try to restore standing to the luck egalitarian ideal – the ideal roughly that persons should not be disadvantaged by circumstances not of their own choosing – and on the grounds of luck egalitarianism defend global egalitarianism. There is potential for new development on equality here. Global egalitarians, given their special sensitivity to distinct problem sets, could be motivated to develop and offer new theories of equality that statist theorists, given their limited problem domain, are not attuned to.

I also think that (ii) global egalitarians will need to say more concretely what kind of distributive commitments and principles they have in mind. For example, some have posited the idea of a Rawlsian difference principle. But I think that more needs to be said as to how this principle is to be implemented and realized and more attention paid to the possible implications of its implementation. For example, what does this mean for national distributive commitments? Will these risk being subsumed by a globalized difference principle? Some of the anti-globalist criticisms have been fuelled by a lack of clarity as to what a global distributive commitment would look like and a clear understanding of its implications for national justice (Freeman, 2006; 2007). Global egalitarians thus have the obligation to do more concrete work.

References

Abizadeh, A. (2007). "Cooperation, Pervasive Impact, and Coercion: On the Scope (not Site) of Distributive Justice". *Philosophy & Public Affairs*. Vol. 35. No. 4. Pp. 318-358.

Barry, B. (1974). *A Liberal Theory of Justice*. Oxford. Oxford University Press.

Beitz, C. ([1979] 1999). *Political Theory and International Relations*. 2nd ed. Princeton. Princeton University Press.

Beitz, C. (1983). "Cosmopolitan Ideal and National Sentiment". *The Journal of Philosophy*. LXXX/10. Pp. 591-600.

Blake, M. (2002). "Distributive Justice, State Coercion, and Autonomy". *Philosophy and Public Affairs*. Vol. 30. No. 3. Pp. 257-296.

Brown, A. (2008) " Are There Any Global Egalitarian Rights?". *Human Rights Review*. Vol. 9. No. 4. Pp. 211-49.

Buchanan, A. (2000). "Rawls's Law of Peoples". *Ethics*. Vol. 110. No. 4. Pp. 697-721.

Caney, S. (2005). *Justice Beyond Borders*.Oxford. Oxford University Press.

Caney, S. (2008). "Global Distributive Justice and the State." *Political Studies* Vol. 56. No. 3. Pp. 487-518.

Cohen, G.A. (2000). *If You're an Egalitarian, How Come You're So Rich?*. Cambridge. MA. Harvard University Press.

Cohen, J. and Sabel, C. (2006). "Extra Republicam Nulla Justitia?". *Philosophy & Public Affairs* Vol. 34. No. 2. Pp. 147-175.

Dworkin, R. (1977). *Taking Rights Seriously*. Cambridge. MA. Harvard University Press.

Fabre, C. (2006). "Global Distributive Justice: an egalitarian perspective". *Canadian Journal of Philosophy* (supplementary vol.) 31. Pp. 139-164.

Freeman, S. (2006). "Distributive Justice and the Law of Peoples". Rex Martin and David. Reidy (eds.) *Rawls's Law of Peoples: a Realistic Utopia?*. Oxford. Blackwell Press.

Freeman, S. (2007). *Rawls*. London. Routledge.

Held, D. (ed.) (1991). *Political Theory Today*. Palo Alto/CA. Stanford University Press.

Jones, C. (1999). *Global Justice*. Oxford. Oxford University Press.

Julius, A.J. (2006). "Nagel's Atlas". *Philosophy & Public Affairs*. Vol. 34. No. 2. Pp. 176-192.

Kant, I. ([1785] 1953). *Groundwork of the Metaphysics of Morals*. Trans. H.J. Paton. New York. Harper and Row.

Kant, I. ([1795] 1991). "Perpetual Peace". Trans. Hans Reiss (ed.). *Kant's Political Writings*. 2nd ed. Cambridge. Cambridge University Press.

Kant, I. ([1797] 1993). *The Metaphysics of Morals*. Trans. Mary Gregor. Cambridge. Cambridge University Press.

Mill, J.S. ([1861] 1977). *Utilitarianism* in *Collected Works* Robson, J. (ed.). vol. X. Toronto. University of Toronto Press.

Miller, D. (1995). *On Nationality*. Oxford. Oxford University Press.

Miller, D. (2000). *Citizenship and National Identity*. Cambridge. UK. Polity Press.

Miller, R. (1998). "Cosmopolitan Respect and Patriotic Concern". *Philosophy and Public Affairs*. Vol. 27. No. 3. Pp. 202-224.

Moellendorf. D. (2002). *Cosmopolitan Justice*. Westview Press. Boulder.

Moellendorf, D. (2006). "Equal Respect and Global Egalitarianism". *Social Theory and Practice* Vol. 32. No. 4. Pp. 601-616.

Moore, M. (2001), *The Ethics of Nationalism*. Oxford. Oxford University Press.

Nagel, T. (2005). "The Problem of Global Justice". *Philosophy and Public Affairs* Vol. 33. No. 2. Pp. 113-47.

Nussbaum, M. (2000a). *Women and Human Development*. Cambridge. Cambridge University Press..

O'Neill, O. (2000). *Bounds of Justice*. Cambridge. Cambridge University Press.

Pogge, T. (1989). *Realizing Rawls*. Ithaca. Cornell University Press.

Pogge, T. (2002). *World Poverty and Human Rights*. Cambridge. Polity Press.

Pogge, T. (2007). *Rawls*. Oxford. Oxford University Press.

Rawls, J. (1971). *A Theory of Justice*. Cambridge. MA. Harvard University Press.

Rawls, J. (1999). *The Law of Peoples*. Cambridge. MA. Harvard University Press.

Rawls, J. (2001). *Justice as Fairness*. Erin Kelly (ed.). Cambridge. MA. Harvard University Press.

Sangiovanni, A. (2007). "Global Justice, Reciprocity, and the State". *Philosophy and Public Affairs*. Vol. 35. No. 1. Pp. 3-39.

Scanlon, T.M. (1975). "Rawls's Theory of Justice". Daniels, N. (ed.). *Reading Rawls*. New York.Basic Books.

Scheffler, S. (1982). *The Rejection of Consequentialism*. Oxford. Oxford Oxford University Press.

Scheffler. S. (ed.) (1988). *Consequentialism and its Critics*. Oxford. Oxford University Press.

Scheffler, S. (2001). *Boundaries and Allegiances*. New York. Oxford University Press.

Tan, K.C. (2004), *Justice Without Borders*. Cambridge. Cambridge University Press.

Tan. K.C. (2006). "The Boundary of Justice, and The Justice of Boundaries". *Canadian Journal of Law and Jurisprudence* Vol. 19. No. 2. Pp. 319-344.

Tan, K.C. (2008, in press), "A Defense of Luck Egalitarianism",.*Journal of Philosophy*. Vol. 105. No. 11. Pp. 665-90.

Cosmopolitanism: Cultural, Moral, and Political

Adam D. Etinson

Introduction

In this paper I tackle the difficult and contested concept of cosmopolitanism. My task divides into three parts. First, I distinguish between three main varieties of cosmopolitanism: *cultural*, *moral*, and *political*. Moral cosmopolitanism's core premise – that all human beings are owed equal moral consideration – sits at the very heart of theories of human rights and global justice, and its philosophical elaboration is therefore of great import to international ethics.

This brings me to my second task, which is to bring order and clarity to the notion of moral cosmopolitanism. I do this by offering a general distinction between the *concept* of moral cosmopolitanism and various *conceptions* of the same. Following Pogge, I make a further distinction between *institutional* and *interactional* conceptions of moral cosmopolitanism. I consider the partiality objection to moral cosmopolitanism, and argue that the resources to overcome this objection are most likely to be found in a conception of moral cosmopolitanism that takes the importance of both political institutions and human interactions into consideration. In particular, I argue that the most plausible conception proposes a moral division of labour between institutions (fulfilling positive duties) on the one hand, and individuals (fulfilling negative duties) on the other.

The third part of my paper argues for a revisionary understanding of the relationship between moral and political cosmopolitanism. The latter has traditionally been understood to be an independent theoretical domain concerned with a single political ideal: that of a world state. Using Kant as a historical example, however, I propose two adjustments to our understanding of political cosmopolitanism. The first is a more developed appreciation of the dependence of political cosmopolitan theorizing on moral cosmopolitan theorizing, and the second is a broadening of the notion of political cosmopolitanism to include not only the ideal of a world state but other strategic institutional ideals as well. All of these comsmopolitan political ideals (i.e., that of a voluntary federation of states, or a patchwork of international institutions dedicated to interpreting and enforcing international law) are linked by their capacity to implement moral cosmopolitan norms such as human rights. I do not argue for a particular cosmopolitan political ideal; which one we choose, after all, may depend on the conception of moral cosmopolitanism we adopt.

Diogenes of Sinope coined the term *cosmopolitan* almost two and a half thousand years ago. When asked where he came from, instead of answering that he was from Sinope or Athens, the ancient Cynic is reported to have answered: "I am a *kosmopolites* [a citizen of the world]"[1]. For us, the word *cosmopolitan* is an adjective that has come to describe pretty much anything that is *of the world* or *worldly*. A cosmopolitan city is one in which people from many different nations or cultures intermingle. A cosmopolitan person is worldly-wise, wears a coat of many *cultures*, feels unrestricted to one, or at home in many. The English language, which is now the most widely spoken on the planet, is what we might even call cosmopolitan. And if there are in fact values which all persons, races, nation and cultures share, then they could rightly be called cosmopolitan as well.

What of cosmopolitan*ism* then? The addition of an *ism* here draws attention to a philosophy or ideology. When philosophers today call themselves cosmopolitan, they are using the adjective in a new sense. They are signalling their allegiance to a particular belief or doctrine. The study of cosmopolitanism is today a burgeoning field in academic philosophy. Most works in the area devote considerable attention to the question of what cosmopolitanism is, trying to delineate the field of inquiry before they delve into it. This paper is, somewhat boringly, primarily intended to be a contribution to that first step: the task of *definition*. The clarity, however, that this effort brings will allow us to make some substantive observations later on.

We can begin by distinguishing between three kinds of cosmopolitan doctrine: the *moral*, *political* (or *legal*), and the *cultural*. In a sense, each variety represents the impact of the ponderous idea of universal membership (or world citizenship) on a different subject: morality, political institutions, and cultural identity.

---

1 (DL, VI 63) This report comes from another Diogenes (Diogenes Laertius) who wrote during the Roman Era. His book, The Lives of Eminent Philosophers, surveys the life and thought of many ancient philosophers, and includes a chapter on Diogenes of Sinope.

1. Cultural Cosmopolitanism

It is perhaps easiest to start with *cultural* cosmopolitanism, as it stays closest to the meaning of the term in common parlance. Cultural cosmopolitanism begins by taking the eclectic, idiosyncratic, culturally mixed-up (i.e., cosmopolitan) lifestyle with which we have become so familiar in modern times, and affirms this as both a possible and fulfilling way of life. By affirming our capacity as individuals to live well in the world by forming pastiche identities that draw from cultures as disparate or as incongruous as we like, cultural cosmopolitanism is a challenge to those strands of liberal thought that defend the importance of rootedness in a single culture for individual well-being and autonomy.[2] It envisions human beings not as rigidly determined products of culture – irrevocably cast into a given cultural mold from birth – but as agents free to roam the earth and assemble (or reassemble) for themselves a unique cultural concoction by choice or by chance. Essential to this idea is the ability of persons to converse and connect *across* cultures; there must be a common human capacity or set of capacities – for language, thought, communication, etc. – that facilitates such cultural transaction.

At the same time, culture itself must be something that can be exchanged, altered, translated, or combined in idiosyncratic configurations if we are to believe in the lifestyle of the cosmopolite. After reminding us that this lifestyle is a viable option, the cultural cosmopolitan can't help but also remind us of the ubiquity of cultural change, interchange, and the resulting indefiniteness of cultural boundaries. In this way, cultural cosmopolitanism moves from a claim about the self and the good life to a claim about the nature, or fluidity, of culture in general.

As Scheffler (2001) has noticed, however, there is a more ambitious claim often tied in with these considerations. This is the notion that cultural cosmopolitanism may be *unavoidable* in modern times, i.e., that it is the *only* possible and fulfilling life choice we can make. Scheffler calls this an *extreme* variant of cultural cosmopolitanism, to be contrasted with its more *moderate* counterpart – the simple affirmation of the While the latter doctrine remains ambivalent, the former looks down on adherence to the values and traditions of a particular community as an outmoded and impracticable life-choice.

2 For classic and influential arguments on the liberal multiculturalist side, see Joseph Raz (1994) and Will Kymlicka (1995). Jeremy Waldron's 1992 article entitled "Minority Cultures and the Cosmopolitan Alternative" remains the stock example of a cosmopolitan challenge to liberal multiculturalism.

Why hold this more extreme view? Stated as such, it's surely too extreme to be acceptable. One way of making sense of this position would be to consider Jeremy Waldron's point that "Cultures live and grow, change and sometimes wither away; they amalgamate with other cultures, or they adapt themselves to geographical or demographic necessity." (Waldron, 1992, pp. 787-788); If immersing oneself in the traditions of a particular community (and only that community), today, requires artificially halting this process by committing our governments to the *preservation* of cultures, then there is indeed a sense in which, as Waldron asserts, anti-cosmopolitanism "is like living in a Disneyland and thinking that one's surroundings epitomize what it is for a culture really to exist" (Waldron, 1992, p. 763).

There is another way of making sense of the extreme form of cultural cosmopolitanism, however, but it involves an adjustment in our conception of the ideal of the cultural cosmopolitan. In a later article, Waldron elaborates on Kant's notion of *ius cosmopoliticus* – which governs the relations between foreign persons and peoples – to show that what makes someone's cultural identity cosmopolitan is not so much its hybridity as the *form of allegiance* that person adopts towards the norms and practices of their culture. Since all human persons, according to Kant, are stuck together on the surface of the earth and thus "destined by nature to [develop], through mutual compulsion under laws that come from themselves, into a *cosmopolitan society*," (Kant [1784] 1991, p. 332) they must fashion a universal coercive law for themselves. Given the scope of this political project, it requires people of different moral, philosophical, cultural, and religious backgrounds to come to terms with one another in a free and open-minded manner on decisions about law. According to Waldron, this makes it important to approach one's cultural traditions not as brute and non-negotiable aspects of their identity – worth practicing simply because they are *yours* – but as norms and practices funded by an array of *reasons* that are open to interrogation. This is what makes agreement (or even debate) about constitutional essentials possible, and it shows how adopting such a rational attitude towards one's cultural beliefs, norms, and practices, is a matter of accepting the modern conditions of an emerging global community.

This way of understanding cultural cosmopolitanism has far more in common with ancient Cynic and Stoic cosmopolitan doctrine of a universal community of rational beings. Exiled from Sinope, then a resident in Athens and later Corinth, we might think that Diogenes the Cynic's migratory lifestyle would have induced him to sing the praises of cultural hybridity. In fact, quite the opposite is true. Diogenes was famous for his complete indifference and even hostility towards local custom and convention. Much like Socrates, the anecdotes surrounding the life of Diogenes depict him as a consistent, ideologically-committed social dissident. While this did make him wildly idiosyncratic, it did not make him a cultural cosmopolitan in the moderate sense of the word: someone who embraces and at times willingly adopts the ways of others.

Of what is known about ancient Cynicism, one certainty is its insistence on life in conformity with universal reason and virtue as opposed to life in accordance with local custom and law. Rather than assemble a coat of many cultures, the ancient Cynics sought to purify themselves, so to speak, of the morally corruptive influence of any local identity or affiliation. The idea of cultural attachment has a patent moral dimension. Does cultural attachment (i.e., being America, being Inuit, being Jewish), for instance, entail giving *preference* to members of one's cultural group, in the same way as one gives preference to the members of one's family? Should this sort of preference-giving be seen as a justifiable, even desirable thing? The ancient Stoics and Cynics thought not. As Nussbaum notes: "Class, rank, status, national origin and location, and even gender are treated by the cynics as secondary and morally irrelevant attributes. The first form of moral affiliation for the citizen should be her affiliation with rational humanity; and this, above all, should define the purposes of her conduct" (Nussbaum, 1997, p. 29). This brings us to *moral* cosmopolitanism.

Moral Cosmopolitanism

The Stoic philosopher Seneca proposed that each of us belongs to at least two commonwealths: the local country of our birth and the universal commonwealth of reason, which includes all human beings regardless of their origin, class, or culture (Seneca, *de otio*: 4, quoted in Schofield 1991, p. 93). I may stand next to some of you as a foreigner, but I also stand next to you as a fellow human being endowed with all the capacities that follow from our common nature. Stoic thinkers fixed on the unique capacity for reason as most worthy of praise in individuals, and founded the fellow citizenship of humanity on its boundless moral value (Nussbaum, 1997, p. 30); since we all possess the divine capacity of reason, the human community is one of moral equals. Stoic world citizenship, then, has at its core an ethical doctrine; it entails first and foremost the equal and fundamental moral status of individuals and obliges us to consider the good of all humankind in our actions (*Ibid.*, pp. 29-30). A favourite and striking visual exercise of Marcus Aurelius' was to imagine the whole human race as a single body (*Ibid.*, p. 34); to disregard one part of humanity is like chopping off one's limb. In some such way, Marcus and the Stoics admirably refused to recognize anything human as alien.

For our purposes, Stoicism is relevant for its offering of the core concept of moral cosmopolitanism: the equal and fundamental *moral* status of all individuals, regardless of race, creed, ethnicity, origin, or geographic location. But how exactly is this status to be understood? There are many options. It might imply some form of globalized consequentialism, where all actions are assessed according to their aggregate benefit or detriment to the welfare of humankind.[3] Or it could imply that we treat each person never merely as a means to an end but as an end in itself, as an equal member in a Kantian universal "*kingdom of ends*"? (Kant [1785]1997, pp. 429-434). It has been said to require the recognition of each person's equal dignity, or their entitlement to a set of central human capabilities that make human flourishing possible (Nussbaum, 2006, p. 76). Does it require that we treat each person as having equal standing as an addressee of moral justification (Beitz, 2005, p. 17)? Is moral equality about securing individual autonomy or observing duties generated by the basic interests and well-being of persons? Or is this rather a theological doctrine, grounded in the idea that human beings are morally equal in the eyes of God their creator?

My assertion is that all of these notions can fit under the rubric of moral cosmopolitanism. One way of making sense of this is to distinguish, as Rawls did, between the *concept* of moral equality and various *conceptions* thereof (Rawls [1971] 1999, p. 5). We may disagree in our *conceptions* of cosmopolitanism while agreeing on the core content of its *concept*. The former develops, interprets, and adds crucial details to the latter, but it does not contradict its formulaic content. A concept is surrounded by a nebula of derivative conceptions, so to speak. In the case of justice, an institutional virtue according to Rawls, the nebula of conceptions surrounds the core notions of non-arbitrariness and the fair consideration of individual claims, which make up its concept (*Ibid.*, p. 5). In order to understand moral cosmopolitanism, we will want to know what lies at the heart of its concept of equality.

Contemporary theorists such as David Miller have located the core of moral cosmopolitanism in the idea that "we owe all human beings moral consideration of some kind... and also that *in some sense* that consideration must involve treating their claims equally" (2007, p. 27). Miller, like many others, recognizes that this core needs further elaboration. He calls this the premise of *weak* cosmopolitanism, to be contrasted with any of its *stronger* counterparts, which add premises that go beyond equal moral

3 Peter Singer (2002) has recently popularized this view (with extension to animals).

concern to argue for a substantive view about what sort of *treatment* it requires, i.e., the globalization of a particular principle of distributive justice (*Ibid.*, 43-44).

One way of isolating the cosmopolitan concept of moral equality is offered by Pogge, who reduces it to three interrelated claims: *individualism, universality,* and *generality*:

> First, *individualism*: the ultimate units of concern are *human beings*, or *persons* – rather than, say, family lines, tribes, ethnic, cultural, or religious communities, nations, or states. The latter may be units of concern only indirectly, in virtue of their individual members or citizens. Second, *universality*: the status of ultimate unit of concern attaches to *every* living human being *equally* – not merely to some subset, such as men, aristocrats, Aryans, whites, or Muslims. Third, *generality*: this special status has global force. Persons are ultimate units of concern *for everyone* – not only for their compatriots, fellow religionists, or suchlike (Pogge [2002] 2008, p. 175).

This seems like a fair rendition of the basic concept of moral cosmopolitanism; however, these principles remain too abstract to be meaningful. If the wrongness of murder is indifferent to borders, race, or ethnicity, this must be because our moral *concern* is focused on some cross-border *feature* of persons: not simply their *humanity*, but some more specific aspect of their humanity that is violated in the act of murder. "Humanity" seems far too vague and trivial an aspect of persons to illuminate the root of this moral prohibition. What might this aspect be then? Again, there are countless ways of fleshing this feature out (*Ibid.*, pp. 175-176). At the risk of smuggling a *conception* of moral equality into its *concept,* we nevertheless have to make a decision here. Following Allen Buchanan, I would argue that the most plausible as well as minimal flesh we can put to the bones of the concept of moral equality is by focusing on basic human *interests* or *well-being* (Buchanan, 2004, pp. 131-137).

In *Justice, Legitimacy, and Self-Determination* (2004), Buchanan argues that the concept of equal moral regard (what he calls the Moral Equality Principle) is not only fundamental to any moral theory worth thinking about (Buchanan, 2004, p. 88), it also provides a foundation for the existence of basic human rights (*Ibid.*, pp. 90-91, 131-135). "One of the most important ways we show equal concern and respect for persons is by acknowledging that there are human rights" (*Ibid.*, 90); and this, via respect for basic human interests. Buchanan appeals to our intuitions here, arguing for this link by listing examples of basic rights that seem to serve or protect basic human interests. So for example, the right not to be tortured, not to be discriminated against on grounds of gender or religion, and the right to resources for subsistence: these rights are rooted in such basic interests as avoiding psychological and physical harm or pain, finding spiritual fulfillment, and living a minimally decent life free of cruelty and oppression (*Ibid.*, p. 134-137).

By itself, this argument does little to rule out the possibility of other, non rights-based manners of respecting equal human interests. For instance, the moral equality principle stated flatly could serve as a basis for some variant of globalized consequentialism that treated individual interests equally but aggregatively, permitting grave harm towards some if it were to lead to enough benefit for others.

Regardless of this indeterminacy, for us, the main attraction of Buchanan's reading of moral equality lies in its ability to accommodate a variety of conceptions thereof, while at the same time adding some much-needed specificity to the original concept. The Kantian emphasis on rational autonomy as a basis for moral equality can now be incorporated as one of several important ingredients in most or even all individuals' well-being; so too can the notions of human dignity and equal capabilities, which can play a parallel role in conceptions of moral equality.[4] In this way, a conception of moral equality as equal concern for basic human interests best mimics the behaviour of a *concept* of moral equality – a common centre of convergence for various *conceptions* of the same.

But if this is our concept of moral cosmopolitanism, then it is even less determinate than Rawls' concept of justice (on which all members of a liberal society can agree). In the latter case, we at least knew what the concept applied to: *social institutions*. Moral cosmopolitanism, on the other hand, seems to apply to the *whole of morality* – all possible moral subject matters or *iudicanda*, as Pogge has called them (Pogge 2007, p. 312). In order to develop more determinate conceptions of moral cosmopolitanism, we need to distinguish between its application as a moral standard for evaluating institutions, on the one hand, and individual or group behaviour on the other. In other words, we follow Thomas Pogge in treating moral cosmopolitanism as a doctrine that holds implications for both *interactional* and *institutional* justice (Pogge [2002] 2008, p. 176).

Once we relegate the scope of moral cosmopolitanism to a specific domain or subject matter, we have already moved away from its concept and into a *conception* of moral cosmopolitanism. We take a more specific stance on what the demands of moral cosmopolitanism are and on whom

4 It should be noted that these very same notions are those most often used in arguments for the existence of human rights (On human rights and autonomy, see e.g., Griffin (2008, Ch. 8) This only bolsters the case for a connection between the concept of moral equality, as we have defined it, and that of human rights. This also fits with Joseph Raz's proposal of an interest-based theory of rights which was intended to illuminate and explain the entire tradition of political and moral discourse about rights (Raz, 1986, p. 166).

they fall. Pogge himself endorses an institutional conception of cosmopolitanism or what he calls *social-justice* cosmopolitanism (*Ibid.*, p. 176; 2007, pp. 316-321). Social-justice cosmopolitanism prescribes norms of social and economic justice on the basis of which we can assess alternative institutional structures at the domestic and international level. What makes these norms cosmopolitan is their ultimate concern for the basic human interests of all persons. Pogge takes the target of such norms to be the institutional protection of human rights (including rights to resources and basic subsistence) via coercive law, for all persons regardless of nationality (Pogge 2002/2008, p. 176).

Before specifying how a just global social and economic order can be practically attained or what it might look like, social-justice cosmopolitans outline the principles of such an order. Thus, Pogge (1989 § III), Beitz ([1979] 1999, p. 170), and Tan (2004, pp. 55-61) have claimed that Rawls' principles of domestic justice, as outlined in *A Theory of Justice* ([1971] 1999, pp. 65-73), are the best principles for determining how to distribute goods and liberties fairly among all members of the world community. Caney (2005, pp. 122-125) has suggested the validity of a patchwork of global principles of distributive justice, and Nussbaum (2000, Ch.2; 2006, Ch.5) argues for the globalization of a *capabilities* approach to distributive justice and human rights.

Part of the attraction of this institutional approach to moral cosmopolitanism is that it focuses the *range* of demands placed on individuals to aid the world's poor, ailing, hungry, and sick. Our duties towards humanity are mediated by the presence of political institutions, and our primary responsibility is to try and promote feasible reforms in *them.* The individual fate of more than six billion earthly inhabitants do not directly intrude into the scope of our lateral moral concern. A purely *interactional* approach to moral cosmopolitanism, on the other hand – one that envisages the moral community of human beings in abstraction from all institutional structures – would make direct and potentially very strong demands on individuals towards other individuals, regardless of relations of geographical proximity, kinship, race, or nationality. If we view all human beings as moral equals to whom we owe direct respect and proper treatment of some kind, then we (especially in the developed world) may be overwhelmed by demands to help those who are suffering all over the world. This would make any constricted focus of our moral and economic energies – say to our friends, family, or compatriots – seem unjustified. But how can such basic forms of partiality be unjust? The claim that such impartiality is unreasonable and subversive forms the *partiality objection* to moral cosmopolitanism.

Peter Singer, who proposes a comprehensive variant of global consequentialism, has become an easy target for such objections. He is famous for pointing out the drastic and in some respects absurd disregard we show towards the fate of others in our everyday behaviour. In one example among many, he asks us to imagine that our duties to suffering persons abroad are as strong as our duties to save a child drowning in a pond that we happen to be passing by (Singer, 1997). Similarly, the money allocated to needless luxuries in the developed world is morally preposterous in light of the good it could do for the global poor (or even the earth's atmosphere) (Singer 2002, pp. 188-189). Although he does not refer to himself as a cosmopolitan, Singer clearly endorses a conception of moral cosmopolitanism. Interestingly, the form that he endorses is neither purely interactional nor institutional, however. Instead, he appears to endorse what Pogge has referred to as a *monistic* or *holistic* approach to moral cosmopolitanism (Pogge 2007, pp. 321-328). According to this view, injustice is primarily a property of *states of affairs*, and only secondarily a matter of individual and group behaviour (interactions) or institutional design (institutions).

As Pogge puts it, "Monistic cosmopolitanism co-ordinates all human agents and all humanly shapeable factors towards one unitary goal [for all *iudicanda*]: to make the world as just as we can make it" (*Ibid.*, 321). This fits the consequentialist spirit of Singer's version of moral cosmopolitanism. All actions, institutions, and choices are evaluated with reference to the overall benefit/harm they produce. It is not my purpose to offer a full criticism of this conception of moral cosmopolitanism, or any other. Nevertheless, there are good grounds for thinking that this conception verges on impracticability. The difficulty with such a view is not simply that, like interactional moral cosmopolitanism, it directly challenges what we tend to think are justified forms of partiality towards friends, family, coreligionists, and co-nationals; in its totalitarian co-option of institutions, individuals, human cultures, and subcultures towards the goal of making the world a better place, it is unable to place a non-arbitrary limit on both the range or strength of the obligations owed towards the whole of humanity. Singer himself only demands that each member of a developed country devote a minimum of one percent of their annual income to a cause that fights world poverty (*Ibid.*, pp. 193-195). We may even intervene on his behalf and propose a maximum – a threshold or target – for this aid in the eventual worldwide protection of basic human rights. But the holistic goal of 'making the world a better place' is too ambitious to properly justify these bare-minimums and bare-maximums. Any limitations to human sacrifice appear arbitrary, and the many impractical and personal goals that make life worthwhile are given no free-reign. Singer is surely able to provide some answers to these criticisms, but I believe we are better off looking towards a conception of moral cosmopolitanism that in spirit is more respectful towards human practice and practicality.

Can an interactional conception of moral cosmopolitanism avoid the partiality objection? One instinct might be to refine the doctrine by restricting it to merely negative responsibilities on the part of individuals not to harm human beings in certain ways. We can plausibly invoke human rights here as the appropriate side constraints. According to this variant then, life can go on as usual, we can act with as much partiality as we like, as long as we don't violate the basic human rights of other persons (*Ibid.*, pp. 328-330). Assuming that we in fact can come up with a slimmed-down list of (primarily negative) human rights that do not make such positive demands, we here have a more workable conception of interactional moral cosmopolitanism, at least one that appears able to face the partiality objection straight-on.

But this adaptation renders the doctrine too anaemic. Surely, the most valuable insight of moral cosmopolitanism is that we do owe something positive to others, be they strangers, foreigners, or the neighbour next door, and human rights are not simply negative rights, they include obligations to educate and provide an adequate standard of living for all persons. What we owe them is certainly more than a policy of simple non-interference or an attempt on our part not to implicate ourselves in any injustice being perpetrated against them. Pogge's institutional conception suggests a path along which we may fulfill these further obligations, i.e., through supporting a more just global institutional structure. But, on its own, the institutional conception is also lacking. It fails to acknowledge the obvious human dimension of moral cosmopolitanism – that there are moral constraints on individual and group behaviour that bind us regardless of the presence of social institutions and a covering law.

The most plausible conception of moral cosmopolitanism, I would suggest, one that still captures the basic thrust of the concept, yet also respects the partialities, normalities, and inane practices of human life, ought to incorporate a focus on both interactions *and* institutions. In this way, such a doctrine could acknowledge the importance of social institutions for securing people's rights and liberties while also acknowledging the person-to-person relevance of the concept of moral equality. In my eyes, the best way of piecing together such a conception would be to call for something like a globalized division of moral labour between persons or groups on the one hand, and institutions on the other. Our positive duties towards others can be mediated via our support for just institutional arrangements and reforms, while our negative duties towards them are satisfied as long as we respect certain non-negotiable side constraints on our conduct. This view, I take it, can easily stem the partiality objection by demanding only minimal duties not to harm others at the lateral, interactional level (where the partiality objection plays out). Whatever other special obligations we wish to take on are up to us. With potentially overwhelming positive duties to humanity removed from the interactional domain of moral concern and displaced onto our relationship with social institutions, we have a conception of moral cosmopolitanism that makes clear and sensible demands on individuals without abolishing their actual habits and practices.

This piecemeal approach to moral cosmopolitanism appears to be that endorsed by Allen Buchanan. The concept of moral equality, according to Buchanan, also entails what he calls the Natural Duty of Justice. Together these two concepts provide us with an outline of our positive and negative duties towards others. The natural duty of justice emerges out of the concept of moral equality because it specifies how we ought to make positive efforts to ensure that the basic rights of others are protected.

Taking the Moral Equality Principle seriously commits us to the Natural Duty of Justice, because a proper understanding of the Moral Equality Principle implies that to show proper regard for persons we must help ensure that their basic rights are protected. The Natural Duty of Justice as I understand it says that equal consideration for persons requires helping to ensure that they have access to institutions that protect their basic human rights. This will sometimes require creating new institutions and will often require reforming existing institutions. (Buchanan 2004, pp. 87-88).[5]

By focusing positive duties towards others on institutions, we do not ignore the importance of genuine kindness, generosity, and universal philanthropy. We simply recognize the undeniable fact that social institutions play the single largest role in determining the life chances of human beings. The attainment of a just global order is a moral aim of first importance for all of us.

Scheffler would have done well to consider some of these finer distinctions in his discussion of moral cosmopolitanism (Scheffler 2001, Ch. 7). There, Scheffler distinguishes between moderate moral cosmopolitanism (which gives free-reign to special obligations between conationals) and its extreme counterpart, according to which our fundamental moral allegiance is to humanity at large and special obligations to others can only have derived or instrumental value (*Ibid.*, pp. 115-116). These are thus two variants of *interactional* moral cosmopolitanism: one that recognizes the ultimate value of partial obligations to friends, family, or conationals,

5 See Buchanan (2004, 85-98) for a more general discussion.

and one that poses a challenge to such forms of partiality by denying them any value beyond their service to the whole of humanity. Scheffler would have had an even easier time defending the former *moderate* view if he had kept a piecemeal approach to moral cosmopolitanism in mind. He considers two objections to the coherence of moderate cosmopolitanism that might force us to retreat to the less compromising extreme cosmopolitan view: one conceptual and the other substantive. The conceptual objection is that a basic commitment to the equality of persons entails a principle of equal treatment, and that special relationships with particular people (i.e., friends, family, and conationals) cannot in themselves justify special treatment (*Ibid.*, p. 120). The implication is that a commitment to moral equality is conceptually incompatible with the non-instrumental justification of special responsibilities. The substantive argument is that "equality and special responsibilities require policies and practices that are diametrically opposed to one another" (*Ibid.*, p. 120). Scheffler has his own answers to these objections (*Ibid.*, pp. 121-124), but the piecemeal conception of moral cosmopolitanism that Buchanan appears to endorse has good answers to each of these objections that a purely interactional conception could not furnish.

With regard to the first objection, Buchanan can argue that a commitment to a principle of equal interactional treatment does not have to entail equal treatment in *all respects.* If we flesh the principle of equal treatment out, as we did above, in terms of a minimum policy of no-harm, non-interference, or (*negative*) respect for basic human rights, then we leave enough room for special responsibilities to build up on top of this minimum level of equal treatment. But Buchanan can go beyond this and claim commitment to equal *positive* treatment of individuals under the *global institutional order*,[6] which is similarly indifferent to interactional partiality and highly morally relevant. With regard to the second objection, Buchanan can claim to specify in a fairly detailed way how nationalistic practices might be reconciled with 'cosmopolitan' ethical practices: citizens can act patriotically and form idiosyncratic bonds, provided they remain consistent in taking their natural duty of justice seriously by making efforts to promote institutional arrangements that will secure the welfare of all human beings.

That a piecemeal approach to moral cosmopolitanism can offer these answers testifies to its promise as a theory about the demands of justice. It is important that matters of institutional justice are included here. The

6 Note that such equal treatment need not entail the flattening out of global resources equally among all nations. We could accept a Rawlsian principle of global distributive justice, which would allow for some global inequalities.

basic insight that all human beings owe each other equal moral consideration has obvious bearings on the shape of domestic and international institutions. Once we begin to consider not just the best moral norms or standards for evaluating the global institutional order, but the best political means for implementing them, we have moved into the territory of *political* cosmopolitanism.

Political Cosmopolitanism

The universal polis imagined by Stoic thinkers was not like any ordinary state. This was a *cosmic* polity (i.e., *kosmo*polites) that did not depend for its existence on human institutional structures or on any means of self-defence. Its boundaries were set by "the sun" and its laws were perfect expressions of the divine norms of reason. Thus, though it may have been *like* a city state, or perhaps the only *true* one (Schofield 1991, pp. 61-63), it was very different from any form of government achievable by mortals. The earthly version of this cosmopolis – a world state wrought by human hands and encompassing all human beings – is the archetype of political cosmopolitanism. Its actual achievement would give very tangible weight to the notion of world citizenship.

Political cosmopolitanism has traditionally been associated with the ideal of a world state encompassing all persons. I propose that we amplify the range of theses that can be entertained under the heading of political cosmopolitanism. I argue for this definitional amplification not because the narrower definition is historically inaccurate, or because there are many self-declared politically cosmopolitan theses that have departed from the ideal of a world republic. Instead, I argue for it because I believe that political cosmopolitanism is best understood as an appendix to moral cosmopolitanism, something patently illustrated in the work of Kant. Given that moral cosmopolitanism can be institutionalized in various ways and in varying degrees (especially in view of the plurality of conceptions of moral cosmopolitanism), this gives us good reason to believe that political cosmopolitanism is a much wider and more interesting field than has previously been thought. We can endorse a thesis in political cosmopolitanism while opposing the ideal of a world state.

As I understand it, moral cosmopolitanism provides an aim, by reference to which the queries of political cosmopolitanism can be answered.[7] In the previous section, we saw that moral cosmopolitanism has strong

7 The distinction bears some resemblance to that of Rawls' Ideal/Nonideal theory distinction (Rawls 1999, pp. 89-91).

implications for global and domestic institutions, prescribing norms of institutional justice that are global in scope. Such ideal moral standards (i.e., the protection of human rights, etc.) provide us with reference points according to which institutional arrangements can be ranked and assessed, but they do not by themselves provide answers to the more practical question of how they are to be implemented. The nonideal conditions of the actual world impose external constraints on what is currently politically realizable and what can reasonably be hoped for. It is the task of political cosmopolitanism to offer concrete political solutions which bear these constraints in mind. Ideals of political cosmopolitanism – which may, for example, include (a) a world republic, (b) a scattering of independent global, regional, domestic, and municipal governance institutions, or (c) a voluntary pacific federation of states – receive their impetus from moral cosmopolitan theorizing about the universal value of human rights, equal respect for individual interests, the benefits of perpetual peace, etc. But less ambitious cosmopolitan political ideals will replace more ambitious ones if the latter are considered to be too unrealistically utopian.[8]

As Pogge notes, moral cosmopolitan theorizing can be applied to the subject matter of social institutions in two ways. First, one can move directly from the basic concept of moral equality to the political thesis that "social institutions ought to be designed so that they include all human beings as equals" (Pogge 2007, p. 313). This straightforward move does yield the archetypal thesis of political cosmopolitanism: a world republic encompassing or at least open to all human beings. Second, one can move indirectly by entertaining a conception of moral cosmopolitanism that does not demand any particular institutional design outright, but that provides criteria for assessing and ranking alternative institutional designs (social-justice cosmopolitanism) (*Ibid.*, p. 313).

Despite acknowledging this dual path of influence from moral to political cosmopolitanism, Pogge defines *political* (or as he calls it: *legal*) (Pogge [2002] 2008, p. 157; 2007 §1) cosmopolitanism as "committed to a concrete political ideal of a global order under which all persons have equivalent legal rights and duties – are fellow citizens of a universal republic" (Pogge [2002] 2008, p. 175). Surprisingly, while recognizing that social-justice cosmopolitanism can indirectly endorse a plurality of institutional arrangements, Pogge confines the topic of political cosmopolitanism to only one ideal: a universal republic. I don't know why Pogge endorses

---

8 Kant, for instance, refers to the ridicule directed at the 'wild and fanciful' ideal of a world republic as put forth by Abbé St Pierre (1658-1743) and Rousseau (See Kant [1784] 1991, pp. 47-48). Surely this is part of the reason why he opts for the surrogate political ideal of a foedus pacificum, as I shall explain below.

such a narrow definition of the term, apart from reasons of historical precedence. Conceptual definitions, terms of art, can be quite arbitrary anyhow. My claim is that it is more useful to amplify the definition of political cosmopolitanism once we acknowledge the variety of manners in which moral cosmopolitanism can be institutionalized or politically implemented.

Pogge's definition runs two distinct ideals together: the institutional realization of equivalent legal rights and duties for every person on the planet, on the one hand, and the ideal of universal citizenship in a world republic, on the other. Stated as such, neither of these ideals (separately or together) fully defines the enterprise of political cosmopolitanism as I have characterized it. But, if we had to choose between the two, we should choose the first. The second ideal is, again, too narrow. As I said above, it constitutes merely one avenue along which to pursue the political implementation of moral cosmopolitanism. On the other hand, the first ideal is more embracing, but this depends on how we interpret the *range* of legal equivalence. If the complete set of legal rights and duties that apply to every person in the world is to be exactly the same *in all respects*, then this ideal would be too demanding. It would rule out any special legal obligations we might incur towards local forms of authority (i.e., our nation of birth) and thereby rule out the possibility of a multinational global political order that might nevertheless realize certain cosmopolitan ideals. If, on the other hand, this universal set of equivalent rights and duties constitutes only a *minimal* set (i.e., of human rights) on top of which we might pile further rights and obligations, then this could be one way of capturing the common project of political cosmopolitanism, which is concerned with the concrete implementation of a global order that takes equal account of the interests of all human beings.

Consider Kant's political thought, for instance, where a cosmopolitical union of humankind constitutes something like the overriding *telos* of earthly political undertakings. What many commentators often underestimate in reading Kant is the extent to which he remains committed to the ideal of a world republic – what he calls a cosmopolitan constitution or society (also a *civitas gentium*) – throughout his political writings.[9] Kant is of course famous for rejecting the ideal of a world state in favour of a pacific league of nations (*foedus pacificum*) on several grounds, the most quoted of which is his professed fear of a global form of despotism.[10] But,

9 See Kant [1795] 1991, pp. 105-106.

10 Rawls (1999, p. 36) misunderstands Kant as unequivocally rejecting a world-state on these grounds, quoting the following passage in Perpetual Peace ([1795] 1991, p. 114; Also see Kant [1793] 1991, p. 90). Monique Canto-Sperber follows Rawls in this respect (See Canto-Sperber, 2006, p. 268).

as Pogge has rightly observed, this rejection is best read as strategic.[11] Though a world state may be difficult or almost impossible to achieve in practice, Kant asserts, "it is nonetheless the inevitable outcome of the distress in which men involve one another" (Kant [1784] 1991, pp. 47-48). Among the strategic obstacles to the implementation of a world government, according to Kant, is the fact that the present nonideal conditions of the world make it such that nations are averse to limiting their sovereignty under the coercive laws of a world republic.[12] Thus, as a pragmatic intermedium, Kant opts for the negative substitute of a voluntary but gradually expanding pacific federation or congress of states that is likely to prevent war: "The latter may check the current of man's inclination to defy the law and antagonise his fellow, although there will always be a risk of it bursting forth anew," (Kant, [1795] 1991, p. 105) he writes. Pogge is right to suggest that Kant really is committed to a world republic as the highest political ideal, but that he "also understands that a pacific league is more easily reachable from the *status quo,* and that a world republic is more easily reachable from a pacific league than from the *status quo.*" (Pogge, *Forthcoming* § 1) Kant has the ideal cosmopolitical society in sight, but understands that acquiescence to the nonideal conditions of the world is an important aspect of any viable political proposal.

For our purposes, the chief value of looking at Kant's work is its illustration of the intimate relationship between the doctrines of moral and political cosmopolitanism. Kant derives the idea of a world republic from his moral doctrine of a possible *kingdom of ends*, a universal moral community of which each human being is worthy of being an equal member (Kant 1785/1997, pp. 41-45). The moral ideal of a kingdom of ends (much like the Stoic's *cosmic* polis) can become a juridical state if all persons are institutionally guaranteed the external freedoms prescribed by universal moral law under a single global sovereign.[13] According to Kant This universal juridical state is not simply a worthy aspiration, but a moral and political imperative for the entire human race (Kant [1798] 2007, p. 332). Due to the practical conditions alluded to above, however, it is an ideal 'constantly threatened by disunion', and that can only be gradually approximated. Kant thus starts out from an ideal conception of moral cosmopolitanism to consider its non ideal implementation in a conception of political cosmopolitanism. He begins by applying the concept of moral

11 For an excellent defence of this strategic reading of Kant's remarks, see Pogge's "Kant's Vision of a Just World Order" (Forthcoming).

12 Kant also mentions the difficulty of governing "too wide an area of land" (1797/1991, p. 171) and the "contradictory" nature of a world state (1795/1991, p. 102).

13 See Pogge (Forthcoming, § 1). Kant briefly mentions the juridical realization of the kingdom of ends in the ([1785] 1997, p. 46).

cosmopolitanism to the subject matter of social institutions in a *direct* as opposed to *indirect* manner. From his basic commitment to the moral cosmopolitan ideal he straightaway derives the political counterpart-ideal of a world state under which moral equality is institutionally guaranteed. But since nonideal conditions do not permit the imminent realization of a world state, he calls instead for a voluntary union of nations.

I would argue that Kant's surrogate political ideal of a pacific federation is no less a thesis in political cosmopolitanism than is his positive ideal of a world state, (although I understand that this claim is somewhat anachronistic when applied to Kant).[14] Both a world state and a voluntary society of peoples constitute political pathways along which the concept of moral equality can (eventually, if not immediately) find concrete institutional realization, and this is Kant's basic motivating aim in considering the merits of both proposals. I think we ought to follow the grain of Kant's thought in our understanding of political cosmopolitanism. With anchoring in a conception of moral cosmopolitanism, it can embrace not just one political ideal, but a range of ideals that may be more or less politically realizable but nonetheless cosmopolitan.

References

Appiah, K. A. (2007). Cosmopolitanism: Ethics in a World of Strangers. W. W. Norton and Company.

Beitz, C. (2005). "Cosmopolitanism and Global Justice". Current Debates in Global Justice, G. Brock and D. Moellendorf (eds.). Berlin. Springer. Pp. 11-27.

Beitz, C. (2004). "Human Rights and The Law of Peoples". The Ethics of Assistance: Morality and the Distant Needy D.K. Chatterjee (ed.). Cambridge. Cambridge University Press. Pp. 193-217.

Beitz, C. (2000). "Rawls " Law of Peoples". Ethics. Vol. 110. No. 4. Pp. 669-696.

Beitz, C. ([1979] 1999). Political Theory and International Relations. 2nd ed. Princeton. Princeton University Press.

Benhabib, S. (2006). Another Cosmopolitanism. R. Post (ed.). Oxford University Press.

Benhabib, S. (2004). The Rights of Others: Aliens, Residents, and Citizens. Cambridge. Cambridge University Press.

14 Kant considered the idea of a congress of states (and the laws that govern it) to be a thesis in international and not cosmopolitan law. The latter is restricted to the law (or right) of hospitality ([1797] 1991, pp. 164-175).

Buchanan, B. (Forthcoming). "Human Rights and the Legitimacy of the International Order".

Buchanan, A. (2004). Justice, Legitimacy, and Self-Determination: Moral Foundations for International Law. Oxford. Oxford University Press.

Caney, S. (2005). Justice Beyond Borders: a Global Political Theory. Oxford. Oxford University Press.

Canto-Sperber, M. (2006). "The Normative Foundations of Cosmopolitanism" Proceedings of the Aristotelian Society. Vol. 106. No. 2. March 2006. Pp. 265-281.

Griffin, J. (1996). Value Judgment: Improving our Ethical Beliefs. Oxford. Clarendon Press.

Griffin, J. (2001). "First Steps in an Account of Human Rights". European Journal of Philosophy. Vol. 9. No. 3. Pp. 306-327.

Griffin, J. (2008). On Human Rights. Oxford. Oxford University Press.

Honneth, A. (1997). "Is Universalism a Moral Trap? The Presuppositions and Limits of a Politics of Human Rights". Perpetual Peace: Essays on Kant's Cosmopolitan Ideal. J. Bohman and M. Lutz-Bachmann (eds.). Cambridge/Mass. MIT Press 1997. Pp. 155-178.

Kant, I. ([1784] 1991). Idea for a Universal History with a Cosmopolitan Purpose. Kant: Political Writings. Trans. H.B. Nisbet. Introduction H. Reiss (ed.). 2nd enlarged ed. Cambridge. Cambridge University Press. Pp. 41-54.

Kant, I. ([1785] 1997). Groundwork of the Metaphysics of Morals. Trans. M. Gregor (ed.). Introduction C.M. Korsgaard. Cambridge. Cambridge University Press.

Kant, I. ([1793] 1991). On the Common Saying: "This may be true in theory, but it does not apply in practice" Kant: Political Writings. Trans. H.B. Nisbet. Introduction H. Reiss (ed.). 2nd enlarged ed. Cambridge. Cambridge University Press. Pp. 61-93.

Kant, I. ([1795] 1991) Perpetual Peace: a Philosophical Sketch in Kant: Political Writings. Trans. H.B. Nisbet. Introduction H. Reiss (ed.). 2nd enlarged ed. Cambridge. Cambridge University Press. Pp. 93-131.

Kant, I. ([1797]1991a) The Metaphysics of Morals. Trans. Introduction and notes Mary Gregor. Cambridge. Cambridge University Press.

Kant, I. [1797] 1991b). The Metaphysics of Morals. Kant: Political Writings. Trans. H.B. Nisbet. Introduction H. Reiss (ed.). 2nd enlarged ed. Cambridge. Cambridge University Press. Pp. 131-177.

Kant, I. ([1798] 2007). Anthropology from a Pragmatic Point of View. Trans. R.B. Louden. Anthropology, History, and Education. Cambridge edition of the works of Immanuel Kant. G. Zöller and R.B. Louden (eds.). Cambridge. Cambrdige University Press.

Miller, D. (2007). National Responsibility and Global Justice. Oxford. Oxford University Press.

Nussbaum, M. C. (2006). Frontiers of Justice: Disability, Nationality, Species Membership. Cambridge. Belknap Press.

Nussbaum, M. (2000). Women and Human Development: The Capabilities Approach Cambridge. Cambridge University Press.

Nussbaum, M. C. (1997). "Kant and Cosmopolitanism". Essays on Kant's Cosmopolitan Ideal. J. Bohman and M. Lutz-Bachmann (eds.). Cambridge/Mass. The MIT Press. Pp. 25 – 58.

Pogge, T. (Forthcoming) "Kant's Vision of a Just World Order" forthcoming in Tom Hill (ed). A Blackwell Companion to Kant's Ethics. Oxford. Blackwell Publishing.

Pogge, T. ([2002] 2008). World Poverty and Human Rights. Cosmopolitan Responsibilities and Reforms. 2nd ed. Cambridge. Polity 2002.

Pogge, T. ([1993] 2007). "Cosmopolitanism". A Companion to Contemporary Political Philosophy. Goodin, P. Pettit, and T. Pogge (eds). Vol. I. 2nd ed. Oxford. Blackwell Publishing.

Pogge, T. (1994). "An Egalitarian Law of Peoples". Philosophy and Public Affairs. Vol. 23. No. 3. Pp. 195-224.

Rawls, J. (1999). "The Idea of Public Reason Revisited". The Law of Peoples. Cambridge. MA. Harvard University Press.

Rawls, J. ([1993] 1996, 2005). Political Liberalism. Expanded ed. Columbia. Columbia University Press.

Rawls, J. ([1971]1999). A Theory of Justice: Revised Edition. Cambridge. MA. Harvard University Press.

Raz, J. (2007). "Human Rights without Foundations". University of Oxford Faculty of Law Legal Studies Research Paper Series. Working paper no. 14/2007. Available at: http://ssrn.com/abstract=999874

Raz, J. (1986). The Morality of Freedom. Oxford. Oxford University Press.

Rorty, R. (1998). "Justice as a Larger Loyalty". Cosmopolitics: Thinking and Feeling Beyond the Nation. P. Cheah and B. Robbins (eds.). Minneapolis. University of Minnesota Press.

Scheffler, S. (2001). Boundaries and Allegiances: Problems of Justice and Responsibility in Liberal Thought. Oxford. Oxford University Press.

Schofield, M. (1991). The Stoic idea of the City. Cambridge. Cambridge University Press.

Singer, P (2002). One World: The Ethics of Globalization. New Haven & London. Yale University Press.

Singer, P. (1997). "The Drowning Child and The Expanding Circle". New Internationalist. Available at http://www.utilitarian.net/singer/by/199704--.htm

Tasioulas, J. (2007). "The Moral Reality of Human Rights". Freedom From poverty as a Human Right: Who Owes What to the Very Poor? T. Pogge (ed.). Oxford. Oxford University Press.

Tasioulas, J. (2002b). "Human Rights, Universality, and the Values of Personhood: Retracing Griffin's Steps". European Journal of Philosophy. Vol.10. No. 1. Pp. 79-100.

Tasioulas, J. (1998). "Consequences of Ethical Relativism". European Journal of Philosophy, Vol. 6, No. 2. Pp. 172-202.

Taylor, C. (1999). "Conditions of an Unforced Consensus on Human Rights". The East Asian Challenge for Human Rights. J.R. Bauer and D.A. Bell (eds). London. New York. Cambridge University Press.

Waldron, J. (2006). "Cosmopolitan Norms". Another Cosmopolitanism. R. Post (ed.). Oxford. Oxford University Press.

Waldron, J. (2000). "What is Cosmopolitan?". The Journal of Political Philosophy. Vol. 8. No. 2. Pp. 227-243.

Waldron, J. (1992). "Minority Cultures and the Cosmopolitan Alternative". University of Michigan Journal of law Reform. Vol. 25. No. 3-4. Pp. 751-92.

Wenar, L. (2006). "Why Rawls is not a Cosmopolitan Egalitarian". Rawls's Law of Peoples: A Realistic Utopia? Rex Martin and David A. Reidy (eds.). New York. Blackwell Publishing. Pp. 95-115.

Arguing for Justice. Global Justice and Philosophical Argumentation[1]

Gabriele De Angelis

Introduction

The following reflections on the argumentative state of the art in the debate on global justice aim to highlight how most of the theories available conflate moral and political arguments and subordinate the latter to the first. Some of the reasons that account for this evolution may be traced back to a relatively concise range of assumptions about the nature of moral argumentation and its objects, although the fact that very few scholars entertain an explicit reflection on the procedures and methods of enquiry makes this critical assessment more difficult to undertake. However, the fundamental assumptions leading the work of the most renown scholars in the debate on global justice can be summed up as follows:

1. Ethical theory is a rational enterprise that aims to discover true principles and norms by means of argumentative enquiry;
2. If well worked out, arguments suffice to decide on moral dilemmas and controversies;
3. Arguments may be based on the objective moral quality of the situations addressed or the persons affected, so that such a moral quality is to be assimilated to the knowledge of states of affairs in the world and, therefore, framed in terms of truth-like claims (Habermas, 1990, pp. 68, 76). Those arguments that stress "moral intuitions" and values make also an appeal to something that is supposed to be "objective" and universalisable beyond cultural boundaries, as the most widespread thought experiments show.
4. Some other arguments refer neither to "intuitions" nor to "institutions". Instead, they seem to take norms and values for granted – expecting the readers to agree on them; those who follow Rawls are

1 I would like to thank Kok-Chor Tan for raising very interesting critical remarks that helped me improve this paper, although I don't think I could answered them all. I am also indebted to Paulo Barcelos for his very useful comments. Responsibility for the content of my paper is of course entirely my own.

even unlikely to be committed to moral intuitionism.[2] This has consequences, however, on the scope of the arguments, for they will depend on what the audience is ready to accept. With taking values for granted and the consequences for philosophical argumentation I deal in the last section of this essay.

It is therefore no wonder that the bulk of the theories make use of ontological arguments and seek in the nature and qualities of objects (human beings) or situations (relations amongst human beings) the reason why certain moral principles and rules should apply. At the same time, most of them also call for a set of potentially universal moral intuitions that ought to allow for an interculturally valid moral theory. Thus, political relationships amongst persons and peoples are assimilated to moral relations, and political institutions as well as legal and social norms ought not only to conform to what is just and right – i.e., morally "true" – from the ethical point of view, but also translate moral principles in practice, as they were just the consequence of what is morally right.[3]

As I would like to argue in this paper, such a conflation of political and moral argumentation is misleading. In fact, moral and political arguments obey to different conditions of agency, circumscribe two different institutional spheres, and require two different forms of argument *and* practice.

For the sake of clarity I will state right away the gist of my argument. As far as contemporary political philosophy underscores the rational character of the enquiry into ethical principles, it disregards an important theoretical and practical achievement of the modern age, the core assumptions of which have also entered the logics of democratic institutions. This achievement consists in replacing moral truth by legal, and in nowadays Western countries also democratic, authority. With regard to the point I attempt to make it will perhaps suffice to point out one key characteristic of this replacement, as it was highlighted a. o. by Kant in his theory of social contract. Kant's theory establishes a contract the adhesion and loyalty to which is never subject to revision from the part of the participants (Kant [1793] 1970, §2).[4] Besides the historical reasons that have led Kant to suggest a model in which political authority is irrevocable, a decisive theoretical reason is tightly connected with the function of social contract, which is – in the last instance – to take the interpretation of norms from

2 I am indebted to Kok-Chor Tan for this remark.

3 This attitude is well exemplified by Simon Caney: "For people to receive their entitlements it is important that there be political institutions in place whose role it is to protect people's rights" (Caney, 2005, pp. 120-121).

4 See also Kant ([1797] 1996 §46), with some substantial differences with regard to the citizen's legal status in the polity.

the hands of those who are affected by their application and to put it in the hands of a third party. Kant's assumption is that, should the interpretation of norms lie by those who have a stake in the controversy that may arise on their understanding, then this would be equal to the absence not only of any polity, but of any institutional order altogether.[5] This is the reason why Kant's theory – as well as in general all those theories that emphasise the institution of a polity as the most necessary trigger of any political order – can be detached from its historical context, which is the establishment of national states as the new, preponderant form of polity as the outcome of a political will instead of tradition or revelation (Kersting, 1994, p. 23; Burgio, 2006, p. 19), and generalised to political phenomena in general. Likewise, Kant's insight can be generalised beyond the establishment of a polity, as it applies to all institutional arrangements that regulate interactions amongst a plurality of actors.[6]

The lesson we can draw from this – as well as from several modern political theories from Hobbes onwards – is that any possible political order must be based on a form of authority, i.e., on institutional and procedural arrangements, the acknowledgement of which precedes any form of substantive "truth". The specific form this arrangement takes in today's Western countries is democratic procedure. As I will attempt to make clear in the following, the acknowledgement that any political order must rest on a procedural structure as well as on a division of political labour rather than on philosophical or any other source of truth is what distinguishes the realm of politics from ethical reflection. Once this is acknowledged, the status and scope of ethical theory is likely to be seen in a different light.

This acknowledgement is independent of whether the norms in question are controversial or not. Indeed, a political instance of decision-making would be necessary even if there would be a thorough consensus on norms. To make this clear, it is important to see that in everyday life norms are understood as generalisations on a socially and historically embedded experience. In other words, in order to understand norms we need to appeal to cases that illustrate their "application", as the latter is what gives us a clue as to the "meaning" of norms. Such an interrelatedness of norm and application has been cleared up within the hermeneutic tradition (Gadamer [1960] 2004), which points out the role of the examples as a set of background assumptions the understanding of which must be presupposed if the norm is to be rightly assessed. This implies that, con-

---

5 Kant's idea was modelled after several preceding examples, including Hobbes's and Pufendorf's.

6 Some hints at this generalisation can be found in Kant's writings themselves, as for instance in the *Critique of Pure Reason* ([1787] 1998, B 373).

trary to common understanding, the formulation of a norm is not so much a guide to correct moral opinions, but the outcome of the rationalisation of such opinions, and is therefore tied up with assumptions whose plausibility is to be empirically assessed by confronting it with the agreement they can earn in decision-making.

This is to be easily noticed in the debate on global justice, as the chief means of argumentation rely either on some form of "intuition" or on what the institutional shape of the national and international society says about what has to count as an accepted norm. Inasmuch as they attempt to ground universal norms (either universal in scope or in justification) (Caney, 2005, p. 27), both the appeal to pure intuitions and the approach based on institutions encounter a similar difficulty: they assume that what is being brought to the fore is a common, potentially universal core of moral assumptions the universal validity of which is granted either by the thought experiments from which intuitions are worked out or by the wide acknowledgement that the examined institutions enjoy. As far as they support relativism, the same theoretical tools are used to highlight the cultural homogeneity of norms as they emerge out of a supposedly closed or at least well-encompassed cultural environment. That they achieve either goals can be questioned in both cases.

I think it important to remark that the following reflections on the forms of argumentation are not to be interpreted as an attempt to take sides for universalism or relativism. Similarly, the point that I will try to make is neither in favour of those who support the pre-eminence of global norms of justice over national boundaries nor in favour of the opposite stance. Inasmuch as I address some of the prominent arguments made in the debate on global justice, this is only meant to highlight some features that are common to all, independently of the normative content they uphold. The idea about the meaning of norms that I have mentioned above is indeed not to be mixed up with the relativist thesis according to which rules ripen within a given cultural environment and are therefore to be interpreted within a common-sense background that excludes generalisations from the very start. Although supporters of relativism have upheld the same or similar theoretical stances to buttress their theses, the question as to which norms can be generalised or universalised is itself empirical, i.e., political, rather than purely theoretical, and relates back to the role we want to assign to intercultural, international, or transnational agreement in the formulation of norms of universal scope, i.e., to the degree in which we want to achieve universalism of justification. As I will try to show later on, such a question cannot be answered on the basis of a purely theoretical, i.e., truth-confident argumentation either.[7]

It is as well important to emphasise that the position I am going to defend is also to be distinguished from *political realism*. Realism consists in the assumption that politics and ethics represent two separate, and not necessarily congruent, spheres of social action, the first hinging upon what Habermas has summarised as "strategic behaviour" (briefly characterised as orientation to the usefulness of actions for the intended goal, negotiation on the basis of diverging interests, and struggle in which the co-actor is seen as an opponent and competitor for the possess of exclusive and individually distributed goods) (Habermas, 1984, pp. 292, 329), the latter revolving around shared norms that regulate the interaction on the basis of shared and ideally "true" convictions.[8] To complicate the picture, realism occurs in two versions, the first being a descriptive theory of political behaviour based on anthropological assumptions about the egoistic nature of mankind, the second insisting on the normative value of the national interest and power politics in the international arena. Thus, power as the "everlasting essence" of politics is opposed to regimes built in terms of legitimacy and international accountability (Dallmayr, 2002, p. 143). Although realism is less liable to the criticisms I set forth in this paper than ethical globalism, what follows is not meant to support realism neither in its descriptive nor in its normative form, and it does not intend to speak to the pre-eminence of power politics over ethics, nor does it rest on a realist anthropology. Instead, it is meant to question the possibility of arriving at "true" ethical principles by means of philosophical argumentation in general, independently if its scope and whatever its aim.

Rather than with realism or relativism, what follows can be associated with the strand of thought known as "anti-foundationalism". Although the leading supporters of anti-foundationalism have been more akin with relativism than with universalism, the points I will be making ought to be distinguished from relativism as well. Indeed, the core question concerns the relationship between politics and the core assumptions of nowadays (normative) political theory. Anti-foundationalism maintains that moral norms are a subspecies of social norms, and that as such they have to be justified by reference to a cultural and historical, i.e., social and – in a way

7 This is the reason why anti-foundationalist stances can be put to the service of different political and moral views (Brint, Weaver & Garmon, 1995).

8 See a summary of the juxtaposition in the history of political thought in Croce ([1931] 1946) and its further development in Bobbio (1984, pp. 15-6). See also Coady (1991) and Shapiro (2003, pp. 1-2), who shows the current reformulation of the classic dilemma of the choice between ethical and "political" behaviour in contemporary political theory.

which is yet to clear better – consensual manner, rather than resting on a-historical and a-cultural presuppositions. In other words, as there is no procedure that enables us to ground them on truth, they have to be grounded on procedures the outcome of which is open to contingency, but the shape of which is limited by what we – in the wake of our historical experience and its self-conscious reflection – have learned to consider as belonging to our political society's core convictions and practices. This comes near enough to the assumptions of relativists, and yet both approaches are not at all the same. While relativism insists that moral norms have no universal validity, but are restricted to the borders of a culture or a national group, anti-foundationalism contends that norms cannot be grounded in themselves, but only made plausible within the boundaries of culturally and historically mediated views of what is right, which does not exclude that their acknowledged validity can be extended beyond them. Since no procedure guarantees that valid rules are arrived at without relying on assumptions which are themselves not granted by any foundation outside the historically and culturally sedimented morality, the ultimate justification of norms lies with a form of decision, as for instance democratic decision-making. Thus, the difference between the approach I will be defending and truth-based accounts of ethics and morals rests on the role of *political decision*. This does not say anything as to the scope of the norm, which can be confined within the range of a culturally or politically defined group or either be universal, if a correspondent procedure is available, but sets the limits to the justification and the foundation of the norm, and has therefore heavy implications as to the role and function of philosophical enquiry into the definition of its validity.

I. Philosophical Arguments on Global Justice

This section will be devoted to the discussion of the ways in which scholars attempt to achieve firm ground under their feet in order to set up a sound argument. This will help to highlight the assumption mentioned above that we best conceive of a norm as an extrapolation from, and a conceptualisation of, experience through which we attempt to make the social world we live in available for intervention. To do so, I will start from two of the most widespread means to set up moral arguments: the use of intuitions and the working out of the normative presuppositions of legal institutions, then I will move on to the so called "moral quality" and the values that scholars suppose to be inherent in a situation, in order to point out the underlying ontological assumptions. Finally, I will juxtapose these kinds of argument with what can be dubbed "pragmatic arguments", which take into account the controversial nature of moral arguments in general and pave the way to a procedural look onto the choices we have at our disposal to deal with, or in the best case to smooth out, ethical disagreement.

I.1. Intuitions and the elementary semantics of morals

Several scholars draw their normative statements back to their coherence with moral intuitions concerning rules and norms that their interlocutors are likely to share. To encounter a methodological justification of this procedure is rare. It seems to be common amongst scholars to take it for granted without questioning its validity or scrutinise its background assumptions. From the use that numerous scholars make of intuitions, they seem to be a sort of equivalent of the "elementary sentences" (Basisätze/Protokollsätze) of logical positivism (Schlick [1925] 1974). They are meant to deliver a starting point for philosophical argumentation, as we need to know which assumptions about shared beliefs are plausible before elaborating any further on our argument. Argumentation based on intuitions is by far the most common in the literature.[9] Nevertheless, it is difficult to properly understand what scholars mean by "intuition". An intuition is usually presented in a statement on the validity of a norm, implying that such a validity can be assumed as buttressed by popular opinion, and usually refers to (mostly fictitious) cases in which we think the common opinion is at no loss as to which behaviour is to be considered as morally correct.

The way it is commonly used, the appeal to intuitions entails an ambiguity. It can either attempt to remind us of a moral common sense we have acquired through socialisation, and thus presupposes a culturally located moral sense,[10] or it can dig out a supposedly universal moral sentiment that leads to assumptions made independently of any cultural tie. It is as far as the latter applies that intuitions fulfil the role of claiming elementary moral truths, and betray therefore an objectivist attitude towards morals, for – as Mackie has pointed out – they include a commitment to "postulating value-entities and value-features of quite a different

9 Is can be exemplified by statements as: "[...] I rely throughout on a common sense of elementary fairness" (Shue [1993] 2008, p. 211).

10 In this respect we can equate with one another "intuitions" and the attitude to take some norms or values for granted with no further explanation, for at the end of the day the argumentative effect is the same: both are means to put the argumentation on a ground that is itself excluded from justification.

order from anything with which we are acquainted", as moral intuition seems to refer to a faculty "utterly different from our ordinary ways of knowing anything else" (Mackie, 1977, p. 34). It is, however, difficult to make out whether and when scholars intend the one or the other use, as an explicit reflection on this point usually stays out. Conclusions can only be drawn from the argumentative context and the scope of the norms addressed. Thus, examples or "thought experiments" such as the beloved "lonely island" bespeak a will to highlight universal moral assumptions, as they seek to figure out situations in which a rule applies when no cultural context seems to be presupposed.

As far as the latter is the case, I think these assumptions problematic (and this independently of whether they are brought in to support universalism, which is usually the case, or relativism). They in fact presuppose the agreement on something which is only apparently contextless, as it will be clear when looking nearer at the content of such intuitions in the following sections.

I.1.a The analysis of institutions

Argumentations based on institutions are more complex. The analysis of institutions is meant to provide a foundation for a "moral common sense", i.e., to work out the norms that everyone who shares the same institutional environment is liable to accept. They rest on the assumption that moral norms are encoded in the institutional arrangements that frame everyday interactions in a political community. The methodological premise is that a society's moral code can be interpreted according to a scheme or a model that resumes the fundamental moral norms that are valid in it and gives a good description of the morally relevant aspects of social life.

Such a kind of analysis, best exemplified by the work of Robert J. Goodin, shows remarkable similarities with the procedures of legal analysis, inasmuch as it treats the institutional arrangements that give shape to social interactions as the basis on which we can rely of we want to work out the moral codex that the participants supposedly share. Thus, institutions are understood as the embodiment of public morals, and as such they allow to test the coherence between our moral theories and opinions on the one hand, and the tacit moral premises on which existing institutions seem to rest, on the other. When international morals are to be investigated Goodin takes international law to be representative of "what we owe to strangers", whereas domestic public law is indicative "of what we owe to countrymen" (Goodin [1988] 2008, p. 259).

Goodin aims to show that we have duties to foreigners, and that the duties we have towards our co-nationals can be best understood as the specification of universal duties that apply generally to everyone and bind mankind in a single moral community. Goodin holds that supporters of the pre-eminence or even the exclusiveness of national duties tend to assume a non-viable model of how society works, and have therefore a flawed picture of both international and national duties. Goodin's considerations entail a criticism of the idea that the "special relationships" that we entertain with our fellow countrymen are the reason why we have towards them special duties that we do not have to discharge with regard to foreigners. Such a model assumes that societies resemble mutual benefit institutions whereas they, in fact, do not fit this mould. Instead, special relationships just strengthen the universal duties that we have towards anyone else. Goodin's argumentation can be summed up as follows.

Scholars who assume that members of the same political community have special reciprocal duties justify their thesis by the special relationship they entertain with one another. Accordingly, political communities are characterised by stronger positive duties than participants have towards one another. At the same time, negative duties towards co-nationals are weaker than the negative duties that foreigners have towards one another. People's gains "from having others' positive duties toward them strengthened exceeds their costs from having others' negative duties toward them weakened, and it is impossible for them to realize the gains without incurring the costs" (*Ibid.*, p. 266). Thus, members of the national community can restrict their countrymen's liberties more than they can restrict the liberties of a foreigner, but they also owe more to the first than to the latter. Therefore, theories of how special relationships work lead to conceiving societies as mutual benefit institutions.

However, Goodin contends that the mutual benefit model does not really work, for the formal status of citizen is not always clearly related to who is benefiting or paying in the mutual benefit scheme. Resident aliens contribute to the scheme while being excluded from many benefits, and handicapped citizens are net beneficiaries. Goodin assumes that mutual benefit schemes allow no one to draw more than she paid in ("the allocation of any surplus created by people's joint efforts may be left open" *Ibid.*, p. 268). Therefore, society is not acting consistently on the moral premises of mutual benefit schemes, and there must be different and more suitable models (or none). Moreover, in the case of the handicapped we are only glad that society does not operate as a mutual benefit scheme.

As the mutual benefit model does not seem to match with the duties we matter-of-factly have towards our fellow citizens, Goodin suggests an alternative model, according to which special duties are the way how general duties are distributed amongst actors, i.e., assigned to particular agents for their implementation. Thus, state boundaries fulfil the function of regulating such a distribution of duties. Therefore, special duties are derivative from, and subordinate to, general duties, although Goodin concedes that the specific way how the first are distributed cannot be deduced from the latter (*Ibid.*, p. 269). The distribution of responsibilities amongst states is the same as in the mutual benefit theory: within states positive duties are stronger and negative duties or liberties are weaker, whereas among citizens of different states the opposite applies. Goodin's model is also able to accommodate the benefits received by those who do not contribute, just because "[...] we have been assigned responsibility for compatriots in a way that we have not been assigned any responsibility for foreigners". "States are stuck with the charges assigned to them, whether those people are a net benefit to the rest of society or not", and this is the reason why they have to grant assistance to the net beneficiaries in some circumstances (the handicapped, etc.) (*Ibid.*, p. 273). Similarly, in case someone is left out without a protection, as for instance a stateless person or a person whose state fails its duties, then this person falls under the residual responsibility of all (*Ibid.*, p. 274).[11] It descends that agents, including states, that are confronted by this task ought to be given enough resources to take care of the needs of those put under their protection. Should this be not the case, then a reallocation is needed.

This argumentative strategy is open to several criticisms. First of all, the reason why we should opt for a coherentist model of morals deserves justification.[12] It is not at all obvious that a model imported from legal theory – and heavily questioned even within legal debate (Grasnick, 2001; Felix, 1998) – suits the needs of ethics. Nothing impedes that we proceed by adding rules and exceptions and forgo any attempt to build a coherent whole out of the currently accepted moral norms, the origin of which usually does not betray any all-encompassing coherentist design. The reason why a rational reconstruction should delete the historical contingency of rule-making needs justification and is not necessarily bound to success. This shows up in the examples quoted above, for the model that Goodin suggests is formulated *ad-hoc* to include some norms the existence of which we can attest, but is neither the only possible model nor the most

11 For an alternative, but equally universal, justification of special duties as a subspecies of universal or cosmopolitan duties see Nussbaum ([2002] 2008, p. 311).

12 In the present context, "coherentist" does not mean that the justification of beliefs about norms descends from their coherence with the rest of our beliefs, as in epistemological coherentism, but indicates only the assumption that we can make sense of legal norms by finding out a single model of morals from which they all descend as a consequence.

plausible in itself. Instead, it seems apt to convince only those who already aim at a universal justification of norms, and raise no claim as to its correspondence to common-sense assumptions about the origin of acknowledged norms.[13]

Moreover, one of the main difficulties inherent in institutional analysis becomes apparent when compared with the opposite strategy, which consists in criticising existing institutions on the grounds that they fail to match the intuitions we have with regard to the moral quality of a given situation.[14] A similar procedure consists in establishing an analogy between society (or international society, or international relations) and an organisational model whose general rules are better known to us and therefore more manageable as a term of comparison. Scholars have used this reverse strategy on several occasions, as highlighted by the following example, taken from the debate on the ownership of natural resources. To ground his thesis that the world's natural resources must be the joint possession of mankind, Brian Barry parallels the distribution of the peoples on earth to a lottery, i.e., to a mechanism of casual allocation of goods deprived of any "moral quality" (Barry [1982] 2008, p. 197). The gist of his argument consists then in rejecting possible objections to this comparison.[15]

The point in such an argumentative strategy is to disregard the current institutional codification of the ownership of natural resources in order to compare it with "intuitions" that appeal to our moral sentiment and tell us, as in Barry's case, that everything which is equal to a lottery produces morally unacceptable outcomes and ought therefore to be redressed. This is a reason not to accept institutional codifications. It speaks rather to the opposite assumption: institutional arrangements (like internationally valid rules of ownership and disposal) can reflect a morally questionable state of affairs.

---

13 For a deeper discussion see Tan (2004, pp. 177-8).

14 Thomas Hurka ([1997] 2008, p. 380) invites us for instance to understand national partiality by similarity with other forms of partiality which may be closer to our common understanding; so we can ask whether national partiality is more similar to familial or to racial partiality as two expressions of the same attitude that we are better acquainted with.

15 The remaining part of his argument is then pragmatic, as his premises do not grant the detailed conclusion he wants to draw. In fact, he suggests that the principle of global ownership be satisfied by means of a tax on the governments of rich countries proportional to GDP per capita; such a tax ought to be distributed among poor countries as a sort of negative income tax, and compounded by a severance tax on extraction of natural resources and a shadow tax on the value of land (Barry [1982] 2008, p. 200). These are of course political decisions that can be backed by the general principle he states, but do not descend from it as an immediate consequence.

The argumentative strategies illustrated above seem to share a common, though mostly tacit, premise, according to which any attempt to reconstruct just arrangements must rely on the coherence of a "moral universum", i.e., on the coherence that our judgements entertain with institutionally codified rules or moral pre-judgements or "intuitions". However, such a coherence can only be the object of *agreement*, for we cannot rely on any fixed philosophical procedure to work it out. The more so, as our moral pre-judgements cannot be expected to be entirely consistent with the social practices we live in.

I.2. The moral quality of a situation

Alongside intuitions and institutions, a second fundamental distinction concerns the objects of argumentation. Scholars can attempt to highlight *natural duties*, *values* that people are supposed to support, or the *moral qualities* that are assumed to be inherent to interactions we entertain with one another.

Scholars who seek after the *moral qualities* that are supposed to be inherent in a situation or relationship that occurs among a given set of actors have to assume that norms are to be discovered rather than stipulated or agreed upon.[16] Indeed, if a certain moral quality lies at the core of a given relationship, then it is independent of the will of the participants. This can be grounded on two distinct reasons: either does the norm implicit in the relation already belong to the commonly shared moral code, or it calls *in itself* for a certain moral conduct, independently of whether the participants have ever agreed that it belongs to the acknowledged moral code they all share. In the latter case, which seems to be the more widespread in the literature, this argument takes the form of an *ontological argument*, as it is the very nature of a relation or a situation that entails the validity of a moral norm. This kind of arguments may be tied up with natural duties, as the latter are shown to emerge out of a situation that imposes on the actors the allegiance to certain norms to which that have never explicitly submitted themselves.[17]

16 This latter strategy can be said to be "cognitive" inasmuch as it treats moral claims as statements about matters of fact, a distinction that has been clarified by Habermas (1990).

17 "Thus, if the basic structure of society is just, or as just as it is reasonable to expect in the circumstances, everyone has a natural duty to do his part in the existing scheme. Each is bound to this institutions independent of his voluntary acts, performative or otherwise" (Rawls, 1971, p. 115).

In the debate on global justice, this kind of arguments is resorted to in order to avoid "morals by consent" as a source of obligation. The moral quality of the interaction is often seen as an alternative to agreement, and is therefore akin to natural duties, values, etc. As to the particular uses of this kind of argument, one of the most frequent forms in which they occur aims to show how a certain relation that people are assumed to associate with a moral responsibility in the national or local community also applies among the inhabitants of the earth. The argument takes therefore the form: "X applies at the national or local level, and it entails – as such, not due to the local scope of its application – a given moral responsibility towards a certain class of actors; but x also applies at the global or international level, so that it then, too, entails the same responsibility". Such an argument is usually set up in order to show that there is indeed a global responsibility (to help foreign poor, to share one's nation health, to relieve famine, to introduce a global ownership of natural resources, etc.). It goes for instance like this: Insofar as we participate in the system of international treatises and institutions that regulate global trade "and share some responsibility for its design, we are morally implicated in any contribution it makes to ever-increasing global economic inequality". Therefore, national borders no longer work as "moral watersheds" (Pogge, 2008a, pp. xvii, xviii). Being the moral relevance of national borders one of the most intensely discussed cases of an object's moral relevance, this will be the case that I stake out here for further discussion.

Charles Beitz argues that wealthy countries have an obligation to restructure the world economic system and to devolve part of their income to developing countries. If there is a global scheme of social cooperation, then states' boundaries have no moral significance and do not mark the limits of social obligations (Beitz [1975] 2008, p. 34). There is a threshold of interdependence "above which distributive requirements such as the global difference principle are valid, but below which significantly weaker principles hold" (*Ibid.*, p. 38). "What cannot be argued is that a wealthy nation's general right to retain its domestic product [to support domestic welfare programmes] always overrides its obligation to advance the welfare of the lesser-advantaged groups elsewhere" (*Ibid.*, p. 42).

A similar argumentative structure has been upheld by Simon Caney: "To establish that principles of justice apply only within the state and not at the global level one would have to supply an account of how the domestic realm differs from the global realm in a morally significant way. More precisely, one must show that (1) all principles of distributive justice apply only when some property (or set of properties) is present; (2) that property (or set of properties) exists at the domestic level; and finally (3) that property (or set of properties) does not exist at the global level" (Caney, 2008,

p. 488). The moral quality of the international arena, which can be either homogeneous or heterogeneous with the national arena, is the basis according to which it must be possible to assert that a responsibility applies or does not apply internationally or globally.

This is the core of the diatribe between Simon Caney and Michael Blake. The argument of the latter goes as such: (4) The state is a coercive actor; (5) States have a duty to justify their policies to those whom they coerce; (6) A commitment to justification entails a commitment to 'relative' principles of distributive justice; (7) States should adopt 'relative' principles of distributive justice in their domestic policy; (8) The global order is not coercive; (9) 'Relative' principles of distributive justice do not apply at the global level (Blake [2001] 2008, pp. 665-76; Caney, 2008, p. 499).

In such a case the dispute will set off right from the start when it has to be decided whether there is coercion at the global level and whether this is such as to allow for or to require a certain commitment.[18] In this case the controversy is not about the normative basis, for the contestants share the same normative assumption according to which coercion, justification and obligation are somehow related (although Caney refuses to restrict obligation to cases of coercion and admits of a brighter concept of coercion than Blacke's), but rather about whether a certain state of affairs subsists or not. Indeed, both scholars accept the morally relevant premise according to which coercion implies a certain moral commitment (x) and then discuss whether y (the international arena) is or is not a case of x.

A further critical point concerns the *meaning of the terms used.* Caney evidently equals coercion with whatever affects people's life as a consequence of somebody else's behaviour, whereas Blake contents himself with direct coercion as exercised by political institutions.

The interpretation of the moral quality of national boundaries depends on further assumptions that scholars make with regard to the national political space. Those who embrace an interactional approach spell it out as a relation of physical proximity and distance to others, whereas

18 "Blake's answer appears to be that whereas the domestic realm directly coerces individuals the global realm does not. The problem with this line of argument is that it is not clear to me why it matters if international legal institutions directly coerce individuals. Why is this a morally relevant difference? Suppose, for example, that institutions exercise coercion over entities like corporations and that, as a consequence of this, they coerce individuals and in doing so jeopardise their standard of living. In these cases A is coercing B who in turn coerces C. On Blake's account there is no need for A to justify his or her conduct to C because his or her coercion is indirect. But this is counter-intuitive: the salient point is that A has led to a disadvantage being coercively imposed on C. The first objection thus stands: Blake has not identified a morally significant difference between the domestic and global realms" (Caney, 2008, p. 500).

those who highlight the political constitution of a national community, i.e., its institutions, highlight the political obligations that citizens have towards one another.

The first approach starts from the general assumption that there is a duty to help the needy if this can be achieved at a reasonable cost on the side of the person who gives aid. Thus, assistance is required if it's urgently needed by one of the parties and if the other can give it without incurring excessive costs (Walzer [1981] 2008, p. 149).[19] Such a duty is also addressed as a duty to behave humanely: "If it's in our power to prevent something very bad from happening without thereby sacrificing anything of comparable importance, we ought, morally, to do it" (Singer [1972] 2008). Nagel makes this attitude explicit when he maintains that help is due to the truly impoverished because of their humanity (Nagel [1977] 2008, p. 56). If we agree on that, then we recognize general duties of humanity. Furthermore, those who assume that physical distance does not affect moral relations also conclude that such duties apply globally, and that there is therefore a global duty of aid.

More problematic is to ground this duty on generalisable reasons. Especially controversial is if such a duty rests on reciprocity, in which case we had to acknowledge a duty of *mutual* aid, or if it subsists without this condition. Thus, Barry distinguishes between a duty bound up with norms that are valid within the range of a certain community and norms that apply generally, without being tied up with expectations of reciprocity. Adopting the widespread example of rescuing a person (often a child) in danger, Barry puts forward the following example: "Perhaps what motivates us in agreeing that there is an obligation to rescue the [drowning] child is that is an unarticulated contextual assumption that the child belongs to our community [...] and that there are norms [...] calling for low-cost rescue from which we stand to gain if ever we find ourselves in need of rescue". If there is a world community, then there is a global obligation of mutual aid. But we had an obligation to rescue someone in danger even if we had no reasonable expectation to be reciprocated in case of need (if we were travelling in a foreign country and saw someone drowning). Barry concludes that obligations of justice are different from obligations of humanity (Barry [1982] 2008, pp. 188-9). The first apply within a given political community whose members nurture legitimate and institutionally codified expectations towards one another, the latter apply

19 See also Miller's Principle of Nearby Rescue: "One has a duty to rescue someone encountered closeby who is currently in danger of severe harm and whom one can help to rescue with means at hand, if the sacrifice of rescue does not itself involve a grave risk of harm of similar seriousness or of serious physical harm, and does not involve wrongdoing" ([2004] 2008, p. 521).

wherever a certain situation is given, as it descends from the mere ability to help at a reasonable cost. In this case, proximity is a positive reason to help, as it is immediately connected with the practical chance to intervene. *The presupposition is that such an intervention belongs to a moral code everyone is expected to agree upon. In such a case, the moral quality of a situation goes along with a recognised value, i.e., the value of human life and the consequent obligation to save it whenever this is possible and reasonable.*

The second relevant application of the rule of proximity or distance concerns the relief of economically caused sufferings worldwide. Scholars who have dealt with the matter have attempted to show the moral irrelevance of physical proximity. A favourite application is famine. Several scholars who have stressed a duty to relieve famine have engaged in the attempt to highlight direct consequences of organised and institutionally backed actions whose direct consequences result in people of less well-off countries suffering severe detriments to their life-conditions or even death for famine. *Such a strategy is based on the assumption that we are responsible for everything that stands in a direct causal relationship with our course of action.* Starting from the assumption that persons have a right not to be killed unjustifiably, and therefore a duty not to kill unjustifiably, Onora O'Neill has shown how the unequal control of resources worldwide directly results in unacceptable outcomes. Even if an actor legitimately exercises her property rights, these cannot override another's right not to be killed unjustifiably. Such a case is for instance given if a company invests abroad, but repatriates most of the profit, leaving the labourers with less than necessary to live on in such a way that their survival expectation is lower than "might have been" (O'Neill [1975] 2008, p. 10) had the company not invested there. The investors are actively doing something for somebody else to die, which is equal to killing her. "Foreign investment that raises living standards, even to a still abysmal level, could not be held to kill, for it causes no additional deaths, unless there are special circumstances [...]" (*Ibid.*, p. 11). Such special circumstances could be given if the investor raises the living standard at the expenses of other people in a developing country, for instance by escaping her duty to give her fair contribution to local development due to the externalisation of transaction costs.

To a similar conclusion comes Nagel ([1977] 2008, p. 52), who starts from the assumption that there must be something morally wrong with a system that allows economic actors to exchange goods in such a way that the prices of what is fundamental for survival raise above the level at which people from less-developed countries can afford them. As the critical point lies with the entitlements and property rights that allow for transactions to take such a dynamic, he maintains that such a system must be subjected to moral scrutiny, as it turns out to be a system with moral characteristics.

Evidently, the success of all of these arguments depend on finding an agreement on what is morally relevant. Several authors seem to agree on the fact that morally relevant is everything that can be drawn back to human intentional action. Accordingly, we ought to shoulder responsibility for anything we contribute to bring about through our actions or omissions, and the degree of our responsibility is assessed on the basis of the values or goods that we either further or damage, the causal relationships we are able to make out, and the chain and the degrees of responsibilities we feel we carry towards others.

On the other hand, the opposite attitude is also widespread according to which situations are morally relevant independently of any kind of agency. Thus, Nagel thinks a social minimum standard of living morally justified inasmuch as morally arbitrary factors have an influence on the distribution of wealth. Development, history, population, etc. are morally arbitrary "as far as the people involved are concerned" (Nagel [1977] 2008, p. 55). The not obvious consequence that several scholars attempt to draw is that situations that subsist in the absence of any intentional action, i.e., not being a consequence of anyone's intentional behaviour, may have to be lifted as "morally arbitrary". So contends Brian Barry that even if past acts or omissions of the population or the government have led to famine etc., the one who suffers this death or starvation is not to be held responsible for it (Barry [1982] 2008, p. 181). Likewise, scholars usually consider the place where a person was born as equally accidental, which implies that the consequences of being born in a place blessed with economic and social advantages or rather fraught with grievances ought to be somehow re-balanced (Nussbaum [2002] 2008, p. 308).

As it emerges out of the preceding examples, rather than being rooted in the "objective" characteristics of a situation the assessment of the occurrences that set off our moral concern depends on the assumptions we make as to the rules that govern responsibility. In the above mentioned examples these relate to the relationship between power (understood as limitation of an otherwise unrestricted individual freedom) and justification; agency, causation and restitution; moral worth, value of human life, and personal responsibility in one's own plight, etc. Evidently, all arguments presented above make appeal to the coherence between some principles that the readers are supposed to share and their application to cases that transcend their usual scope. This is especially the case when the issue revolves around international or global justice, for scholars intend then to show that what is relevant within the national sphere is also relevant in situations that take place outside these borders. However, such a relevance can only be assessed on the basis of shared assumptions: if proximity is held irrelevant to moral behaviour, then it should indeed be irrelevant in general, if responsibility depends on causation, and causation only, and causation connects events across borders, then responsibility should extend across borders also, etc.

Thus, all the examples illustrated above rest finally on the coherence of a set of moral rules given some general principles that establish a link between agency and responsibility. The underlying expectation is that the audience can be convinced of the validity of certain norms that represent the application of general principles to more specific cases, and such expectation is (implicitly) justified by the fact that those principles are thought to belong to an already established moral code. As far as the assumptions are accepted, they can serve as the basis for further conclusions as long as the specific cases can be subsumed under them. In other words, the positions presented above start from the assumption that the coherence with some general principle is enough to motivate an audience to accept certain norms. This implies that a consensus can be achieved on: the premises – i.e., the general principles –, the description of the situations to which they should apply – i.e., the characterisation of what is morally relevant to it as well as the empirical assumptions that justify the causal nexus –, and (implicitly) on the absence of any limiting conditions and rules (which often remains implicit or not immediately thematic). In no case is the assumption justified that the moral quality of a situation is inherent in the situation itself (besides, such an agreement does not mean that the norms are stipulated, but that they are *acknowledged*, whatever their source). That the allegiance to a (supposedly anterior) moral code is essential to moral argumentation is particularly evident when values are discussed.

I.3. Values and intuitions

Starting from their definition, *values*, a further premise of most moral arguments, are in themselves controversial. As a first approximation they can be spelled out as a concern that we have for something or somebody.[20] They can also define what is worth striving for and are addressed in the

20 So defines Pogge different moral attitudes towards others according to the scope of our moral concern: individualism is thus characterised by our "ultimate concern" with "humans beings rather than families, tribes, ethnic, cultural, or religious communities"; universality by our "ultimate concern" with "every living human being *equally*" rather than with members of specific groups; and generality by the "global force" that universalists ascribe to the latter attitude, so that everyone should be concerned with everyone else, not just with friends, countrymen, etc. (Pogge [1992] 2008b, p. 356).

literature in the form of beliefs.[21] In the literature on global justice, values tend to be understood as *a term which is meant to describe a widely shared attitude towards what is of importance in individual life. A value is an interpretation of what people cherish as belonging to the foundations of their life-project.* A further strategy consists therefore in taking a value for granted and to show how its coherent pursuit implies certain norms of moral conduct. The first part of Blake's argument quoted in the former section can illustrate this:

(1) Autonomy is valuable; (2) Each person is entitled to attain a decent standard of living (where this is defined in absolute terms)/each person is entitled to the material resources necessary for autonomous action; (3) A commitment to autonomy entails that a coercive political system which restricts persons' autonomy needs to be justified to those whom it coerces; (4) The state is a coercive actor; (5) States have a duty to justify their policies to those whom they coerce; (6) A commitment to justification entails a commitment to 'relative' principles of distributive justice; (7) States should adopt 'relative' principles of distributive justice in their domestic policy (Blake [2001] 2008, pp. 678, 686; Caney, 2008, pp. 498-9).

The value called on here is "autonomy", understood as the ability to shape one's own existence according to one's own preferences by exploiting the resources available to the person, and is then spelled out as, or boils down to, a limitation on public taxation and a duty to justify whatever amount the government wants to exact from the citizen. Consider also the following example.

When developing his argument for the global ownership of natural resources, Steiner contends that peoples have rights prior to any distribution of goods, and theories of equal distribution must identify in these rights what is to be equal from the start. To these rights belongs also the right to untransformed and untransferred things allotted in equal domains towards which all others have a duty of forbearance. These things are our bodies and raw natural resources, as access to things external to our bodies "is a necessary condition to the occurrence of any action" (Steiner [1999] 2008, p. 640). The basis of such an argument are theories of social contract, which presuppose the original, pre-social ownership of, i.e., the prior right to, what is object of contract or restitution (posterior rights) (*Ibid.*, 2008, p. 639). A person owes restitution if she received more than her initial share. All earth resources constitute a global fund. Therefore, "liabilities to

21 In order to simplify the matter, I will focus exclusively on how values are defined and discussed in the literature on global justice, but we need to bear in mind that philosophical and sociological discussions of values usually go well beyond this. On the sociological traditions see Hechter (1992), Alexander & Smith (1993), and Powers (2000).

pay into the fund accrue to owners of territorial sites and are equal to the value of the site they own, and claims to equal shares of that fund are vested in everyone" (*Ibid.*, p. 641).

A stronger version of the allegiance to values subordinates the scope of the validity of norms to some goods that are to be preserved within a certain political or cultural community. In the debate on global justice, some scholars subject norms that are to be acknowledged as valid among a community larger than the national one to the maintenance of local customs and conditions of cultural integrity.

Michael Walzer has argued in these terms when defending the normative priority of the national sphere over international or global duties. He maintains that, in order to increase the likelihood of a peaceful coexistence of national communities while preserving their internal cultural differences, state borders are to work as a shield that deflects the cultural and social pressures that may come from abroad: "Neighbourhoods can be open only if countries are closed, or rather, only if countries are potentially closed" (Walzer [1981] 2008, p. 153). It is under this condition only that states can grant loyalty, security, and welfare, and only then can neighbourhoods be indifferent associations built according to market capacities and personal preference, in which people are able to overcome or do without rigid parochialism towards one another: "To tear down the walls of the state [...] is not to create a world without walls, but rather to create a thousand petty fortresses" (p. 153). The distinctiveness of cultures and groups is a value most people believe in, Walzer concludes, and in order to safeguard them closure must be permitted somewhere else.

One of the principal difficulties with value-assumptions is that they in fact already presuppose, rather than grounding, a specific application as well as a historical, institutional, and cultural frame. Thus, the first difficulty that argumentations based on shared values encounter consists in the assessment and definition of the values themselves. Values are often tacit and culturally rooted, as is the understanding of the fundamental concepts scholars make use of as well as the taken-for-granted character of the assumptions they rely on. This kind of biases is well known at least since the communitarian critique of liberal morality.

As a matter of fact, the interpretation of the concepts used in the argumentation has an impact on the cultural scope of the latter. To illustrate this we can take up once more the Blake-Caney controversy. A point of convergence between the two is the idea that coercion and individual autonomy generally stand opposite one another. This is the reason why both scholars require that power be justified, as opposed to power is the private sphere, especially intended as the individual property owned by those who could be affected by the enforcement of the norm that the political community agrees upon. As distributive justice obviously affects individual property (either positively or negatively, but what needs to be justified is especially its negative incidence), the diatribe boils down to paying taxes, how much and in order to achieve what.

It is important to remark that this is a specifically north-American approach to the matter, the underlying assumption being that the individual assigns to political authority just so much legitimacy as it is produced by a universalist moral argument stating either what everyone owes to others or what is due to political authority (both argumentative strategies can converge). Willingly or not, Anglo-Saxon (and increasingly European scholars as well) tend to assign to the political system only a residual role: the state or the international arena are not a (factual, hypothetical or possible) space of collective political responsibility in which the people concerned by the consequences of the decisions ought to be at the same time recognised as their authors, but as a sort of provider of services that charges us with costs for which we demand an account.

Thus, when Miller spells out the foundation of right and wrong in apparently functional ways as something that satisfies a social demand he does in fact nothing else than softening up the liberal principle of individual autonomy – understood as a right to personal, unshared possession of private goods – through a principle of universal mutual respect: "The terms of self-governance in virtue of which someone conducts herself in a morally responsible way are terms that she could want all to share while respecting all. [...] an act is wrong just in case it violates every code that all could self-respectfully share" (Miller [2004] 2008, pp. 510-511). Thus, what actually is an ad-hoc solution to accommodate both the supremacy of individual needs and the universal duty to help the needy appears to be a consequence that descends from two more abstract principles on which people are supposed to agree. However, as it becomes clear when it comes to spelling out what is meant by "self-governance" and "equal respect for all", these principles are in fact but the distillation of a historical experience, and are therefore "void" without the examples and applications that illustrate their consequences. In this respect, it is the "consequences" of their "application" that – pragmatically – clarify both their meaning and the degree of agreement they are likely to encounter among the audience.

The cultural bias of moral argumentation has been addressed in a synthetic and impressive way by MacIntyre, who points out how actors learn their moral code in a specific cultural context. As highlighted above, norms have to be illustrated by reference to moral goods, very much like the debate on global justice is replete with cases and example that are supposed to immediately speak to our moral conscience, as in the case of the drowning child or the starving poor. However, the moral goods by reference to which moral rules are to be justified are tied up with a particular kind of social life, relationships, etc. As a consequence, MacIntyre highlights how even the moral irrelevance of my birthplace as well as of the life conditions I found in the society I was born into is an ultimately poor argument. In fact, the hypothetical assumption that if I were born somewhere else I would also enjoy some other goods does not diminish the cultural specificity of what I actually enjoy and of the person I am, for goods only exist as particularised ones. Therefore, "detached from my community, I will be apt to loose my hold upon all genuine standards of judgement" (MacIntyre [1984] 2008, p. 128).

Such a conclusion can be understood in two different ways: as a plead for relativism and localism or as the claim that whatever meaning we ascribe to a "value", the examples that we need to make in order to illustrate it will usually be accessible only or preferentially to people who share with us a certain "moral" and institutional history, and therefore cherish some moral goods, are receptive to determinate associations, and grasp the terms in which we frame the debate ideally without any further effort. How far this is the case is, however, a purely empirical question.

I.5. Pragmatic arguments

A further kind of arguments, that deserves to be called "pragmatic", is worth special consideration. Pragmatic arguments respond to a problem that arises in practical controversies on a given issue, and aim to encounter a solution even in the absence of a shared justification in order to ensure some goods. To do so, pragmatic arguments attempt to take into account the distribution of moral opinions within a political community or across different communities, and ask how the distance between the conflicting cultural convictions can be bridged in order to achieve certain results, as for instance the securement of environmental standards or the protection of fundamental rights. Thus, these arguments are goal-oriented and ad-hoc. Although they may rely on value-orientations and thus resemble some arguments treated before (I.3.), their specific difference consists in their forfeiting any assumption about the philosophical justification or the cultural generalisability of the goods they aim to secure. For instance, in defending specific duties amongst co-nationals as part of a political "collective project" in which all participants are supposed to engage, Miller sets up a multifaceted argument a central element of which concerns the relationship between special duties and the stability of national governments. Accordingly, compatriots are part of a "life-determining collective project" in which I have a duty to participate; if a government's stability and effectiveness depend on the citizens' participation in a common "life-determining collective project", then every participant has to show all others special loyalty, the exact cost of which is to be weighed against other commitments (e.g., familiar) and other projects (Miller [2004] 2008, p. 514). Miller qualifies these demands as "political", and I take this to mean that they depend on political decision rather than on properly moral norms. They in fact go back to the desirability of a certain political arrangement, the maintenance of which depends on the satisfaction of some given empirical conditions to which moral demands are to be subordinated. Some ultimate goals decide therefore on the scope of moral arguments.[22] He makes use of a similar argument in favour of the duty to help the needy worldwide, which would descend from the fact that we are likely not to want to live in a world in which the reliability of international norms depends on fear of retaliation (of the poor against the rich), but on self-respectful loyalty based on concern for others (*Ibid.*, p. 516).

Charles Taylor argues in a pragmatic way when he contends that no "adequate terms for whatever universals we think we may discern between different cultures" are at present available to us. And yet, this would not be an insurmountable hindrance to establishing some universally acknowledged and enforced means to protect human life and life-conditions, as what we need to formulate for an overlapping consensus are certain norms of conduct. "[...] One can presumably find in all cultures condemnations of genocide, murder, torture, and slavery, as well as of, say, "disappearances" and the shooting of innocent demonstrators" (Taylor [1999] 2008, p. 407).[23] The context of Taylor's remark is the debate on whether there are moral universals, whether it is possible to detect or achieve a cross-cultural agreement on them, and whether the content or the form of human rights are such as to be convincingly applied in all cultures generally. His strategy consists in affirming the supposedly universal aversion from certain conducts independently of the legal form or the exact philosophical justification of the ban we wish to put on them. The readiness to step back from the adhesion to either philosophical-cultural convictions or institutional forms when it comes to discussing the possible worldwide protection of human life represents a pragmatic attitude that looks at the concrete results in terms of factual standards of personal safety and integ-

---

22 This does not rule out that the political project may itself be defined in moral terms, as Miller does when he maintains that we must be concerned with others as persons (rather than in the pay-off of my participation) and ought therefore to help others even in case they are not able to contribute to the common project (Miller [2004] 2008, pp. 507, 515).

23 For a similar account of "fundamental human interests" to be protected by human rights see Buchanan, (2004, pp. 134-7).

rity rather than taking for granted the complex of doctrines and institutions that made the history of human rights in Western countries. Although Taylor wants his thesis to be understood as the quest for an "overlapping consensus", his suggestion is as a matter of fact not to be easily distinguished from a "modus vivendi", inasmuch as both the modes of justification and the ethical form of the results he aims to achieve are left to the political imagination of the peoples involved.

A further remarkable attempt to allow for pragmatic arguments to win out over more fundamental opinions is suggested by Charles Beitz (2001), who weds himself to a position that echoes the realist interest in unilateralism when he maintains that the function of international law is to constrain the states' behaviour in the international arena. Universalist human rights are thus supposed to set a standard that does not necessarily correspond to the lowest common denominator of all cultures. Instead, Beitz sees human rights as "a political construction intended for certain political purposes", which "is to be understood against the background of a range of general assumptions about the character of the contemporary international environment" (Beitz, 2001, p. 276). As such, human rights ought to fulfil three functions: putting a constraint on domestic constitutions of states and the rules of international organisations, describing goals of development applicable to all contemporary societies, and finally furnishing grounds for political criticism on the part of international and transnational actors, including NGOs and citizens of global civil society. If such a pragmatic and unilateral approach is taken, neither a doctrine of natural rights nor any comprehensive doctrine is needed, although in accepting the doctrine we might be moved by such beliefs (*Ibid.*, p. 277).[24]

This kind of arguments forsake a general philosophical account of norms and opt for a convergence on results on the basis of some functional considerations. They furthermore give different weight to *consent* as a presupposition for valid norms and – what is more important – make thematic the *audience* to which they address their claims (national communities in Miller's, the world populations in Taylor's, liberals as the ideal-type of the common political opinion in affluent countries in Tan's, and that part of the international community that stresses human rights in

24 All in all, Beitz's theses are far from being purely "pragmatical", as his statement about the unacceptability of genocide testifies. Thus, if we were to draft human rights according to the culturally specific moral codes of the different societies, we might turn out allowing genocide if we encountered into a racist and violent society. This is not acceptable inasmuch as we assume that "[...] the ground of our belief that genocide is a great wrong has to do not with the fact that other people agree it is so, but with the nature and consequences of genocide itself" (Beitz, 2001, p. 274; Beitz quotes Scanlon 1998, pp. 337-8).

Beitz's case). As I hope to make clear in what follows, although both elements may seem peripheral to any "pure" normative interest, they are indeed of the utmost importance for argumentation in general.

II. Moral arguments and political decisions

The former overview of the most common kinds of arguments used in the debate on global justice casts light on the fact that the allegiance to a shared moral code, rather than the inherent ontological quality of moral occurrences, is a (usually unstated and in most cases underestimated) presupposition of argumentation. Furthermore, the former reflections draw our attention to the following, also as a rule unstated, assumptions that I think lie at the basis of the attitude of most scholars towards moral questions. First of all, political decision is seen as a subspecies of moral judgement: it must be led by knowledge of what is right. Moral judgement, as philosophically informed judgement, states the conditions at which political decisions are legitimate. Politics ought to be at least in accordance with moral principles.

The last assumption is not at all obvious. In fact, in the history of democratic theory legitimacy has been conceived of either as the realisation of a set of ethical principles which ought to inform decision-making processes or as a procedure the correct application of which grants the legitimacy of the outcome. The philosophical arguments mentioned in the previous paragraphs seem to support the first stance, inasmuch as they aim to restrain the range of possible outcomes while binding their legitimacy to moral conditions that are apparently independent of any procedure. As a matter of fact, democratic theory has also attempted to trace the limits that encompass democratic legitimacy, for instance in that it tries to define the concept of fairness that political decision-making is to satisfy.

In the light of this widespread attitude towards political institutions, it is worthwhile to remind of the existence of a line of thought that draws a sharper distinction between the scope of moral arguments and democratic decision-making. Several examples can be made, but I will sketch just three of the most relevant, delivered by Ernst Tugendhat, John Rawls, and Richard Rorty.

II.1. Tugendhat

Tugendhat's ethical theory moves from the assumption that moral and legal norms, and customs, are to be interpreted as restraints on the search for one's own good (likewise Rawls [1989] 1999, p. 449). Thus, he explicitly puts his theory in the context of a society in which individual autonomy is understood as the ability to decide one's own course of life according to a rule an actor prescribes to herself. Such an actor gives priority to her own judgement rather than to inherited norms, and subjects the latter to her own scrutiny and interpretation or is at least expected and has a concrete chance of doing so. In such a context, whilst in the case of legal norms and customs the question as to what the ruling norm is can be decided on purely empirical grounds, moral norms address the question as to whether a given ruling norm is also right. "Right" can a norm be either with reference to one's own personal good, in which case we are confronted with a subjective preference, or in general, in which case we are facing a claim of generalisability. Again, it is an empirical question which one of the two is the case in actual interactions. The decision depends on the form of the sentence, i.e., on the degree of generalisability expressed by the use of the copula and its possible restrictions within the sentence. The rationale of a norm *in itself*, as opposed to the judgement as to whether the validity of a norm is good *for me*, consists then in its generalisability. The canonical form of a moral judgement is then "It is good that the norm x is valid". This stage of moral judgement, in which the convergence of individual preferences on the validity of a norm is to be sought, depends on a preceding stage in which everyone is called to decide whether she subjectively approves of the norm. As a correct and thorough assessment of the individual preferences through third parties is unlikely to be delivered, the participation of all actors interested in, or affected by, the validity of the norm is an indispensable condition of moral dialogue. As Tugendhat himself concedes, this is, however, a political choice rather that a direct output of his reasoning, for his argument goes just as far as to show that individual preferences play a role in the definition of a norm's validity, if the validity is intended as generalisability. Nevertheless, he has good reason to see the latter as granted by the understanding and the current use of moral statements (Tugendhat, 1992, pp. 285-308).

A weak point in Tugendhat's analysis consists in the numerous presuppositions he has to make, chiefly the assumption that there is as a matter of fact a discursive procedure that enjoys the confidence of all participants in the (virtual or factual) dialogue through which we can decide on the generalisability of a norm. However, Tugendhat's point is to show how moral sentences can be dealt with in a certain historically and institutionally given context of decision, and he does not intend to ground in any way the fairness of the procedure itself, although the political preference for an inclusive decision-making somehow descends from the conditions of generalisability he linguistically makes out.

What is of interest for my current purposes is Tugendhat's point on the undecidability of moral sentences beyond the joint expression and harmonisation of individual preferences, whenever the individualistic expectations he illustrates are at work in collective moral life. As far as this is the case Tugendhat's conclusion supports the priority of procedure over philosophical restrictions to legitimacy and validity of norms. Moreover, his theory takes into account a model of the political and cultural environment in which ethical claims have to be disentangled, and shows how the moral principles that work as an argumentative premise have to reflect what can be presupposed as a self-understanding of the people who share a certain social space. So is for instance the individualism that lies at the bottom of Tugendhat's assumptions a *social fact* rather than an ethical option, and such a fact poses certain questions to ethical theory – for instance as to the way to solve ethical conflicts amongst people who share a certain self-understanding. Tugendhat also highlights what it means to make appeal to a certain kind of *consensus* when we argue on ethical questions: the argumentative premises must be such as to reflect the assumptions that our potential or factual audience makes on the basis of a certain social experience. This should also clarify that consensus is not to be seen primarily as a source of normativity, but as a premise for the *understanding* of moral claims.

II.2. Rorty and Rawls

It may well be said that the importance of John Rawls's idea of a priority of democracy over philosophy (Rawls, 1985) has been underrated in scholarly debate until Richard Rorty took it up and painted its main features with brighter colours. This idea's general point has been widely understood, and since then addressed, as the neutrality of democratic institutions to conflicting conceptions of the good life. Acknowledging that the political communities of the West are characterised by the fact of value-pluralism, Rawls's theory is intended to answer the question as to "how we [can] design our defence [of a constitutional democratic regime] so as to achieve a sufficiently wide support for such a regime" (Rawls [1989] 1999, pp. 471-2). Rawls's idea of "justice as fairness" is framed in such a way that those who already support the constitutional, democratic regime should also be able to endorse the political conception. Justice as fairness spells out what has a concrete chance of turning into an overlapping consensus. Thus, the intuitive idea that lies at the foundation of this conception, which consists in "idea of society as a fair system of cooperation", is meant not so much as an unquestioned starting point that has its roots in any intuition about the just or the right, but as an idea of which we can hope that it "can be part of an overlapping consensus" (*Ibid.*, p. 472).

In making this assumption and formulating this practical programme Rawls moves from the empirical assumption that "[...] as a practical political matter no general moral conception can provide the basis for a public conception of justice in a modern democratic society". The historical conditions that have brought to democratic political institutions as an outcome of the European religious wars through the principle of toleration and the establishment of constitutional governments has brought to bear the idea that a currently affordable conception of political justice "must allow for a diversity of doctrines and the plurality of conflicting, and indeed incommensurable conceptions of the good" (Rawls, 1985, p. 225). Rawls's idea aims to transform a "modus vivendi", i.e., a political practice and an institutional tradition that produce a certain form of political life without making it explicit, into an "overlapping consensus", i.e., into a consciously formulated and acknowledged philosophy of public life. Such a mutation would allow the citizens of a liberal polity not only to share the enjoyment of certain goods – which they do anyhow –, but to express their allegiance to the corresponding values and institutions and to consciously manage their development (Rawls [1989] 1999, p. 471). Thus, Rawls acknowledges the difference between a political practice and the explicit formulation of its moral and political premises, so much so, that his appeal to the principles we live by is far from being an appeal to something already enclosed in the mind of the participants in the polity. The principles he formulates are rather an attempt to establish a link between what we think we know about our collective political life given the institutions we live in and what we are able to systematise and theoretically buttress in order to make it to a coherent whole.

However, Rorty gave Rawls's thesis a further twist by pointing out an apparently weaker, but as a matter of fact even stronger version of it, which consists in spelling out this conclusion about the historical conditions for democratic communities as the necessity to come to an "accommodation" amongst citizens instead of relying on the truth of moral certainties. Likewise, rather than being a philosophical expedient to come to well-balanced conclusions, Rawls's "reflective equilibrium" ought to be intended as a substitute for philosophical accounts of the morality of norms – Rorty dubs them as accounts of self or rationality. In this point Rorty departs from a strictly interpretive understanding of Rawls's ideas and downplays the role of "public reason" as framed by Rawls: if we acknowledge that, given the current state of ethical pluralism in contemporary Western societies, no knock-down argument is expectable in moral argumentation, it becomes evident that what we need to achieve is not so much a standard of philosophical decision, but a form of public consciousness and discussion such as it allows us to cease to feel the need for general principles and philosophical accounts and gives way to a pragmatic attitude of reciprocal accommodation (Rorty, 1991).[25] With regard to cross-cultural encounters with interlocutors who do not share such a pragmatist attitude Rorty just suggests to consciously draw a culturally biased limit to the acceptability of arguments: "We have to insist that not every argument needs to be met in terms in which it is presented. Accommodation and tolerance must stop short of a willingness to work within any given vocabulary that one's interlocutor wishes to use, to take seriously any topic that he puts forward for discussion". If we discard the idea that there is a single "moral vocabulary" and a single "set of moral beliefs" suitable "for every human community", then the consequence to be drawn relates much more to the limits of discussion than to the scope of universal arguments (*Ibid.*, p. 190).

II.5. The priority of democracy over philosophy

As I hope to have made clear thus far, moral arguments are rooted in a cultural environment on which we have to rely if our premises and goals have to be understood. Before going any deeper into the conclusions that we can draw from the above considerations, it is worthwhile to consider some objections commonly raised against so called "anti-foundationalist stances". I will focus on three of them and show why I think that the approach illustrated so far can effectively fend them off. So contends Simon Caney that "[...] people do not construe their their moral convictions as valid because they conform to their community's way of life. Rather, they believe that these convictions [...] are valid because they are supported by cogent arguments" (Caney, 2005, p. 43).

However, the point is that arguments are not raised in a cultural void, but need to be illustrated by means of examples that make clear the consequences that they would have for social behaviour. Incidentally, this still says nothing as to their acceptance, as they can still hope to achieve a universal scope of justification, but says something as to the way I have to

25 Caney comes to a similar assessment of the role of authority (i.e., institutions) when we face disagreement in the case of the decision over a "just war": "[...] we need to have a legitimate authority because there is often dispute about whether a war is justified" (2005, p. 206). It is not immediately intelligible why such an insight does not affect his views of other, both domestic and international, questions of justice. I am, again, indebted to Kok-Chor Tan for encouraging me to draw a sharper distinction between Rorty and Rawls.

deal with my interlocutors if I want to interact with them: I need to rely on instruments that be able to secure agreement. A further claim of Caney's concerns the supposed cultural insensitivity of universalism: "A universalist moral theory can be sensitive to context if it factors these into the application of its principles" (*Ibid.*, p. 40). For sure, this is likely to be the case, but not for the reason he adduces, as the distinction between a norm and its application is finally untenable. If the norm reads: "Do not kill", without any further, then there is as a matter of fact nothing to add to it, but when it comes to more complex norms, its possible outcomes will irremediably enter the process of justification.

A further, frequently raised objection to anti-foundational positions contends that they be self-refuting. Summarising the most effective, Caney concludes that claiming that universal moral norms cannot exist because they cannot be justified to all is equal to claiming a transcultural normative principle, i.e., that it is wrong to impose a principle on somebody without her agreement or without the principle being justified to her (*Ibid.*, p. 50). The argument, so concludes Caney, is therefore self-refuting. However, besides the fact that agreement is an option the alternative to which consists in conflict as a further option, whether a norm can be justified to anyone is an empirical question rather than a normative one. Whether we should strive for that and at which conditions is a different matter. Those who stress the importance of agreement usually do so as an alternative to violence, and invite others to share this preference. It turns into a norm once people agree that agreement is preferable to violence. I don't see why such an argument should be self-refuting.

This implies that the quest for a certain sort of agreement is implicit in every argumentation – even though we may aim to set up an argument that brackets out consensus as a source of normativity, as several scholars seek to achieve. What can replace this latter kind of consensus, with which we are acquainted from theories of social contract, is nothing but a different kind of agreement, i.e., an agreement on the premises on which we put the normative conclusions we want to draw, if we want coherence to govern our moral behaviour. Indeed, the source of normativity that we make appeal to in such a case is determined by the force of the norms that we and our audience have already accepted as inherited by our collective history or the social environment in which we grew up.[26] This opens up a further question as to the assessment of such an agreement as well as of the

26 Some scholars acknowledge the importance of such an agreement, as highlighted by their effort to make sure that their claims combine with other cultures' scales of values. See for instance Caney (2005, pp. 46, 74), Vincent (1986), Walzer (1994), and Tan (2004, p. 135).

consequences that we want to draw from the premises on which we agree. It is exactly at this point that a procedural concern comes in, the more so, the less we can take such an agreement for granted. Thus, the question that we have to answer in order to make any headway in moral argumentation relates to the political structure that allows us to check out or create such an agreement, and to transform it into collectively binding decisions. The pre-eminence of the institutional side of politics has a long-standing tradition in political thought. As in the context of the present essay I can hardly give a satisfactory account of it,[27] I will present the following thesis as hypotheses for further research.

If we take seriously the idea that procedural tools are what we need in order to assess scope and content of the agreement on norms that may be present amongst the audience to which we address our claims, then we should also conclude that, contrary to most scholars' tacit assumption, political procedure has a priority over whatever theoretical criterion of legitimacy. In other words, any concern with legitimacy ought to presuppose the participation in collectively binding decision-making the outcome of which has pre-eminence over the theoretical concern. Especially as long as ethical positions are controversial, philosophically informed opinion turns out not to go beyond a political opinion to be publicly discussed and fed into the process rather that being an external instance to test political legitimacy. As illustrated above, this is fundamentally Rawls's and Rorty's point.[28]

---

27 In order to encompass the scope of the theories I presently refer to, it must suffice to mention that the contemporary tradition has a peak with Kant's idea of a "state of devils" (Kant [1796] 1992), has been impressively continued by Hannah Arendt (1993, Fragment 1), and has dominated democratic theory both from within the Anglo-Saxon tradition that started at the turn of the century (Bentley [1908] 1967) and from the contributions that German scholars brought in the aftermath of the Nazi takeover (see Schumpeter [1942] 1996, pp. 242, 250, 269; and De Angelis, 2009 with regard to Hans Kelsen's political theory in the context of the Weimar Republic), also influencing contemporary "pluralist" theories.

28 Bader comes to a similar conclusion with regard to national fundamental controversies on values. He suggests to further "the duties of civility, such as the duty to explain positions in publicly understandable language, the willingness to listen to others, fair-mindedness, and readiness to accept reasonable accommodations or alterations in one's own view" (1999, p. 614), and expresses himself against all attempts to regulate "philosophically" what belongs to public reason or what does not (however, he understands his position as an objection to, rather than as a development of, Rawls's thesis).

As a matter of fact, some of the scholars that participate in the debate on global justice take pains at assessing the role of moral arguments in political debates and in the context of democratic legitimacy. However, the priority of political decision over moral argumentation stays often in the background, which might account for the

The conclusion that some scholars have drawn after acknowledging this state of affairs privileges the effort to construe our cultural and political history as coherently as possible in order to establish the largest possible consensus on the ethical foundations of our societies. For sure, this "our" is itself difficult to narrow down to an easily identifiable set of categories or reference groups. However, be it the nation, one's own fellow-citizens, a social class or milieu, it is important to remark that such an identification is not related to what within the debate on global justice is discussed as the moral significance of national or cultural boundaries. Instead, the effort to clear up the cultural and political history in which we grow up is usually aimed at choosing the course of action most apt to preserve what we have learned to value. Unfortunately, the effort to picture our cultural and political history as a coherent whole underrates the sources of tension as well as the ideological and political struggle that characterise all groups, countries, or nations.[29]

However, as far as moral argumentation highlights either "institutional ethics" or widespread "intuitions" or principles we expect every rational agent to agree upon, it works as a facilitator of public discussion. This is the public task achievable by working out the political conceptions that seem to be implicit in the political environment we live in. However, instead of relying on such an analysis for appointing unquestionably valid norms, this operation can reasonably aim to sort out the historically sedimented normative and moral content in order to identify what is most likely to yield a widespread agreement, and then submit it to rational proof.[30] With regard to the debate on global justice, this should also help to remind us of the historical origin of the bulk of our moral concepts as well as of their rootedness in a (or even several) political culture(s).

---

seemingly skimpy consideration that scholars afford democratic institutions. Nevertheless, moral arguments may support an explicit call for a larger inclusion of democratic procedures on global justice issues. So affirms Pogge that the ultimate responsibility for the decisions to be correct "should lie with the persons concerned" ([1992] 2008b, p. 372).

29 The temptation to emphasise the commonality of values and cultural codes is common to political studies in general, and especially to the branch specifically devoted to "political culture" (Wildavsky, 1989, p. 21). And yet literature on democracy as a "culture of conflict" is also well present in the history of social sciences. See for instance Schwartz (2007, pp. 132-4) for a sketch of different concepts of solidarity and models of social security in contemporary US.

30 MacIntyre belongs to the scholars who have emphasised this latter aspect of moral analysis: "One of the central tasks of the moral philosopher is to articulate the convictions of the society in which he or she lives so that these convictions may become available for rational scrutiny" ([1984] 2008, p. 119).

In order to do so, moral argumentation should also clearly identify its addressee. As pointed out above, independently of whether their scope is universal or particular, moral premises implicitly target a culturally defined audience. To make this clear in setting up the argument from the very start (as for instance Tugendhat explicitly does) helps to better orient our expectation as to the agreement that we may experience.[31]

A further consequence relates to our methodological presuppositions. As far as arguments are put forward as universally valid due to the ontological nature of their object, such a public function of philosophical argumentation is difficult to fulfil, for we loose sight of the context within which our argument can reasonably get some hearing. As Rorty has pointed out, to replace the question about the nature of things (for instance human beings) with the question about the purposes we want to support means to abandon theological, scientific, or metaphysical descriptions (Rorty [1996] 2008, p. 316) in favour of a reflection on how to reconstruct what we think we have learned from our collective historical and cultural experience in order to make it available for further discussion with people who come from a different background (may they be co-citizens or foreigners). This paves the way to assessing the historical value of the norms and institutions we have given our allegiance to and to orient ourselves at goals we wish to achieve both in the national and the international arena. Such a goal-oriented conception of morals shows through the "pragmatic arguments" sketched above.[32]

As long as the public function of philosophical argumentation takes the form of a reflection on the cultural presuppositions and political history of our societies, the goal that it can more easily achieve is to influence our national institutions and decision-makers. Such a goal shows through the efforts of those who plea for a global redistribution of income and welfare, as they reasonably enough seek to influence those who detain the bulk of the world's wealth.

However, those scholars who strive for a global dialogue on norms and values are usually far worse off. First of all, a decisive hindrance in playing

31 Some scholars make this attitude explicit in that they address political commitments inside their own political community and cultural environment. So states Tan (2004, pp. 7) that whoever accepts egalitarian liberalism in its general form, which states that all persons deserve equal respect and concern, "ought also to be a cosmopolitan liberal".

32 Theoretically, such a preference can be clarified by pointing out the role of hypothetical imperatives – i.e., of goal-dependent norms that explicitly presuppose a set of preferences and (cultural, personal, or political) choices – in the construction of moral arguments (Foot, 1978). For an analysis of hypothetical imperatives see Grice (2001, p. 52).

a role in democratic institutions on issues of global justice evidently consists in the absence of any such institutions in the international arena. As far as theories of democratic decision – making are addressed, they rather support claims about the special responsibility towards fellow-citizens and the moral and political relevance of national borders (Miller [1988] 2008, p. 248; Miller [2004] 2008, pp. 513-5).[33] However, research on transnational social movements and civil society highlights the worldwide efforts to promote forms of democratic inclusion in international and supranational decision-making as well as attempts to forge a worldwide dialogue on global ethics and politics. Although research on global civil society emphasises once more the importance of shared values and political culture, and thus throws us back into the dilemma of how we can have institutions if we do not find out the "right" norms in the first place, there is still a remarkable line of thought that sets this alternative aside, forgoes the pre-eminence of "normative", i.e., philosophical, legitimation and points out a chance of intertwining a global dialogue without giving priority neither to universal nor to "local" principles. This line of thought has been sketched out above under the heading of "pragmatic arguments" and is well present especially beyond academic boundaries amongst the so called actors of "global civil society". This is a promising field of research if we want to assess the degree of intercultural normative agreement.

References

Alexander, J., Philip S. (1993). "The Discourse of American Civil Society: A New Proposal for Cultural Studies". *Theory and Society*. Vol. 22. No. 2. Pp. 151-207.

Arendt, H. (1993). *Was ist Politik? Fragmente aus dem Nachlass*. Ursula Ludz (ed.). Munich. Piper .

Bader, V. (1999). "Religious Pluralism. Secularism or Priority for Democracy?" *Political Theory*. Vol. 27. No. 5. Pp. 597-633.

Barry, B. ([1982] 2008). "Humanity and Justice Global Perspective". Thomas Pogge, Darrel Moellendorf (eds.). *Global Justice: Seminal Essays*. St. Paul/MN. Paragon House. Pp. 179-209

Beitz, C. ([1975] 2008). "Justice and International Relations". Thomas Pogge. Darrel Moellendorf (eds.). *Global Justice: Seminal Essays*. St. Paul/MN. Paragon House. Pp. 21-48.

33 See also Waldron, who attempts to combine political considerations on the pre-eminence of territorial institutions and obligations over global, unlimited duties with universalist arguments ([1993] 2008, pp. 403, 411).

Beitz, C. (2001). "Human Rights as a Common Concern". *The American Political Science Review*. Vol. 95. No. 2. Pp. 269-282.

Bentley, A. F. (1908/1967). *The Process of Government. The Study of Social Pressures*. Peter H. Odegard (ed.). Cambridge/MA. The Belknap Press of Harvard University Press.

Blake, M. ([2001] 2008). "Distributive Justice, State Coercion, and Autonomy". Thomas Pogge, Darrel Moellendorf (eds.). *Global Justice: Seminal Essays*. St. Paul. Mn. Paragon House. Pp. 657-695.

Bobbio, N. (1984). "Etica e politica". Walter Tega (ed.). *Etica e politica*. Parma. Pratiche Editrice. Pp. 7-17.

Brint, M., William G. W., Meredith G. (1995). "What Difference Does Anti-Foundationalism Make to Political Theory?"*New Literary History*. Vol. 26. No. 2. Pp. 225-237.

Buchanan, A. (2004). *Justice, Legitimacy, and Self-Determination: Moral Foundations for International Law*. Oxford. Oxford University Press.

Burgio, A. (2006). *Per un lessico critico del contrattualismo moderno*. Napoli. La Scuola di Pitagora.

Caney, S. (2008). "Global Distributive Justice and the State". *Political Studies*. Vol. 56. N. 3. Pp. 487-518.

Coady, C.A.J. (1991). "*Politics and the Problem of Dirty Hands*". Peter Singer (ed.). *A Companion to Ethics*. Oxford. Basil Blackwell. Pp. 373-383.

Croce, B. ([1931] 1946). *Politics and Morals*. Trans. Salvatore J. Castiglione. London. Allen & Unwin.

Dallmayr, F. (2002). "Globalization and Inequality. A Plea for Global Justice". *International Studies Review*. Vol. 4. No. 2. Pp. 137-143.

De Angelis, G. (2009). "Ideals and Institutions: Hans Kelsen's Political Theory". *History of Political Thought*. Vol. XXX. No. 3. Pp. 524-546.

Felix, D. (1998). *Einheit der Rechtsordnung*. Tübingen. Mohr Siebeck.

Foot, P. (1978). "Morality as a System of Hypothetical Imperatives". *Virtues and Vices and Other Essays in Moral Philosophy*. Berkley and Los Angeles. University of California Press.

Gadamer, H-G. ([1960] 2004). *Truth and Method.*. Trans. revised by Joel Weinsheimer and Donald G. Marshall. 2nd ed. London-New York. Continuum.

Goodin, R. E. ([1988] 2008). "What Is So Special about our Fellow Countrymen?" Thomas Pogge, Darrel Moellendorf (eds.). *Global Justice: Seminal Essays*. St. Paul/MN. Paragon House. Pp. 235-253.

Grasnick, W. (2001). "«Einheit der Rechtsordnung». Zur Zukunft einer Illusion". *Merkur*. Vol. 55. No. 1. Pp. 62-66.

Grice, P. (2001). "The Carus Lectures on the Conception of Values". *The Conception of Values*. Oxford. Clarendon Press.

Habermas, J. (1984). *The Theory of Communicative Action*. vol. I. Trans. Thomas McCarthy. Boston. Beacon Press.

Habermas, J. (1990). *Moral consciousness and communicative action*. Trans. Christian Lenhardt and Shierry Weber Nicholsen. Cambridge/MA. MIT Press.

Hechter, M. (1992). "Should Values Be Written out of the Social Scientist's Lexicon?" *Sociological Theory*. Vol. 10. No. 2. Pp. 214-230.

Hurka, T. ([1997] 2008). "The Justification of National Partiality". Thomas Pogge, Keith Norton (eds.). *Global Ethics: Seminal Essays*. St. Paul/MN. Paragon House. Pp. 379-403

Kant, I. ([1787] 1998). *Critique of pure reason*. Trans. Paul Guyer (ed.). Cambridge. Cambridge University Press.

Kant, I. ([1793] 1970). "On the common saying: "This may be true in theory, but it does not a apply in practice"". *Kant's Political Writings*. H. Reiss (ed.). Trans. H.B. Nisbet. Cambridge. Cambridge University Press. Pp. 61-92.

Kant, I. ([1796] 1992). *Perpetual peace*. Trans. introduction and notes M. Campbell Smith. Bristol. Thoemmes Press.

Kant, I. ([1797] 1996). *The metaphysics of morals*. Trans. Mary Gregor (ed.). Cambridge. Cambridge University Press.

Kersting, W. (1994). *Die politische Philosophie des Gesellschaftsvertrags*. Darmstadt. Wissenschaftliche Buchgesellschaft.

MacIntyre, A. ([1984] 2008). "Is Patriotism A Virtue?" Thomas Pogge. Keith Norton (eds.). *Global Ethics: Seminal Essays*. St. Paul. Mn. Paragon House. Pp. 119-137.

Mackie, L. J. (1977). *Ethics: Inventing Right and Wrong*. Harmondsworth & New York. Penguin.

Miller, R. W. ([1988] 2008). "The Ethical Significance of Nationality". Thomas Pogge, Darrel Moellendorf (eds.). *Global Justice: Seminal Essays*. St. Paul/MN. Paragon House. Pp. 235-253.

Miller, R. W. ([2004] 2008). "Moral Closeness and World Community". Thomas Pogge. Keith Norton (eds.). *Global Ethics: Seminal Essays*. St. Paul/MN. Paragon House. Pp. 507-530

Nagel, T. ([1977] 2008). "Poverty and Food: Why Charity Is Not Enough". Thomas Pogge, Darrel Moellendorf (eds.). *Global Justice: Seminal Essays*. St. Paul/MN. Paragon House. Pp. 49-59

Nussbaum, M. ([2002] 2008). "Patriotism and Cosmopolitanism". Thom Brooks (ed.). *The Global Justice Reader*. London. Blackwell. Pp. 306-314

O'Neill, O. ([1975] 2008). "Lifeboat Earth". Thomas Pogge, Darrel Moellendorf (eds.). *Global Justice: Seminal Essays*. St. Paul/MN. Paragon House. Pp. 1-20

Pogge, T. ([1992] 2008b). "Cosmopolitanism and Sovereignty". Thomas Pogge, Darrel Moellendorf (eds.). *Global Justice: Seminal Essays*. St. Paul. Mn. Paragon House). Pp. 355-390.

Pogge, T. (2008a). "Introduction". Thomas Pogge, Darrel Moellendorf (eds.). *Global Justice: Seminal Essays*. St. Paul. Mn. Paragon House. Pp. xiii-xxiv.

Powers, W. R. (2000). "The Harvard Study of Values: Mirror for Postwar Anthropology". *Journal of the History of the Behavioural Sciences*. Vol. 36. No. 1. Pp. 15-29.

Rawls, J. (1971). *A Theory of Justice*. Cambridge/MA. Harvard University Press.

Rawls, J. ([1985] 1999). "Justice as Fairness: Political, Not Metaphysical". Rawls. *Collected Papers*. Samuel Freeman (ed.). Cambridge/MA. Harvard University Press. Pp. 388-414.

Rawls, J. ([1989] 1999). "The Priority of Right and Ideas of the Good". Rawls. *Collected Papers*. Samuel Freeman (ed.). Cambridge. MA. Harvard University Press. Pp. 449-472.

Riedel, M. (ed.). (1972). *Zur Rehabilitierung der praktischen Philosophie*. Vol. I Freiburg. Rombach.

Riedel, M. (ed.). (1974). *Zur Rehabilitierung der praktischen Philosophie*. Vol. II Freiburg. Rombach.

Rorty, R. (1991) "The Priority of Democracy to Philosophy". Idem. *Objectivity, Relativism and Truth: Philosophical Papers I*. Cambridge. Cambridge University Press. Pp. 175-186.

Rorty, R. ([1996] 2008). "Who Are We? Moral Universalism and Economic Triage". Thomas Pogge, Keith Norton (eds.). *Global Ethics: Seminal Essays*. St. Paul/MN. Paragon House. Pp. 313-323

Scanlon, M. T. (1998). *What We Owe to Each Other*. Cambridge. MA. Harvard University Press.

Schlick, M. ([1925] 1974). *General Theory of Knowledge*. Trans. Albert E. Blumberg Wien. Springer.

Schumpeter, J. ([1942] 1996). *Capitalism, socialism, and democracy*. New York, London. Harper & Brothers.

Schwartz, J. M. (2007). "From Domestic to Global Solidarity: The Dialectic of the Particular and the Universal in the Building of Social Solidarity". *Journal of Social Philosophy*. Vol. 38. No. 1. Pp. 131-147.

Shapiro, I. (2003). *The Moral Foundations of Politics*. New Haven & London. Yale University Press.

Shue, H. ([1993] 2008). "Subsistence Emissions and Luxury Emissions". Thomas Pogge, Keith Norton (eds.). *Global Ethics: Seminal Essays*. St. Paul. Mn. Paragon House. Pp. 207-231

Singer, P. ([1972] 2008). "Famine, Affluence, and Morality". Thomas Pogge, Keith Norton (eds.). *Global Ethics: Seminal Essays*. St. Paul/Mn. Paragon House. Pp. 1-14.

Steiner, H. (1999/2008). "Just Taxation and International Redistribution". Thomas Pogge, Darrel Moellendorf (eds.). *Global Justice: Seminal Essays*. St. Paul/Mn. Paragon House. Pp. 637-65.

Tan, K.-C. (2004). *Justice Without Borders. Cosmopolitanism, Nationalism and Patriotism*. Cambridge. Cambridge University Press.

Taylor, C. (1999/2008). "Conditions of an Unforced Consensus on Human Rights". Thomas Pogge, Keith Norton (eds.). *Global Ethics: Seminal Essays.* St. Paul/Mn. Paragon House. Pp. 405-430.

Tugendhat, E. (1992). "Sprache und Ethik". Idem. *Philosophische Aufsätze.* Frankfurt am Main. Suhrkamp. Pp. 275-314.

Vincent, J. R. (1986). *Human Rights and International Relations.* Cambridge. Cambridge University Press.

Waldron, J. ([1993] 2008). "Special Ties and Natural Duties". Thomas Pogge, Darrel Moellendorf (eds.). *Global Justice: Seminal Essays.* St. Paul. Mn. Paragon House. Pp. 355-390.

Walzer, M. ([1981] 2008). "The Distribution of Membership". Thomas Pogge, Darrel Moellendorf (eds.). *Global Justice: Seminal Essays.* St. Paul. Mn. Paragon House. Pp. 145-177.

Walzer, M. (1994). *Thick and Thin: Moral Arguments at Home and Abroad.* Notre Dame/IN. University of Notre Dame Press.

Wildavsky, A. (1989). "Choosing Preferences by Constructing Institutions: A Cultural Theory of Preference Formation". Arthur Asa Berger (ed.). *Political Culture and Public Opinion.* New Brunswick-Oxford. Transaction Publishers. Pp. 21-46.

II. Normative Theory

Global and Statist Egalitarianism and Their Woes

Daniel Kofman

Introduction

As views proliferate about both the nature and scope of distributive justice, so does the complexity of implications of one for the other. Egalitarian views alone differ on whether the equalisand should be an aspect of outcome or some prior advantage – and whether income, resource, wealth, welfare, primary goods, access to advantage, or opportunity; and whether justice should equalise the effects of brute luck. Others reject egalitarianism in favour of prioritarianism, sufficientarianism, or a hybrid or pluralist approach, and then multiply again on the question of the appropriate distribuend. The question of scope of distributive justice is not unaffected by the substantive view one adopts. Generally speaking, the weaker the requirements of a conception to redistribute the pattern-upsetting effects of liberty or choice, or the more responsibility attributed to individuals for their own welfare, the less problematic to consider the scope as globally wide (or alternatively, the less relevant or important the question of scope). One can think of theories on a rough continuum: at one end a libertarian entitlement doctrine that shuns pattern-sensitive distribution outright, then a social minimum or guaranteed subsistence doctrine, next a sufficientarian requirement that a more substantial level of welfare or resources be secured for all, then approaching the other end a prioritarian concern always to benefit the worst off, and at the far end various egalitarian doctrines. The libertarian extreme renders the question of scope irrelevant, since any redistribution for the sake of altering an emergent pattern, even in the domestic arena, is ruled out; social minimum and sufficientarian doctrines can perhaps rely on universal humanitarian grounds and finesse the debate about associational grounds of justice, while prioritarian and egalitarian doctrines land squarely in the midst of such debates.

The rival positions on scope are statism[1] and globalism. It is philosophically easier to be a globalist, I have just suggested, the farther one is from the egalitarian end of the spectrum.[2] One can readily see why: the weaker the distributive duties, the more plausible that humanitarian considerations alone, as opposed to relational or associational ones, can account for them.[3] Even associational theories – which hold that distributive justice is grounded in the participation by members in a common association, whether because the association uses coercion against rule-breakers, is self-ruling, mutually benefits members, or some combination[4] of these – usually grant that rich countries or individuals have humanitarian duties to try to raise everyone globally to a minimum level of basic health and subsistence.[5] Thus it is widely accepted that such duties are justifiable by non-associational considerations alone. A higher sufficiency threshold may be somewhat more vulnerable to controversy; yet it is difficult to see how a statist egalitarian who accepts humanitarian duties to raise everyone to a

1 Sangiovanni (2007) weirdly labels this the 'internationalist' view. While one can imagine what he means by mentally inserting a hyphen every time the word comes up, I prefer a less arduous term.

2 I have no stake in making this point too literally. I readily accept that it is possible for some doctrine x to be more egalitarian in some important sense than another doctrine y, but less problematically globalist. The spectrum is in any case rough, the notion of being philosophically problematic vague, and the point about implications for scope merely suggestive at this point. I shall try to show, however, that certain objections to globalist egalitarianism actually tell against the domestic application as well; that is, what seems like a scope problem is really a problem for the doctrine per se.

3 Of course this does not mean, if the weaker theory is correct, that associational grounds have been refuted; merely that they will have been rendered superfluous; it is still possible that the weak duties in the domestic case are overjustified. I use 'associational' for common institutional arrangements, while 'relational' includes both associational as well as mere causal relations. Pogge, for instance, justifies globalism by alleging that rich countries are (in part) causally responsible for other countries' poverty, and also benefit from it. This causal relational can be more (as with Pogge, 2008) or less systemic, depending on one's view of global economic relations.

4 Nagel (2005), for instance, holds that the combination of being self-ruling and coercive accounts for associational duties of justice that do not obtain toward nonmembers of the association.

5 Thus Sangiovanni writes that he will "assume that all plausible criteria of distributive justice, whether national, international, or global, must at least require raising all human beings to a minimal threshold defined in terms of access to basic goods, including clothing, shelter, food, and sanitation. ... all of the major forms of 'internationalism' [i.e., statism] ... accept it as a starting point" (Sangiovanni, 2007, p. 4, fn. 5). He goes on to observe that this is less "controversial" among philosophers, while the "philosophically more difficult and controversial question is how to identify the level or domain to which we should assign equality as a demand of justice, and, more importantly, why." The answer defended in this paper is that we shouldn't be egalitarian either globally or domestically.

minimum threshold can consistently resist a further demand to enable people to be at a level where they could realise reasonable aspirations to lead a decent life. Why should humanitarian concerns require provisions for subsistence and basic health, but not a chance to live a decent life (no matter how rich the would-be benefactor)? Since the egalitarian recognises the intrinsic moral worth of either distributed outcomes or distributed opportunities to outcomes (as the entitlement libertarian does not) and since they further acknowledge humanitarian duties of provision to achieve global basic thresholds, fixing the threshold of concern at a level sufficient for people to lead decent lives would seem fairly compelling.

The real controversy begins, it would then seem, further across the spectrum toward the egalitarian extreme. For purposes of this essay I shall generally ignore the difference between prioritarian and egalitarian theories and focus on the question of whether the associational aspect of states grounds duties beyond sufficientarian ones. I begin, however, with some remarks about justice and fairness in order to undermine the belief that one can draw sustenance for statism through an analysis of the concept of justice. I then move to my main argument: that statist egalitarianism faces a dilemma: either its associational justification of statism is too weak, in that it cannot explain distributive duties to unproductive co-citizens such as the disabled, or it is too strong and cannot contain itself to state borders as proponents would wish. I examine four arguments for statism. The most persuasive is that societies bear a large responsibility for the welfare of their own members because the decisions they make with respect to investment, controlling corruption, and efficiency have far greater and more direct effects than anything outsiders do. But an egalitarian who accepts this consideration as a reason to limit the external scope of distributive justice cannot then consistently resist limiting the internal stringency; that is, they cannot object to the claim that individuals within a society bear large responsibility for their level of welfare. The objection to external scope thus carries over to an objection to internal stringency, or to the substance of the theory, and points toward a less stringent redistributive goal. I then argue, in part following Goodin, that duties of justice are general and that practical statism is justified only insofar as there is a tacit global agreement to divide global responsibility along state lines to execute duties of justice. This explains state responsibilities for unproductive members, without elevating states to the hallowed status of an independent moral source of justice. I end with some brief remarks about how the substance of justice should be conceived in light of the preceding considerations of both the global and domestic cases. I shall argue that sufficientarianism cannot, despite its self-understanding, entirely avoid interpersonal comparisons of welfare, but that its real attraction is its aspiration to increase the responsibility of agents – both individuals and states – for their own welfare, including for the pursuit of rewarding and satisfying lives under circumstances not entirely chosen by themselves.

The concept of justice

I begin with some general remarks about justice. Since Rawls distinguished between a concept and a conception, and then defended his 'conception' of justice as fairness, many have used these with the same critical caution as cultural revolution Maoists incanting from the little red book. I do not deny that a concept-conception distinction can be useful, but it is not hard and fast. If one tries to draw it on the basis of what is not controversial (the concept) and what is (the conception) counterintuitive results quickly follow. Nor should this be surprising, since controversy is a contingent social phenomenon. A very detailed fleshing out of a concept might lack controversy because no one has bothered to challenge it, while even a thin construal of a concept might still be 'contested' for any number of reasons. The point for current purposes is that discussions of the scope of justice seem invariably to presuppose a consensus about the concept, as if all controversy about substance is at some other level: the conception. But the question of whether justice holds between non-relational individuals is very much a question of what one thinks (the concept of) justice is.[6] Those inclined toward statism frequently hold that two individuals separately stranded on the same island bear no duties of justice toward each other. Of course if this were merely a stipulation, there could be no quarrel with it. But then, if one further has a conception of justice as fairness, it is certainly not the case that justice exhausts fairness, for there is no reason to suppose that fairness between the island's two inhabitants ought not to obtain.

6 Nozick (1974) raised the point that the very concept of 'distributive justice' is biased toward a patterned view, which he rejects. One might think there is still a thin concept of justice shared even by an entitlement theorist and a Rawlsian, since even the former is answering the question of how goods ought be distributed, namely, by however the free transactions of people continually redistribute them. But even this formulation is still misleading, since there is no libertarian prescription that people ought however freely to distribute goods this particular way rather than that. The thin formulation, therefore, purchases (the appearance of) commonality at the price of ambiguity. One might then seek a family resemblance account, but it suffices merely to try listing the semantic properties some of which the concept must have to realise how 'contestable' the concept, not just the 'conception', really is.

Let us dwell on this longer. It seems intuitively obvious, at least to this writer, that if Mr Greedy quickly seized the island's best land by placing a fence around the perimeter, leaving 'enough' but not nearly 'as good' or 'as much' to Mr Decent, then this would be unfair, all the more so if Decent had good-naturedly presumed that the two would share equally, or according to need, both land and produce. Some might go along with this but nevertheless argue that the unfairness stems from this being a zero sum game, where Greedy's seizure was Decent's privation. What if, on the other hand, the land was divided equally in quantity and quality, but one produced far more by his greater industriousness? Here, it is held, duties of justice do not arise since there is no common association between the two people.

But this analysis misinterprets the issue at hand. If, on the one hand, the greater industriousness merited the greater share, why should it not do so were they in common association? On the other hand, if the industriousness was not merited, say because one takes a hard determinist view of the matter (as Rawls seems to have) then how does the greater industriousness differ morally from the greater piece of land seized? Or put another way, what should be the baseline of fairness admitted in the first instance with respect to land? Why presume it unfair that Greedy take more than half the island (if this time we assume uniform quality), but fair that he take fully half? A fifty-fifty division is arbitrary with respect both to the parties' natural endowments and needs, so if one does think there is an issue of fairness, why not count everything that matters, including endowments both external and internal? One cannot distinguish between the two cases by saying that the first is zero sum: so is the second, since on the hard determinist denial of desert for industriousness and its products, the relevant sum is the land plus its total produce given the differential productivity of each. One might, I suppose, deny the original intuition that the greedy land seizure is unfair in the absence of a prior agreement or common association, but if that is so I must confess not to know what is fairness. Rather, I suspect that such a view would be allowing the values of autonomy and consent to flood the space of other values – a not uncommon foible in liberal writing – in this case fairness.[7]

7 David Heyd explicity denies that fairness obtains beyond a contractual community. But the question remains whether this is mere stipulation (or assertion). After all, the intuition lingers that Greedy's land seizure is wrong. Call the issue related to the judgment *shmairness*. If Greedy is wrong because unshmair (though not unfair) – that is, acting greedily by taking a larger share than anyone else in a non-contractual situation – the ethical point remains. (Unshmairness would resemble the Greek *pleionexia*). David Heyd (2007).

A temptation might persist to analogise to a scenario that is not zero sum. After all, my rejection of the relevance of industriousness to marking the difference between associational and non-associational fairness was based on the disjunction that either industriousness merits a greater share, whether within or without an association, or that it is within a zero sum game where fairness should prevail. But what if the game was not zero sum and the differences that arose were not based on industriousness? Suppose, for instance, that there were two islands, each with a sole inhabitant. On Abundance Mr Lucky has a better living for less effort than on Infertile, where Unlucky has to work arduously and constantly to eke out bare subsistence. One might wish to say that if the two were unaware of each other, justice evidently could not be implemented, and since 'no can' implies 'no ought'(the Modus Tollens version of Kant's dictum) there are no inter-island demands of justice. But even if this is true, it offers no support to the idea that justice must be associational. All it shows is that justice must be implementable, and that sometimes a separation between people or associations prevents implementation. Suppose that one or both of the islanders built a boat and discovered the other island. If Lucky insists that Abundance is his and his alone, and he need not alleviate Unlucky's predicament on Infertile, it is difficult to see a morally relevant difference between this and the single island seizure by Greedy. The only new element of possible moral interest is that both have entrenched expectations and adaptations; indeed it might well be that this ought to be factored in, but that doesn't show that justice does not apply, nor that those sorts of factors need not be considered when determining justice within an association. In all these cases one must be careful not to vacillate in a way biased toward the associational view. Just as industriousness raises a challenge for any egalitarian theory, so does the possibility that expectations and adaptations affect justice (to which I later return). It begs the question of whether the scope of egalitarian justice is associational to raise these objections against egalitarian justice only in non-associational contexts such as dissociated hypothetical islands.

If questions of fairness can arise beyond association, an associationalist view of justice obviously faces a problem. One might persist in holding that justice, even justice as fairness, is still different from fairness beyond justice.[8] The 'circumstances of justice', according to Hume and following him Rawls, include common association. The trouble is that while Hume

8 Alternatively one can speak of different levels of justice, each with its own demands, as Murphy (2007), Nagel (2005), and Sangiovanni (2007) do. The substance, not the terminology, is important. I wish only to establish here that considerations of fairness can obtain without associational relations, whatever one chooses to call the ensuing duties.

didn't think of justice as fairness (or if he did, didn't think of fairness as equality) Rawls and his followers do. So Hume can plausibly argue that the island case might well be one of unfairness but not of injustice, since justice in any case does not require equal distribution. Hume can thus say with Nozick: Sure it's unfair; so is life – What has that to do with justice? (Recall Nozick's analogy between market distributions and marital choices that deprive some of equally attractive conjugal options: unfair maybe, but not unjust.) Rawls and other associational statists, on the other hand, would have either to deny that Greedy is being unfair, which I have suggested seems implausible, or else to concede that justice does not exhaust fairness. But then, why should justice as fairness not extend to cases of fairness outside associational bounds? In Rawls' case, unlike Hume's, a separation of justice as fairness from non-associational fairness would seem to require a special defense; otherwise it would be in danger of appearing to be merely a stipulation. One can see that the problem here is to get a grip on the very concept of justice. If the scope of the concept were decided merely by stipulation, obviously that could come only at the price of depriving the question of any lingering interest; the interesting normative question would be displaced to the nature and scope of other duties, such as (extra-justicial) fairness and humanitarian beneficence.

Statism

I turn now to an examination of specific arguments in favour of a statist conception of justice. As mentioned previously, I shall argue that justifications of statism face a dilemma of being either too weak to account for state duties to non-contributing citizens, or, if they do manage to account for them, too strong to contain duties within state boundaries. The dilemma arises naturally by the presence within state boundaries of people who stand in a crucial respect in relation to their working and producing cocitizens as do people outside the state boundaries: as non-participants in the productive life of the particular citizenry. Some egalitarians bite the bullet and deny that duties of justice obtain between contributing and non-contributing citizens. But embarrassed by the juxtaposition of such demanding content (their egalitarianism) next to seeming callousness, they then assert that duties of humanity explain why these people should be cared for. One problem for such a view is to explain why such duties should be borne by the state in question, as opposed to anyone else, or perhaps the richest state (until no longer the richest, at which point the new richest state would carry on, etc.); I shall have more to say about this below. The second problem, however, is a variation on the second horn of the dilemma, or perhaps a third horn of a trilemma, for it now appears again that humanitarian duties are poised to go far enough as to render the question of the scope of justice uninteresting. After all, egalitarians and prioritarians are unlikely to say that duties to the disabled should be exhausted at subsistence, while everyone else should be raised to the benchmark of equality. If these duties are to provide the disabled with more than a bare minimum, and if they are duties of humanity rather than justice, then duties of humanity beyond borders are presumably robust enough to render the scope of duties of justice irrelevant.

Let us consider more closely what seem to be the four main arguments for statism. I shall argue that three risk goring by the first horn above: they face difficulty accounting for state duties to non-contributing citizens. The fourth is the most plausible, or contains the most plausible elements, but ultimately at the price of undermining the case for egalitarianism even domestically. The four are (1) non-voluntary membership of a coercive politico-legal system; (2) participation in a common cooperative system engendering reciprocity in the mutual provision of domestic public goods; (3) a Nagel–Rousseauean argument from the will being engaged as both author and subject of the laws; (4) membership in a single centralised system of power and decision-making.

(1) *Non-voluntary membership of a coercive politico-legal system*

The prevalence of this argument is somewhat surprising. The idea is that since the system is coercive – punishing those who fail to comply with its laws – and membership in it is non-voluntary, so that one cannot easily remove oneself from its coercive purview because of the burdens involved, it is incumbent on such a system to treat its coerced members fairly. The argument is surprising given how much the contract tradition from Hobbes to Rawls has tried to conceptualise the just polity as being, in the latter's words, "as close as a society can to being a voluntary scheme". For Rawls justice is intimately bound up with the society being a voluntary cooperative scheme. Coercion is adopted to prevent freeriding and to demonstrate publicly one's commitment; there is a direct line here all the way back to Hobbes' dictum that words without swords are but empty. But the coercion is itself chosen, on this conception, and in order to buttress the already agreed scheme; it is not itself a justification of adherence to principles of justice.

The point can be exemplified by imagining people in a contractual situation before they have decided to add coercion against freeriders. They have agreed principles of justice, and now someone who has gained an unfair advantage refuses to give it up. He would have no moral leg to stand on if he replied that the system is not (yet) coercive so he is not bound by principles of justice. If he were to respond honestly, he would have to say that the other members were suckers for not yet having enforced their principles with coercion, and that he was now going to take advantage of this while he could still get away with it. The reason one needs coercion is to prevent violations of justice; coercion is not the reason why one needs justice.

There is a persistent misunderstanding about this point that is worth analysing further. Michael Blake, who develops the coercion argument for statism, might reply to the above as follows: the actual social contract is a myth, while the hypothetical contract, as Dworkin observed, is not just a pale form of an actual contract; it is no contract at all. Real societies have real laws and real enforcement. Since a citizen is coerced to pay her taxes, she has a right that the taxation system be justifiable by principles that, if she is reasonable, she can accept as just. It may well be that some version of Rawlsian constructivism can identify what those principles should be. But it is the fact that these or some other principles are being coercively imposed on people that creates the requirement that they had better be just. If the system is working to the unfair advantage of some over others, the further fact that members of it have no choice in the matter gives them legitimate grounds for complaint.

This possible reasoning mistakes what can be an additional reason for being just – that coercion is being applied – for a necessary reason: that without coercion justice need not apply. My invocation of the contract tradition was not intended as an endorsement of the view that contractualism is the correct approach to determining principles; only that it is one influential approach that illustrates that duties of justice obtain prior to (and independently of) coercion. The fact that someone is coerced into complying with a principle could be all the more reason to treat her justly, all the more reason for her to complain if treated unjustly. But it is certainly not necessary for there to be duties to treat her justly, nor necessary for her to have legitimate grounds for complaint.[9]

Sangiovanni seems on the verge of making this point, and indeed makes it in part with respect to coercion. In his counterfactual thought experiment, a coercive state with progressive taxation – presumably on grounds of justice – suddenly ceases to be coercive, but people continue voluntarily to comply with state laws. It is counterintuitive, Sangiovanni suggests, that duties of justice no longer obtain simply because the system

9 Imagine a child being stopped from playing somewhere by an adult. The reason given by the adult ought to be a good one, given that the child is being coerced. However, if it is a good one, it presumably ought to be complied with whether or not coercion is employed; presumably it is better that it be complied with for a good reason, and if the adult's is a necessary and sufficient reason it had better be that one.

has ceased to be coercive. This would seem just a complement to my point above that it is counterintuitive to say there are no duties of justice before coercion is used. But Sangiovanni then shifts to the claim that non-voluntary membership in the society – understood as the inability of people to leave without undue burden – avoids this objection.[10]

I would make two points in reply. First, there is an element of truth in the claim, but it is a trivial one that does not support statism. In this sense of non-voluntariness, everyone globally is in a non-voluntary situation not only with respect to their own societies but with respect to global divisions into societies and polities, and the global distributions of goods that ensue. There does seem something intuitive in the claim that if someone could pick themselves up without any burden to themselves and reinstall themselves in another society, one might be justified in saying to them: if you don't like the way things are done here, why don't you move to X?[11] The fact that they cannot do so defeats the force of the taunt. But this same point applies to the non-associated islanders discussed above. Both Decent and Unlucky can say to Greedy and Lucky respectively, 'If I could get easily back to civilisation I would make no claim against you; in fact I would be happy to leave your entire island to you. I have no choice in the matter of my being here, yet there is a choice about how we divide the available goods. But secondly, there is a deeper misunderstanding in the non-voluntary membership justification of statism that resembles the problem with the coercion-based justification. Sangiovanni construes the non-voluntariness of residency (probably following Rawls, who in turn was probably following Hume's critique of Locke's tacit consent) in terms of the degree of burden that would be incurred by someone who tried to leave. What exactly constitutes this burden? In part, no doubt, being deracinated, leaving one's attachments and familiar environment of experiences, possibly language and culture, and so forth. So why not impose this burden on whoever dislikes the local distribution? Presumably because

10 Sangiovanni (2007) doesn't endorse this position; in fact he thinks it is ultimately unpersuasive and prefers a reciprocity-based argument to be discussed below. My criticism is just that he thinks non-voluntary residency a coherent defense of statism that is immune to the criticism just made of coercion. But both are subject to the same objection: that they either presuppose the duties of justice they claim to make necessary, or they generate entirely counter-intuitive examples of reasons to apply justice.

11 This was a familiar taunt in the Cold War, where X was the questioner's favourite communist enemy. This could be understood against the background of a different issue, that of the relativism of justice. Different societies might have different standards or values, each of which is defensible on general grounds, and this could give rise to different principles of justice in each society. I cannot pursue this here, except briefly below.

doing so would be *unfair*. So it is presupposed that considerations of fairness already apply to the person in question. This can be seen in the following example. Suppose a person had no attachment to her country or anyone in it, and would be quite willing to try something new by emigrating if a suitable place could be found. But suppose the only available place was a barren desert like Infertile where, instead of having available to her the conditions of a modern industrial society, she would have to struggle like Unlucky just for subsistence. Would it be fair to tell this person, If you don't like the way things are done here, why don't you move to Infertile? Presumably the decline of living standard here would itself be an unfair burden that it would be wrong to impose on her. If that is correct, then the concept of non-voluntariness of membership is itself parasitic on an antecedent conception of justice, or at any rate fairness. Suppose, for instance, that one was a sufficientarian. If the person were, as stated above, willing to emigrate to a suitable place, and there was one that enabled her to have 'enough' for a decent life, then her first residency would be voluntary and justice need not apply. But that is only because justice has already been applied; the person will be getting 'enough' no matter what. Or suppose one was an egalitarian. Then if the only available alternative was a place where her life would be significantly worse off, even if meeting standards of sufficiency, from the standpoint of egalitarianism it should still be unfair to force her to accept being worse off; hence it would be an unacceptable burden, hence her residency would be non-voluntary, hence justice between her and her original society should apply. Non-voluntariness is therefore not an independent necessary and sufficient condition for the need for justice to apply, but in fact circularly presupposes the application of justice to determine non-voluntariness. (There is an affinity here with Hume's discussion of coercion).

(2) *participation in a common cooperative system engendering reciprocity in the mutual provision of domestic public goods*

Sangiovanni, and arguably Rawls, adopt this reciprocity-based defense of statism. Justice is owed between members of a common cooperative system because each benefits from the contribution of all the other members in the joint production of public goods. I have already suggested, with the examples of isolated islanders, that it is counter-intuitive that duties of justice require this associational basis. A close reading of Sangiovanni shows that it is not the association per se, but the degree each benefits from the contributions of the others, that grounds the duties of justice; that is why he calls his a reciprocity-based view. But there are two questions that can be raised about this account. First, why should only jointly produced public goods ground duties of justice? Sangiovanni's answer is that only these put each in everyone else's debt. But while this might provide a motivation for each, and especially the better off, to comply with distributive principles, that cannot be the only reason for considerations of justice to apply, unless one wishes to reduce justice to a Hobbesian-Gauthierian scheme of mutual advantage. This leads to a second point, mentioned at the beginning of this section. The reciprocity-based view has difficulty accounting for obligations toward non-working residents such as the disabled. Sangiovanni handles those who are willingly unemployed by saying that arguably nothing is owed them (Sangiovanni, 2007, p. 28 fn. 45), but the disabled are obviously in a different category. His answer is that if they are still, say, law-abiding, voting, tax-paying, and otherwise involved in their community, then they are still contributing to the public goods that enable even a wealthy entrepreneur to pursue her life-plan. But this seems strained to the point of implausibility. Suppose someone was so disabled that she didn't vote or participate in the community. She doesn't work so doesn't contribute taxes. She may not break the law, but couldn't even if she wanted to. Her only interaction with society is as a recipient of aid from health and care agencies. It strains credulity to tell an entrepreneur or anyone else that they owe her aid because of her contribution to the production of public goods. In cases like this, Sangiovanni says that such people "do not have any claims deriving from a conception of distributive equality", but they do "have claims deriving from their equal moral worth and dignity as human beings, which include claims to the alleviation of suffering and pain" (Sangiovanni, 2007, p. 31 fn. 50).

This argument is deeply problematic in the context of reciprocity-based statism. If the suggestion is that the more disabled someone is, the less they should receive, and that someone prevented from making any useful contribution should receive the barest subsistence and medication to alleviate pain, the view will seem counterintuitive to all but the most tough-minded libertarians and Gauthierians. If that was not the intended position, but rather that the humanitarian duty should be able to account for why the severely disabled might receive as much or more than the less severely disabled or the able-bodied, the challenge will now have been displaced to the question of why reciprocity supports statism. For now two more questions arise: (a) if humanitarian concerns alone can account for duties to raise a severely disabled person to levels comparable to those of members of a reciprocity-based system, has not the case for statism just gone by the boards? After all, what makes the severely disabled an object of humanitarian concern is that they cannot help being in the state they are in. That is the morally relevant aspect of their situation that does the work of grounding duties to them, but the global poor are equally in a state of poverty not of their choosing, as globalist luck-egalitarians observe.

(b) If the duty to the severely disabled is purely humanitarian, why is the political state that they are in the agency that must assume the duty to help them. Oddly, in the same footnote where Sangiovanni explains duties to the severely disabled as based on humanitarian considerations, he cites Robert Goodin's essay "What is So Special About Our Fellow Countrymen?". But Goodin uses this example precisely to argue that all duties of justice within states are derivative of universal moral duties – which Sangiovanni's associational statism denies – and that otherwise one cannot explain why states are responsible for their own (severely) disabled residents. The alternative that Goodin suggests now appears entirely convincing: that there is a global division of responsibility along state lines to carry out universal duties of justice, such that each state assumes responsibility for its citizens and residents.[12] This division of responsibility makes sense up to a point: states are unrivalled concentrations of power and agencies of control, and they are consequently the most appropriate agents to implement justice among their citizens. But when states fail to do so, whether because their governments are corrupt and unjust, simply incompetent, or because the poverty of their state is beyond their control due to global economic factors or bad luck, then there is reason to consider other states and individuals secondarily responsible. The view is analogous to one which holds parents primarily responsible for their children's welfare and upbringing. When the parents fail to discharge this duty for whatever reason – death, incompetence, neglect, or abuse – the duty must be assumed by someone else. The right of the child is not diminished by the failure of the primary duty-bearer, nor should it be automatically the case that the rights of the global poor be diminished by the failure of their governments.

The difficulty of accounting for duties to the disabled also is faced by the first view discussed above, the coercion-based account. It again seems implausible to suggest that someone who is bed-ridden and not paying taxes (so not coerced in any significant way) should be cared for by the state because she is still in the purview of a coercive system.

Luck egalitarians would of course have no difficulty accounting for obligations to the disabled. But then it is difficult to see why this view should be contained within national borders; after all, being born in an impoverished country is bad brute luck of vast significance in terms of one's prospects for well-being (Beitz, 1983). Both main views examined thus far face the dilemma delineated above: either they cannot adequately

---

12 I am indebted to Rekha Nath for pointing out to me the similarity between Goodin's view and my own, and I have recast this section to attribute the view to Goodin (1988).

account for duties of states to their non-contributing residents, or in accounting for them they cannot then contain the duties so justified to the boundaries of the state, but must on pain of inconsistency extend them to the world's needy.

(3) *Nagel's Rousseauean argument that citizens are both authors and subjects of the laws.*

This argument I think can be dealt with briefly. Being subject to the law has already been addressed in the section on coercion, for what else does being subject to law mean? The novelty in the argument is the claim that citizens make the law. But while one might think jointly making laws can create special associational duties, there seems nothing in the argument to show that this is necessary for there being duties of justice. Moreover, the notion that citizens make the laws, even in democracies, is somewhat idealised. Whatever moral weight the notion has seems derived from good old actual contract theory. People who consent to govern themselves in a certain way should perhaps, within some reasonable bounds, be so governed; what else can jointly making the laws morally amount to? But even among those who really did consent (and putting aside whether unanimity would be required) this doesn't really show what the content of the laws should be. If consent is doing work here – and if not I do not see what is significant about jointly making laws – then it would seem that a range of content-options from across the spectrum, including individual-risky utilitarianism, should be permissible. With respect to coercion – being 'merely' subject to law – it makes sense to say that one ought to be able to justify the law to the worst off. But with respect to makers of the law far less needs to be justified: if someone complains that he is badly off, one need only ask him why in heaven he consented to such an arrangement, and whether he should not think twice about it the next time. If, on the other hand, non-unanimity is presumed, then the relevance of jointly making the law disappears. And to reiterate, even if I have misconstrued Nagel's argument and joint authorship of the laws is *sufficient* to create some special duties of justice, this gives no support to a claim that joint authorship is *necessary* for justice to obtain.

(4) *membership in a single centralised system of power and decision-making*

This argument, versions of which can be found in David Miller's version of statism, has I think two related elements: that the welfare of citizens is affected primarily by the policies (and general character) of their state, and that therefore moral responsibility for ensuring justice for people lies primarily with their states. There is some merit, I think, to this argument. If a state's poor investment policies lead to its being badly off, it seems wrong to hold other states primarily responsible for redressing the inequality. Miller himself draws attention to the parallels between holding states as collectivities and individuals within societies responsible for self-inflicted predicaments. He is aware, as well, that individuals within societies are not equally responsible, and many not responsible at all, for policies of their state. This is evident with dictatorships, but is arguably to some extent true with democracies as well: some people might have opposed the sitting government, and in any case governance is nowhere by referendum. But the point I wish to emphasise is the other side of the coin: if responsibility can defeat the applicability of egalitarianist justice globally it should do so domestically as well.

No doubt it is important to clarify what is now meant by egalitarianism. Luck egalitarianism, after all, aims precisely to render justice responsibility-sensitive. Responsibility, however, can mean many things. It can refer to the control one exercises over the acquisition and use of wealth, income, resources, or primary goods. But it can also denote the control one has over the significance one attributes in one's life to different goods. This is a sensitive point. A long-standing criticism of utilitarianism is that it seems to count adaptive preferences to various levels of privation equally with other preferences, and that is thought to be one of the ways it is at odds with considerations of justice (Elster, 1982). On the other hand, there is a well-known phenomenon of exemplary adaptations – not solely of preferences, but an entire reorientation of value and lifestyle – to extreme hardship or deprivation (what Saul Smilansky calls 'fortunate misfortune': where a tragic situation or very difficult condition that befalls someone – a death of a loved one, a near-fatal disease, loss of limb, disability – or more morally troublesome cases of man-made suffering such as wrongful imprisonment, racist persecution, torture or even incarceration in a concentration camp – leads to a radical transformation in their life and the finding of new 'meaning' (Smilansky, 2007). Think, for example, of a Helen Keller, Elie Weisel, Stephen Hawking. What stance should justice take in the face of such situations?

On the one hand it seems obvious that one ought to continue to condemn mistreatment, wrongful incarceration, persecution, in short injustice in general, however much there remained a chance that a victim might ultimately and indirectly benefit from the wrong. Similarly, adaptations to injustice and exploitation of the 'false-consciousness' variety must be discouraged, insofar as they encourage actions that are wrong in themselves. Finally, disability, suffering, disease, loss of livelihood, and other disadvantages of the sort that would likely prevent one from leading a normal life, would seem to be grounds for compensation with the aim of enabling as normal and decent a life as possible.[13] Poverty that was severe enough would fall into this category as well. For one thing, successful adaptations to such significant adversity are rare and unpredictable; for another, even many who adapt brilliantly to adversity might have suffered needlessly. (Might Stephen Hawking have done as well or better without suffering disability?)

All the above is on the side of compensating for severe disadvantage. But as for adaptation to merely unequal shares of particular goods or bundles of goods, it would seem undesirable to adopt principles for the sake of discouraging them. That is, it is desirable that justice not undermine the incentive for individuals and distinct societies to pursue a satisfying and worthwhile life in the non-ideal circumstances (and unequal advantages) that the complexities of real life normally generate. In other words, adaptations to inequality should not be automatically assimilated to false consciousness, as egalitarian conceptions would encourage one to think. Thus the notion of responsibility to which justice should be sensitive ought to include a wide range of control the individual should retain for finding a meaningful life within the vast and possibly infinite complex of circumstance and value. There are reasons to wish to avoid too much interference by government institutions in this individual control, not least of which is the old worry of undermining self-reliance. And similarly, there is a degree of parallel responsibility that governments and their respective societies should assume in the face of inequalities between nations. A conception of global justice that placed the onus on the wealthiest nations always to raise poorer nations to their level would have a pernicious effect on the adoption of sound development policies.[14]

Sufficiency

Some of Frankfurt's strictures against the egalitarian ethos mesh with the thrust of the previous paragraph. But it is not only the encouragement of envy, of looking over one's shoulder at how others are doing, that is a

13 'Normal' is admittedly both vague and subject to various kinds of relativity. Nevertheless, I think in the context of this brief account sufficient sense can be made of it: someone confined to a wheelchair, struggling with leukemia, or possibly having been psychologically scarred by serious abuse, would be a typical case of a person prevented from leading a normal life without material and other help.

14 A burgeoning literature of development studies make this point. Dambisa Moyo identifies an "aid curse" similar to resource curse African countries. Dambisa Moyo (2010), *Dead Aid: Why Aid Is Not Working and How There Is a Better Way for Africa.* See also William Easterly (2006), and Stephen Knack (2001).

perverse incentive of this ethos. In fact, implementation of a sufficiency doctrine might require considerable comparison, *pace* Frankfurt (1987; 1997; 2000), Crisp (2003), and even sympathetic critics such as Casal (2007). This is for two reasons: first, because raising up to the sufficient threshold those below requires taxation of those above, and some further principle, presumably, to determine whom to tax more and whom less. Secondly, sufficiency would seem at least partially relative to the general aggregate of available goods, services, and technology. A century ago what might have been thought to be sufficient to lead a decent life could be considered poverty today, and this is an inherently 'comparative' point: a poor person today must compare herself to her contemporaries, or at any rate the contemporary technological capacity and aggregate wealth, to know if she has sufficient opportunities and sufficient welfare generally. If medical breakthroughs lead to a two hundred year average life expectancy for the many who can afford access to the relevant treatment, others with an eighty or even one hundred year life expectancy would not have enough.

Thus the merit of sufficiency doctrines is not that they repudiate comparative judgements encouraged or required by egalitarian and prioritarian thinking, and hence the morally valueless envy such judgements allegedly engender. Rather, their merit, and what perhaps in part motivates their proponents without them fully recognising it, is their attempt to increase the scope of responsibility of people for their own general well-being (whether or not those people are envious of those better off than them).

The earlier point about adaptation is that an egalitarian ethos would seem to encourage people to look to government to make their lives better, instead of striving themselves to discover from the multitudinous available life paths one that would be satisfying and meaningful. Are you ugly? (Nietzsche might say to Socrates). Then become a philosopher. Are you bad at sports? Learn to play an instrument. Neither of these succeed? Try being exceptionally kind – surely anyone can do that.

The importance of self-reliance is just as acute with regard to the collectivities known as states. Miller's emphasis on responsibility is no doubt heightened by an awareness of how the Asian tigers, more importantly China and India, and following them Pakistan, Vietnam, Bangladesh and others are beginning to achieve for their citizens decent levels of income and welfare. But some degree of adaptation should likely also be accepted and encouraged here. Societies with scarce resources at least have the potential to become industrious; the incentive to do so should not be undermined.

These remarks take justice in an opposite direction from where the late Jerry Cohen would have taken it. It is of course possible to treat justice as an abstract ideal that approaches equality, but if the remarks above have merit, the result would be the further normative principle that justice should never be implemented. Whether this 'rescues' justice or condemns it to relative irrelevance is an open question. One might think it rescues its pristine purity at the cost of irrelevance. The alternative view I have been proposing is a conception of justice that incorporates psychological facts, circumstances of the plurality of avenues of meaningfulness and satisfaction, and incentive effects. Cohen would call the principles that emerge from consideration of these factors principles of regulation, not justice. For present purposes I am happy that those in agreement with Cohen treat my entire discussion as actually about principles of regulation and not justice.

To return to the case of the island refugees with which I began, it seems intuitive that issues of fairness arise between them even if they do not share an association, and it further seems arbitrary to hold that these considerations of fairness are irrelevant to justice. But the industriousness of one as against the laziness of the other is arguably not arbitrary, and while the determinist question of responsibility and desert is debatable, the general value of encouraging 'compatibilist' responsibility – even if something like determinism is true – is not. Again, even a Cohenian who would reject 'tainting' justice with considerations of its incentive effect might agree with principles of regulation taking these into account. The incentive effect of a scheme of justice is itself a consideration in favour of or against that scheme, and I have tried to suggest in this paper that at both a global and a national scale there are important reservations about adopting any egalitarian conception.

References

Anderson, E. (1979). "What is the Point of Equality?". *Ethics*. Vol. 109. No. 2. Pp. 287-337.

Beitz, C. (1979). *Political Theory and International Relations*. Princeton. Princeton University Press).

Beitz, C. (1983). "Cosmopolitan Ideals and National Sentiments". *The Journal of Philosophy*. Vol. 80. No. 10. Pp. 591-600.

Brooks, T. (2008). *The Global Justice Reader*. Oxford. Blackwell.

Casal, P. (2007)."Why *Sufficiency* is not Enough." *Ethics*. Vol. 117. No. 2. Pp. 296-326.

Crisp, R. (2003). "Equality, Priority, and Compassion." *Ethics*. Vol. 113. No. 4. Pp. 745-763.

Crisp, R. (2004). "Egalitarianism and Compassion." *Ethics*. Vol. 114. No. 1. Pp. 119-126.

Easterly, W. (2006). *The White Man's Burden*. Penguin. Oxford.

Elster, J. (1982). "Sour Grapes". In B. Williams & A. Sen. Eds. *Utilitarianism and Beyond.* Cambridge. Cambridge University Press. Pp. 219-38.

Frankfurt, H. (1987). "Equality as a Moral Ideal." *Ethics*. Vol. 98. No. 2. Pp. 21-43.

Frankfurt, H. (1997). "Equality and Respect." *Social Research*. Vol. 64. No. 1. Pp. 3-15.

Frankfurt, H. (2000). "The Moral Irrelevance of Equality." *Public Affairs Quarterly*. Vol. 14. No. 2. Pp. 87-103

Goodin, R. (1988). "*What* is *So Special* about Our Fellow Countrymen?". *Ethics*. Vol. 98. No. 4. Pp. 663-686.

Heyd, D. (2007). "Justice and Solidarity: The Contractarian Case Against Global Justice". *Journal of Social Philosophy*. Vol. 38. No. 1. Pp. 112-130.

Jones, C. (1999). *Global Justice: Defending Cosmopolitanism*. Oxford. Oxford University Press.

Knack, S. (2001). "Aid Dependence and the Quality of Governance". *Southern Economic Journal.* Vol. 68. No. 2. Pp. 310-329.

Miller, D. (1999). "Justice and Global Inequality." A. Hurrell and N. Woods (eds.). *Inequality, Globalization and World Politics*. Oxford. Oxford University Press.

Miller, D. (2004). "National Responsibility and International Justice." D. Chatterjee (ed.). *The Ethics of Assistance: Morality and the Distant Needy*. Cambridge. Cambridge University Press.

Miller, D. (2007). *National Responsibility and Global Justice*. Oxford University Press.

Moellendorf, D. (2002). *Cosmopolitan Justice*. Boulder. Westview.

Murphy, L. (1999). "Institutions and the Demands of Justice". *Philosophy & Public Affairs*. Vol. 27, No. 4. Pp. 251-91.

Nagel, T. ([2005] 2008). "The Problem of Global Justice". *Philosophy and Public Affairs*. Vol. 33. No. 2. Pp. 113-147. Reprinted in Thom Brooks. *The Global Justice Reader*. Oxford. Blackwell.

Nozick, R. (1974). *Anarchy, State, and Utopia*. New York. Basic Books and Oxford. Basil Blackwell.

Parfit, D. (2000)."Equality or Priority?". Matthew Clayton and Andrew Williams (eds.). *The Ideal of Equality*. London. Macmillan.

Pogge, T. (2008). *World Poverty and Human Rights*. 2nd ed. Cambridge. Polity.

Rawls, J. *A Theory of Justice*. Rawls, J. (1971). *A Theory of Justice*. Cambridge. MA. Harvard University Press.

Sangiovanni, A. (2007). "Global Justice, Reciprocity, and the State". *Philosophy and Public Affairs.* Vol. 35. No. 1. Pp. 3-39.

Scheffler, S. (2002). *Boundaries and Allegiances: Problems of Justice and Responsibility in Liberal Thought.* Oxford. Oxford. Oxford University Press.

Smilansky, S. (2007). *Moral Paradoxes.* Malden/MA. Blackwell Publishing.

Tan, K. C. (2004). *Justice Without Borders.* Cambridge. Cambridge University Press.

Walzer, M. (1983). *Spheres of Justice.* New York. Basic Books.

Wenar, L. (2001)."Contractualism and Global Economic Justice". *Global Justice.* Thomas Pogge (ed.). Oxford. Blackwell.

Wenar, L. (2003 [2008]). "What We Owe to Distant Others". *Politics, Philosophy, Economics.* Vol. 2. No. 3. Pp. 283-304. Reprinted in Thom Brooks. *The Global Justice Reader.* Oxford. Blackwell.

What is so Special about the State?

Rekha Nath

Introduction

For many, justice, or at least an important sub-species of justice, is concerned with what we owe to others with whom we share an association. In this spirit, John Rawls (1999a, p. 3) called justice the 'first virtue of social institutions' and for Hume (1966 [1777], p. 25) the bounds of justice grow in accordance with the bounds of interaction. In light of this connection between justice and associations, the state has come to occupy a central role in political philosophy as the primary association to which assessments of justice apply. Claims of justice, as a result, are often phrased in terms of what *citizens* rather than simply *individuals* are owed. Without any doubt, the state is an important association for most individuals in this world, and this fact is unlikely to change any time soon. Yet, taking seriously the relationship between justice and interaction requires that we pay attention also to the normative implications of global interdependence. In particular, we ought to ask how the high levels of interaction through transnational institutions like the World Trade Organization (WTO) and the International Monetary Fund (IMF) influence our moral obligations to individuals outside of our own states.

A view that has been frequently defended both in public discourse and political philosophy drives a wedge between the normative relevance of states and the global order with respect to what is owed to individuals in each domain. On this view, which I follow others in calling 'statism', the state plays a special role in generating duties of justice that apply exclusively among citizens.[1] Citizens of a state are in a special relationship that

1 The following are a representative sample of statist views: Richard Miller (1998), John Rawls (1999b), Michael Blake (2002), Thomas Nagel (2005), and Andrea Sangiovanni (2007). For ease of language I, and most of the statists, use the term 'citizen' rather loosely. For all intents and purposes, certain groups of non-citizens like long-term and permanent residents are included in the scope of statists' egalitarian concern. See Blake (2002, p. 266n8) and Sangiovanni (2007) the latter of whom uses the phrase 'citizens and residents' throughout his defense of statism.

gives them claims of egalitarian justice upon each other. That egalitarian justice should be restricted to the state is driven by the claim that inequality is morally troublesome only when attached to certain forms of institutional interaction. In this way, duties of egalitarian justice are generated as a result of the unique relationship among citizens. And although global interaction is recognized as influential and ever-growing, it is nonetheless regarded as markedly different in character from the interaction among state citizens. Consequently, statists oppose extending principles of egalitarian justice, which are suited for the state, to the global domain.[2]

This paper is devoted to examining the merits of the statist position. It proceeds as follows. In the first section, I discuss the three main strategies employed by statists in defense of restricting the scope of their theories to the state. The second section criticizes this scope restriction on the grounds of the statists' reliance upon a faulty empirical characterization of the institutional relationships that transcend state borders. In the third section, I turn to the statists' normative claims that the particular institutional relationships claimed to be unique to the state are capable of generating claims of egalitarian justice. I suggest that the statists fail to provide a satisfactory account of why, and consequently where, inequalities generate claims of justice. I conclude, then, that the restriction of egalitarian justice to the state, at least according to the explanations considered, is unjustified.

I: The Statist View

In this section, I examine the statist argument for restricting duties of egalitarian justice to the state. Essentially, the statist claims that the particular form of institutional interaction found in the state generates mutual duties of egalitarian justice among citizens. The statist further argues that these same types of duties are not owed to foreigners because the global domain lacks the requisite characteristics to generate concern for inequalities between individuals from different states. The idea that citizens are in a unique relationship with one another that generates member-specific claims of justice is two-part (Sangiovanni, 2007, p. 8). First, is the empirical claim that some particular type of institutional relationship that is found among citizens does not exist outside of the state. Second, is the normative claim that the given form of interaction unique to the state

---

2 Some statists, particularly Nagel (2005) argue that *no* principles of justice whatsoever obtain beyond state borders. Instead, only humanitarian duties that target individuals' absolute levels of deprivation apply outside of the state.

generates obligations of egalitarian justice. Consequently, individuals owe duties of egalitarian justice to, and *only* to, their fellow citizens. As such, for the statist to maintain that inequalities require attention only within the state they must successfully defend the following two claims: (1) a relevant empirical disanalogy exists between the state and the global domain, and (2) this disanalogy entails that certain forms of domestic inequality are unjust while those same forms of global inequality are not.

In what follows, I explore three competing explanations for restricting duties of egalitarian justice to the state that have recently been put forward. Each of these focuses on a different aspect of the state's institutional structure to support the claim that it uniquely triggers concern for equality. These different aspects of the state that act as 'triggers' (that is, they trigger claims of egalitarian justice among those bound up in the given type of institutional relationship) are: (1) the coercive apparatus of the state; (2) citizens' co-authorship of the state's coercive regime; and, (3) and the state's provision of basic goods.

First, according to the *coercion argument*, egalitarian duties are exclusively owed to citizens of the state due to their subjection to the state's coercive regulations that significantly violate their autonomy (Blake, 2002; see also Miller, 1998). Through both criminal and civil law, the state regulates numerous areas of citizens' lives. Moreover, it possesses an unrivalled capacity to enforce its legal regulations through punitive measures, such as fines and imprisonment. State coercion is distinct not only in its magnitude, but also for the domain of citizens' lives over which it governs. Through its legal apparatus, the state plays a significant role in defining property entitlements and regulating taxation.[3] From a liberal perspective, Blake claims that we ought to be concerned by state coercion precisely because it violates citizens' autonomy. Not all types of coercion or autonomy-violation stand in need of the same justification as that which the state enforces over its citizens. Rather that the state subjects its citizens to a regime of private law, and is thus in the business of defining and maintaining a predictable system of distributive holdings for its members distinctly gives rise to the special justification they are owed. Drawing on Rawls's hypothetical contract reasoning, Blake argues that the only form of justification that will suffice is the implementation of the difference principle. After discussing the other two statist arguments, which also

---

3 Blake uses the term 'private law' (in contrast to 'criminal law') to refer to all legal protections of private entitlements, including 'the law of contracts, torts, and property' which as a collective body 'defines how property will be understood and held, and what sorts of activities will produce what sort of economic holding' (Blake, 2002, p. 281).

draw on Rawlsian reasoning to justify the need for egalitarian duties in the state, I will say a bit more about this type of argument.

A second account of statism also focuses on state coercion, but it draws on something different from autonomy-violation to ground the need for justification through egalitarian duties. Its focus is on the role of citizens as joint authors of the terms they coercively impose upon one another. Call this the *co-authorship argument.* In addition to the moral significance of citizens' *subjection* to state coercion, it is emphasized that they are also the *joint authors* of those terms since they have political authority over them (Nagel, 2005, pp. 128-130). Due to their twin role as subjects and authors of the state's coercive terms, all citizens share a collective responsibility for them. It doesn't matter for this account that some states are not democratic or that many citizens even in democratic states vehemently oppose particular policies adopted by their governments.[4] Instead, insofar as the state association is largely inescapable, what matters is that citizens cannot help but uphold and consequently perpetuate its coercive terms through their compliance therewith and tax contributions. Each citizen thus inherits the duty to his fellow compatriots to only coercively impose upon them terms that they would reasonably find acceptable, both as recipients of such treatment and in their role as joint authors of the same.

Despite both focusing on state coercion, there is a significant difference between how this account and the previous one explain how egalitarian duties are generated within the state. Blake's coercion argument focuses on the ways in which state coercion thwarts individuals' autonomy, and it claims that equality among citizens is needed to justify this infringement of autonomy. The co-authorship argument, by contrast, draws on citizens' responsibility for the rules that they unavoidably play a role in enforcing in their co-citizens' names. Only if the state adopts egalitarian principles of distributive justice can this project be justified to its members in virtue of this special relationship. A third argument for limiting egalitarian concern to the state differs from the previous two in its focus on what the state does *for* its members in beneficial terms as opposed to what it does *to* them as a burden. According to this account, which we can call the *basic goods provision argument,* the state uniquely provides its members with the essential goods they need to live autonomous lives.[5] Citizens in

4 This much is clear from Nagel's (2005, p. 129n14) statement that even colonial powers and occupying forces give rise to this form of collective authorization since under these regimes subjects are expected to uphold the laws that are enforced, which are at least purportedly enacted to serve their interests.

5 As Sangiovanni (2007, p. 4) puts it: Citizens of a state provide one another with 'a central class of collective goods, namely those goods necessary for developing and act-

the state enjoy, or typically expect to enjoy, such goods as physical security, legally protected rights, and a stable market and property rights system (Sangiovanni, 2007, pp. 20-21). Since the state provision of these goods depends on citizens' legal compliance and their financial and social support, it can be said that indirectly citizens vitally depend on one another. As a result of each citizen's role in sustaining the state, she has a claim on her fellow citizens to be treated with reciprocity for her contributions. And, in this way, all citizens of the state owe another duties of egalitarian justice in return for their mutual efforts to uphold the state. Unlike Blake and Nagel's accounts, egalitarian justice is not seen as a form of compensation for the burdensome aspects of the state but rather is owed as a form of fair reciprocity for making possible the very conditions that enable members of society to flourish.[6] Since the distribution and the accumulation of wealth generally within the state are made possible by the cooperation of all citizens, they are all owed an explanation for the relative distributive shares that ensue.

Despite the different focal points of statists – on coercion, co-authorship, and basic goods provision – these accounts nonetheless arrive at the same conclusion: that egalitarian justice applies exclusively in the state. This may come as a surprise. For one thing, what does each of these different triggers have to do with equality? Furthermore, how is it that the same requirement, egalitarian duties of justice, follows from such different types of institutional relationships?[7] These questions can be answered by pointing out that regardless of the important differences between these accounts, they share an underlying normative rationale. None of these triggers actually has much to do with equality *per se*. Instead, the demand for egalitarian claims among citizens is generated by the following two-part argument:

(1) The given trigger *x* demarcates the group of persons to whom some form of special justification is owed. In particular, the trigger gives rise to

---

ing on a plan of life'. They 'constitute and maintain the state through taxation, through participation in various forms of political activity, and through simple compliance, which includes the full range of our everyday, legally regulated activity' (p. 20).

6 Sangiovanni (2007, p. 26) writes that 'Your talents, efforts, and skills, that is, have been able to win you social advantages only through the cooperation and contributions of other citizens and residents'. Due to reciprocity, 'others are owed a fair return for what they have given you, just as you are owed a fair return for what you have given others'.

7 Of course, none of the proponents of the different accounts argue for the mutual compatibility of their accounts, but the fact that they all seek to derive the same normative requirement from different sources is interesting.

the need for distributive justice within the state since the state plays a significant role in regulating distributive holdings through property rights and taxation schemes.

(2) The presumption towards equality is cashed out in Rawlsian terms drawing on what distributive principles would be chosen in a hypothetical contract. From this reasoning we get the difference principle, which stipulates that the state's basic structure only permit inequalities that maximize the position of the representative worse-off group.

In grounding his egalitarian account, Rawls focuses on how distributive inequalities can have harmful effects on citizens' social and political relations with one another, as well as (and arguably to a lesser degree) the moral arbitrariness of permitting luck-derived inequalities (Freeman, 2007, chapter 4; Scheffler, 2003). The statists considered above defend their endorsement of the difference principle almost exclusively on the basis that inequalities traceable to morally arbitrary factors are unjustifiable in the state context, while mostly ignoring the impacts of inequalities on relationships.[8] Sangiovanni (2007, pp. 22-29) points out that citizens' joint provision of goods like education and a stable property rights system enables those with favored morally arbitrary characteristics like talent to make greater returns than their less talented compatriots.[9] Insofar as the ability of the better-off to do so well depends on their fellow citizens' contributions to the state system, the luck egalitarian impulse only applies in such goods-providing systems like the state. Proponents of the coercion and co-authorship accounts claim that state coercion can only be justified by hypothetical consent if it does not allow morally arbitrary factors to allow the talented and the like to benefit more from the coercive system than others (Blake, 2002, p. 283; Nagel 2005, pp. 127-129).[10] In sum, these different arguments respectively claim that pervasive coercion, joint authorship of pervasive coercion, and the provision of basic goods trigger claims of egalitarian justice to justify the given form of institutional interaction to participants of the state.

---

8 The one minor exception to this is Blake. Although he gives most of his attention to this idea of hypothetical consent, he mentions an alternative consideration in support of restricting egalitarian considerations to the state: 'Those who share liability to a coercive government, after all, must have relatively equal abilities to influence that government's policies under any plausible theory of liberal justice' (2002, p. 284).

9 Talent is just one example among a number of different morally arbitrary factors that can be cashed in upon to translate into economic gains. See Sangiovanni (2007, pp. 25-29).

10 It may seem that there is a missing link here – namely, why *equality* is the only way to justify such a system. I agree that it is not obvious and develop this criticism in the following section.

II. Challenging the Statists' Empirical Claims

Having outlined some of the recent arguments that have been put forward in defense of restricting egalitarian concern to the state, I now consider whether this restriction is justified. Both the statists' empirical and normative premises must be correct for their claim that egalitarian justice is confined to state boundaries to hold. Rejecting either their empirical or normative claims would suffice to refute the statists' claim about the scope of egalitarianism. In what follows, I show that the statist accounts can be challenged on both fronts. Turning first to the empirical claim, we can consider the accuracy of the depiction of the state as a unique domain of institutional interaction. In a number of respects, it is glaringly obvious that the state is a unique form of association; but my concern in this section is limited to the empirical claim that the global domain lacks the particular triggers – coercion, co-authorship, and basic goods provision – as claimed by the respective statist accounts.

Proponents of the statist approaches considered in the last section all readily admit that the incidence of each of these triggers, in some form or another, is not limited to the state.[11] However, they qualify in the following four ways that the institutional interaction found in the state versus in the global domain possess some morally relevant and unique characteristics.[12] The first point, which applies only to the coercion and co-authorship arguments, states that whereas the state compels and threatens its citizens to behave in particular ways, what appear to be instances of global coercion are in actuality action-guiding incentives that individuals are free to abide by or to reject. In this way, the influence of the global order is voluntary, while state influence is coercive. Second, the state is thought to be special insofar as it is necessary for the realization of its citizens' autonomy while the global order is not. Third, the global order has an indirect relationship with individuals, as its influence is mediated through states. A relevant feature of this indirectness is that the global

11 Blake (2002, p. 265), for instance, appreciates that exploitative international trade relations might be coercive. See also Sangiovanni (2007, p. 21) and Nagel (2005, pp. 137-139) for statements of the appreciation that *similar* relationships exist globally as to in the state.

12 The empirical disanalogy between the state and the global order has been widely discussed – both by statists and their critics. As such, much of what I say in this section rehearses objections that have already been made by others. In particular, the four points I discuss here that seek to show the uniqueness of the state have been considered by Matthias Risse (2006, pp. 679-681) in which he criticizes Blake's account. Other critiques of statism that inform my own are Joshua Cohen and Charles Sabel (2006), A. J. Julius (2006), and Arash Abizadeh (2007).

order *depends* crucially on states for both coercive enforcement and goods provision such that the global order's influence on individuals is reducible to the influence of individuals' own states and does not stand in need of independent justification. The fourth point concerns the unique domain of individuals' lives over which the state regulates in comparison to that of the global order.

Turning to the first claim, the global order is alleged to be a voluntary association in contrast to the state, which is coercively imposed and collectively authorized by all of its members. The relevant difference between the two domains, according to this claim, relates to global order lacking the means to compel individuals to obey (Blake, 2002, p. 265, 280, and 293; Nagel, 2005, pp. 138-140). Unlike states, global institutions do not have sanction-based enforcement schemes (based either on financial sanctions or other punitive measures) that have authority over individuals. With regards to international organizations like the United Nations and the WTO, they rely on states for the domestic enforcement of their rules.[13] Due to their lack of coercive instruments, the global order's imposition of any rules or regulations does not seem to require the same sort of justification that the state's rules do to their members.

While it is true that states voluntarily sign up to international agreements and have the formal option of exit, individuals within those states that assent to these organizations are nonetheless non-voluntarily subject to the terms that follow this initial sign-up.[14] The statist might respond that states have freely signed up to organizations like the WTO, whereas individuals have had no such choice in joining their state. But, this point is irrelevant as the statists do not rely on claims about the historical origins of the state as to whether the formation of any given state association was voluntary (Cohen and Sabel, 2006, pp. 157-158). But, in a similar fashion, once a state has signed up to international organizations, it cannot usually abandon its newfound institutional commitments with ease because the terms of the relationship entered set up incentive structures that make the cost of exit increasingly higher for the state. As such, entire

13 To make this point Nagel says 'political institutions are different, because adherence to them is not voluntary: Emigration aside, one is not permitted to declare oneself not a member of one's society and hence not subject to its rule, and other members may coerce one's compliance if one tries to refuse. An institution that one has no choice about joining must offer terms of membership that meet a higher standard' (2005, p. 133).

14 One might claim that since individuals are represented by their states they do have some say over their subjection to various global regulations. This might be the case for some individuals, but a great number of others both in undemocratic states or those whose interests are underrepresented within democratic states will be faced with non-voluntary subjection to global rules.

populations and future generations of individuals within states face terms dictated by the global order that define many of the options open to them. Once locked into the terms of many global associations, citizens of states that voluntary sign up to such agreements hardly have a meaningful exit option. There is still a difference between 'non-voluntary' and 'coercive' influence – even if it is clear that the influence of the global order is hardly voluntary for individuals – and through the remaining points in this section I examine the relevance of this difference.

Turning then to the second claim, the state is regarded as unique insofar as it enables its members to live autonomous lives while the global order lacks the role of being necessary for individuals' autonomy-preservation (Blake, 2002, p. 280; Sangiovanni, 2007, pp. 34-35).[15] Due to this role, citizens have a unique dependency on their state. Undoubtedly, many states play an important role in the autonomy preservation of their citizens. But, not all states do so.[16] For some individuals in states that are unable to or choose not to provide the conditions for autonomy to citizens, this capacity is instead sometimes made possible by the United Nations, or through loans administered by the World Bank, or in some cases through private means (Risse, 2006, p. 681). These observations reveal that not only is it the case that states sometimes fail to provide their citizens with conditions for autonomous existence, but moreover there are other bodies besides states that can and do step in to fill this role. For this disanalogy to hold, the statist must be able to show that there is actually something special about the specific class of autonomy-enabling goods that only states provide for their citizens, which will be considered in the fourth point below. The general point, though, that states exclusively provide individuals with the conditions for autonomous life seems patently false.

According to the third claim, the global domain does not trigger duties of egalitarian justice because it is not directly imposed upon individuals (Blake, 2002, p. 280; Nagel, 2005, pp. 139-140; Sangiovanni, 2007, pp. 21-22). What is relevant about this indirectness is that the global order depends upon states for both financial support and legal enforcement, and

15 Blake says, 'Only the state is both coercive of individuals and required for individuals to live autonomous lives. Without some sort of state coercion, the very ability to autonomously pursue our project and plans seems impossible' (p. 280). This objection does not apply to Nagel's argument since he does not draw on the state's provision of autonomy-enabling goods for citizens.

16 Sangiovanni (2007, p. 4, 20, and 21) mentions occupied, weak, and failed states as exceptions to his account. He says, 'citizens and residents, in all but the most extreme cases, provide the financial and sociological support required to sustain the state' (p. 20).

so whatever it does to and for individuals around the world is thought to be reducible to states' actions. If the global order cannot coerce individuals or provide them with basic goods without the help of states, then it would not seem to stand in need of independent justification for the reasons that the state does.

To assess whether the mediated nature of the relation matters in determining the boundaries of egalitarian justice, it makes sense to consider the rationale for the statist claims that coercion or basic goods provision trigger a special demand for justification. Turning first to Blake's account, the reason he thinks that state coercion stands in need of justification is that it violates individuals' autonomy. According to this rationale, however, we should oppose subjection to global terms that infringe autonomy regardless of their mediated and/or uncoercive nature (Risse, 2006, p. 681).[17] This is because one's autonomy may be reduced both by indirect and direct forces that have similar effects on reducing the reasonable choices available to an individual.

Let us turn then to see how the co-authorship argument deals with the fact of mediation. Citizens' collective authorization of their state's institutional structure through their compliance with its laws generates a claim on behalf of each citizen for justification for those specific terms. If she finds the state's terms to be unjustified, then she has a complaint against her fellow citizens. By contrast, Nagel's point about the indirectness of the global order is that if individuals have a complaint about the way that global rules influence their lives then it should be targeted to their own government. In such cases despite the enormous potential influence of the global order on individuals' lives, it is seen as up to states ultimately to control the influence upon their own citizens that results from cross-border interaction. Any seemingly coercive global influence can, on this view, be seen as a product of coercive state influence since the state has at least some say in how open it is to transnational interaction. After all, state governments and indirectly their citizens give authority to global rules, and if states are unable to bring about the changes in global rules that they desire then they are free to abandon that particular institutional commitment. Now, this point is only plausible if we regard global organizations like the WTO and IMF as ones that can easily be left – but this is not

17 Ryan Pevnick (2008, pp. 406-409), in illustration of this point, shows that the two main reasons that coercion is opposed are for impeding autonomy and expressing disrespect. Both of these objectionable factors result from other, non-coercive, behavior that should also by the logic of the coercion argument give rise to the need for justification. He discusses the ways in which states' policies (for instances, regarding immigration or agricultural subsidies) can be shown to infringe the autonomy of foreigners, and arguably show disrespect for them.

true, as once states join these organizations the costs of leaving are very high.[18] Moreover, the influence of global rules is not fully reducible to one's own state's coercive enforcement. To explain: although the global order may not have its own coercive apparatus and must as a result rely on its member states' for domestic enforcement of its regulation, in addition often states other than one's own use *their* internal mechanisms to enforce global rules (like intellectual property rights or trade penalties) against other states. In this way, through citizens' financial support of their respective states and compliance with global rules, individuals world-wide do collectively authorize those terms that would not be perpetuated without their support.[19] Through this authorization, according to Nagel's logic they would owe justification for those terms to foreigners and compatriots alike.

We can turn, then, to the relevance of Sangiovanni's claims about the indirect nature of the global order's provision of basic goods. He notes that the global order cannot provide any goods without working through states. This has to do with both the lack of a global coercive authority and of an independent revenue-generating body (Sangiovanni, 2007, p. 21). Two points can be made in reply. First, states' ability to provide citizens with basic goods depends on compliance with certain global rules and norms. These include rules that are often taken for granted but are certainly not natural or necessary facts, like each state enjoying sovereignty over the natural resources in its territory and being able to exercise full control over its borders thus dictating who may enter and under what circumstances. These rules, and global compliance with them contribute greatly to enabling states to provide basic goods for their own citizens. A state's very ability to provide its citizens with a stable property rights system depends on the global order's prior recognition of what even counts as that state's property. Second, setting aside this relationship of dependency between states and the global order that is inverse to the one claimed by Sangiovanni, it is furthermore unclear why the global order's provision of

---

18 Cohen and Sabel ((2006, p. 168) forcefully express this point as follows: 'Opting out is not a real option (the WTO is a "take it or leave it" arrangement, without even the formal option of picking and choosing the parts to comply with), and given that it is not, and that everyone knows it is not, there is a direct rule-making relationship between the global bodies and the citizens of different states'.

19 If we look at real-world examples of individuals' dissatisfaction with global rules, it appears that in some cases citizens have directed their complaints to their own governments while in others individuals have directed complaints of fairness at international institutions themselves. Consider recent South Korean protests upon the government to reject imported foreign beef (which would violate WTO rules) for health and safety reasons; in contrast, the famous 1999 Seattle trade protests indicate that individuals do see global institutions as responsible to *them*.

certain goods is diminished by its partial dependence on states. Even if the enforcement of an international property rights system like the Trade-related Aspects of International Property Rights (TRIPs) regime depended on states for financial support and legal implementation, nonetheless new forms of reciprocity-based good provision that cross state borders come about through it. Through their compliance with global rules and through their financial support thereof (even if both occur at the state level), individuals gain important basic goods from this activity that depend in turn on the cooperation of both compatriots and foreigners.

A final posited difference between the state and the global domain brings attention to the different domains of individuals' lives over which each regulates. In particular, two exclusive roles of the state are highlighted: (1) it maintains a stable system of property holdings and entitlements (Blake, 2002, p. 281; Sangiovanni, 2007, p. 20)[20] and (2) it provides security from physical attack (*Ibid.*, p. 19).[21] With regards to both of these domains, global analogues can be found. Intellectual property rights are regulated internationally through the TRIPs system; furthermore, the 'international resource privilege' and 'international borrowing privilege' respectively recognize those who seize government power (by whatever means) as the rightful owners of the natural resources within that state's territory, and these individuals are able to borrow money on behalf of the given state's citizenry (Pogge 2002, pp. 113-115). These are clear examples of global rules that determine the distributive property holdings and entitlements of individuals. Turning to the claim that the state uniquely protects its citizens against physical attack, we find counter-examples of transnational military alliances such as NATO that fill this role, as well as United Nations peace-keeping forces that protect individuals from physical harm in cases where their states fail to do so. In defense of the statist position, one might note that states *typically* carry out these roles for their citizens, and their influence in these domains is more pervasive and profound than that of the global order. This idea, which asserts that the difference between the state and the global order is a matter of degree rather than a categorical difference, is not endorsed by any of the statists whose

20 Blake and Sangiovanni disagree on what about the state system of property rights and entitlements matters. For Blake, its *coerced* nature as backed by penalties is key, whereas for Sangiovanni it is the fact that citizens' contributions support this autonomy-enabling system. See Sangiovanni (2007, pp. 13-14n20) for criticism of Blake's assertion that this domain of activity is exclusively regulated by the state.

21 The point about different domains of activity is connected to the assertion above that only the states provide citizens with autonomy-enabling conditions. Yet, regardless of their connection with autonomy, we can separately examine whether these types of goods are provided only by the state.

views are under consideration.[22] The points made above have challenged the statists' empirical claims by showing that global instantiations of the different institutional relationships thought to be unique to the state can be located.

III. Challenging the Statists' Normative Claims

In addition to the empirical challenges of the previous section, our examination of the statists' arguments must also consider whether they provide a sound normative account of why egalitarian concern obtains only among individuals linked in these particular ways. A difficulty that appears to confront all three of the statist arguments considered above relates to how they establish the connection between the given institutional relationship and egalitarian duties. Against all of these accounts, we might ask, 'Why does violating someone's autonomy, or collectively authorizing a system of coercion, or benefiting from a system of basic goods provision give rise to concern for inequalities among those so connected?' The fit between these triggers and justification via egalitarianism is not obvious, at least not initially. My main task in this section is to understand how egalitarian duties follow from these specific triggers. I conclude that even if statists can make the case that the relationship between citizens generates concern for equality, they fail to show that *only* this relationship does so.

I will begin by considering why egalitarian duties are thought to apply among those bound by institutional coercion before turning to the other triggers. What is morally problematic about coercion is that it violates the autonomy of the coerced. According to the coercion argument associated with Blake, justification of the state's large-scale violation of its citizens' autonomy requires that they enjoy egalitarian shares of some good. This view requires some investigation into why egalitarianism would be the appropriate response to the violation of individuals' autonomy. Instead it seems that either coercion is justified by 'its results and rationale' or that it is simply unjustified.[23] To explain this point, we might think of, on the one hand, forms of 'ideal state coercion', in which the state engages in coercive practices that can be justified by their benefits for citizens. Examples include state laws regulating traffic violations or the criminalization of assault. In that the goods of safe traffic and lower crime rates serve the

22 See Risse (2006, pp. 683-89) for development of this argument.
23 See Pevnick (2008, pp. 402-403) on use of this phrase. This and the rest of the discussion in this paragraph closely draws on Pevnick's understanding of ideal and non-ideal state coercion – also framed as a critique of the coercion argument.

public benefit, citizens should not regard their autonomy as unjustly violated by these regulations – indeed, their autonomy is likely to be increased overall by such rules. On the other hand, 'non-ideal state coercion' refers to those coercive practices that can neither be justified by their results nor rationale. For instance, Pevnick provides an example in which a state government conscripts its citizens to fight in an unjust war. Extending egalitarian concern towards all citizens would be a misguided form of compensation for this particular instance of autonomy-violation. Even worse, as Pevnick suggests in this case, egalitarianism would seem to be a bribe for forced participation in what is an unjustified form of coerced activity.

For most instances of state coercion, I think this point about coercive policies requiring a built-in justification holds. Principles of egalitarian justice are an illegitimate response to many of the different forms of coercion that the state could potentially exert upon its citizens. Distributive egalitarianism simply cannot justify the autonomy infringement of such things as unjust war conscription, racist policies, or cruel and unusual punishment. Conversely, egalitarian principles are unnecessary to justify goods like the state's tax-funded provision of a health-care system or public roads. If we focus just on one narrow domain of state coercion – the coercively imposed laws that determine property rights and entitlements – the coercion argument gains some plausibility. In coercing individuals to abide by a system that predictably controls the distribution of benefits and burdens among them, it makes sense that concern for distributive justice obtains. The argument for *egalitarian* shares, then, does not serve as a justification of autonomy-violation generally, but instead to justify more specifically the coercively enforced distributive scheme by which all citizens must abide. In response to this way of understanding how the call for equality would follow from state coercion in this domain, it should be noted that there is nothing about coercion over the domain of distribution that stands in favor of any given scheme of distributive justice. Coercive regulation of this domain simply gives rise to the need to justify the resulting distributive pattern to those upon whom it is imposed, but plausibly this justification can be cashed out in any number of ways. As such, the particular call to eliminate the influence of morally arbitrary factors on individuals' relative shares requires an independent argument (which the use of Rawls's original position provides, but we should note that it does not follow directly from coercion itself). In sum, then, the coercion argument can be partially rescued from Pevnick's worry about incoherency by specifying that only a coerced system of property rights and entitlements must be justified to all individuals who are expected at risk of penalty to abide by it. But, as we can recall from the points made in the first and fourth objections to the statists' empirical characterization of the global order above, we find the non-voluntary existence of a property rights and distributive entitlement scheme internationally too. Insofar as the effects of this imposition and the domain of activity over which it regulates are comparable to that of the state's such system, this understanding of the coercion argument gives rise to global duties of egalitarian justice. More to the point, though, there is reason to doubt that the imposition of these global rules is simply non-voluntary rather than coercive. Border control is backed by force, and so is ownership of natural resources found within a state's territory. In response, one might note that that the unique property of state coercion is its enforcement by a legal system that is accountable to those over whom it assumes jurisdiction, whereas international property rights schemes and immigrations rules are not enforced through any such legal system.[24] This line of argument leads to the following perversity seen in Arash Abizadeh's (2007, p. 351) ironically posed explanation to a foreigner for why she has no claims to egalitarian justice upon us: 'We not only coerce you, but we coerce you without subjecting our ongoing coercion to the constraints of a legal system and the rules of law, and therefore we have no responsibilities of comparative distributive justice to you'.[25] Not only is it perverse to deny the unlawfully coerced any justification, but it is moreover inconsistent with the underlying rationale of concern for autonomy-violation.

This point about perversity, although it has so far been developed in response to Blake's account, also highlights precisely what it problematic about the normative premise of Nagel's co-authorship account. Excluding foreigners from having a say in the conditions that they are subjected to both by other states and global rules, is the very action that serves to justify their further exclusion from the scope of justification (via egalitarian or other duties of justice). In this way, the need for a justification of the terms we play a role in imposing upon others depends entirely on the existence of formal legal institutions that regard both us and them as its members. Yet, these accounts make no attempt to consider the prior issue

---

24 Blake (2002, p. 280n30) suggests this point briefly in a footnote: He says, the justification for 'the coercive exclusion of would-be immigrants [...] would be significantly different from that offered to a present member for the web of legal coercion within which she currently lives.' See also Nagel (2005, pp. 129-130), who writes that 'Immigration policies are simply enforced against the nationals of other states; the laws are not imposed in their name'.

25 On this point about the perversity of excluding those *not* subject to lawful coercion from the scope of egalitarian justice, see Julius (2006, pp. 179-184) who argues that this view entails that a tyrant owes less justification to those he rules over than does a leader who attempts to be accountable to his citizenry.

of the conditions under which bringing about such institutions are *necessary* in virtue of the particular types of interaction that exist among the concerned individuals. Instead, individuals from well-off countries maintain that they owe no justification to worse-off foreigners because they choose not to create the institutions necessary to give rise to such justification, and it is at the same time only in their power to bring them about.[26]

Let us turn now to the case of the basic goods provision argument and how it attempts to justify egalitarian duties. As with the coercion and co-authorship arguments, the connection between the trigger of reciprocity in goods provision and the normative requirement of egalitarianism stands in need of explanation. If I contribute to the collective provision of basic goods for my compatriots, isn't what I am owed in return simply the enjoyment of those same basic goods? Reciprocity, the normative ideal central to the basic goods provision argument, does not seem to further require that all members of the state are owed egalitarian shares above and beyond each enjoying the basic goods provided by the state (that are made possible by their joint contributions). Take the case of security from physical attack – which is a key good that Sangiovanni emphasizes is provided *only* by the state. All citizens contribute through the tax system to support the state provision of security; certainly, some individuals fare better than others within the state, but the fact that every citizen enjoys physical security appears to serve as sufficient justification for each member's contribution to the system. To convincingly defend egalitarian shares as a normative requirement stemming from collective basic goods provision, something more is needed. Such an explanation for why reciprocity requires egalitarian duties rather than just the mutual provision of the same basic goods for all citizens is available. Yet, as I go on to show, this explanation comes at the cost of sacrificing the claim that only the state gives rise to this special relationship. To understand how egalitarian claims are derived from basic goods provision, we need to think about two different aspects of basic goods. In one respect, enjoying physical security and access to decent health-care and education are valuable things in and of themselves. In a second respect, enjoying these goods has instrumental value in enabling individuals to achieve many other ends that would not otherwise be possible. The good of education, for example, endows its holder with the ability to participate in a competitive work-force and to earn a greater income than would otherwise be possible.

26 See Pevnick (2008, pp. 403-406) on the idea that the ability to bring about a global coercive authority depends mostly on the willingness of well-off state actors, and insofar as it is in their power to block the formation of such an authority the worse-off are doubly disadvantaged if we restrict claims of justice to coercive domains.

That the state's provision of basic goods for its citizens gives rise to egalitarian duties draws on the second capacity of these goods – to enable different relative gains between individuals – rather than the first capacity in which each citizen can be said to enjoy the goods for their own sake. In this way, well-off citizens within the state actually owe *more* than just the provision of basic goods to their worse-off compatriots in the spirit of reciprocity. The basic goods provided by the state – like a health-care system, a stable property rights system, a system of education, a stable market, and a legal order – enable all of its citizens to pursue their goals and flourish in ways that would not be possible in the absence of these goods (Sangiovanni, 2007, pp. 25-29). As a result, those with talent and other favorable natural abilities are enabled to make higher returns than others in society. The ability of the talented to make comparative gains in the market depends crucially on the contributions of all members of society in providing them, through their government, with these important basic goods. The underlying rationale for obligations of egalitarian justice specifically is that cooperation gives rise to justification for the distribution of benefits and burdens that follow from it among all individuals subject to the scheme.

Understanding why reciprocity in the context of mutual basic goods provision triggers egalitarianism in this way, however, makes it difficult to maintain the claim that the state is a unique context of reciprocity. Recall, Sangiovanni claims that global inequality should not be considered problematic insofar as individuals world-wide do not contribute to a common institutional system that provides basic goods.[27] Yet, this seems odd since regardless of whether global institutions provide basic goods, they certainly provide a number of other (non-basic) goods that enable individuals to make use of their morally arbitrary characteristics. According to the rationale of the basic goods account, the global provision of goods that allow some to make greater returns than others should give rise to egalitarian claims on the part of all those individuals world-wide who contribute to maintaining that system. Consider the following example to demonstrate this point. In the case of a wealthy American CEO, the basic goods provision argument claims that he has egalitarian duties towards his worse-off compatriots because without their support of the state system he would not be able to achieve these high levels of financial success. Assume further that it can be shown that the CEO would not be able to amass such great wealth were it not also for the enforcement of international intellectual

27 For the moment, we can set aside my suggestion to the contrary from the last section and tentatively grant the empirical premise endorsed by Sangiovanni that only states provide individuals with basic goods.

property rights regulations and trade agreements that allow him access to developing country markets. Thus both the contribution of his compatriots and of foreigners allow the CEO to make use of morally arbitrary characteristics in order to make relative monetary gains. As such, it proves inconsistent to maintain that the CEO has egalitarian obligations only to his compatriots insofar as the conditions that enable his relative benefits depend on the compliance of members of his own state and of foreigners. In both domains, regardless of the provision of *basic* goods, we still find the provision of some goods that allow the naturally well-endowed to secure higher returns than others. It is true that the global order does not in most cases directly provide a number of intrinsically valuable goods that are necessary to live an autonomous life, like the fulfillment of basic needs, access to health-care, and a system of education.[28] Yet, the global order does provide a wide range of goods that enable individuals to make use of morally arbitrary characteristics for personal gain. International regimes that define and seek to protect intellectual property rights and trade regulations are good examples of such global public goods. Essentially, then, for the normative claim of the basic goods provision argument to make sense, it must drop its focus on the provision of basic goods and instead focus on those goods that enable differential benefit. In doing so, however, egalitarian duties cannot be restricted to the state.

Conclusion

In this paper, I have assessed the reasons offered in favor of restricting the scope of egalitarian concern to the state and have concluded that this scope restriction is unjustified on two independent grounds. First, with regards to the statists' empirical claims, it has been shown that the global domain possesses the features that are thought to be exclusive to the state and uniquely capable of triggering egalitarian concern. Second, I have

28 As in the case of failed or weak states considered above, there are important exceptions to this rule. One interesting question that requires further examination concerns states that (for whatever reason) become unable to provide their citizens with basic goods, and whether this vitiates citizens' prior egalitarian commitments to one another. Without offering a definitive argument for this conclusion, it seems perverse that inequalities in this circumstance should be permissible among the members of the state who continue cooperating with one another though they are unable to fully secure mutual basic goods provision. A further puzzling questions concerns the relationship between bodies (like the United Nations) that sometimes provide individuals with basic goods when their states are unable to – does this relationship also trigger egalitarian duties, and if so among whom?

argued that we have reason to doubt that the respective factors that generate egalitarian concern, according to the arguments considered (from coercion, co-authorship, and basic goods provision) are actually able to show us where, or only where, inequality is problematic. I conclude, then, that we should reject the statist claim that the scope of egalitarian justice ought to be limited to the state.

References

Abizadeh, A. (2007). "Cooperation, Pervasive Impact, and Coercion: On the Scope (Not Site) of Distributive Justice". *Philosophy & Public Affairs*. Vol. 35. No. 4. Pp. 318-58.

Barry, C. & Valentini, L. (2009) "Egalitarian Challenges to Global Egalitarianism: A Critique". *Review of International Studies*, Vol. 35, Pp. 485-512.

Blake, M. (2002). "Distributive Justice, State Coercion, and Autonomy". *Philosophy and Public Affairs*. Vol. 30. No. 3. Pp. 257-96.

Cohen, J. and Sabel, C. (2006). "Extra Republicam Nulla Justitia?". *Philosophy & Public Affairs* Vol. 34. No. 2. Pp. 147-175.

Freeman, S. (2007). *Justice and the Social Contract: Essays on Rawlsian Political Philosophy*. Oxford. Oxford University Press.

Goodin, R. E. (1988). "What Is So Special About Our Fellow Countrymen?" *Ethics*. Vol. 98. No. 4. Pp. 663-686.

Hume, D. ([1777] 1966). *An Enquiry Concerning the Principles of Moral*. Open Court/Ill. Free Press.

Julius, A.J. (2006). "Nagel's Atlas". *Philosophy & Public Affairs*. Vol. 34. No. 2. Pp. 176-192.

Miller, R. (1998). "Cosmopolitan Respect and Patriotic Concern". *Philosophy & Public Affairs*. Vol. 27. No. 3 Pp. 202-24.

Nagel, T. (2005). "The Problem of Global Justice". *Philosophy and Public Affairs* Vol. 33. No. 2. Pp. 113-47.

Pevnick, R. (2008). "Political Coercion and the Scope of Distributive Justice". *Political Studies*. Vol. 56. No. 2. Pp. 399-413.

Pogge, T. (2002). *World Poverty and Human Rights: Cosmopolitan Responsibilities and Reforms*. Cambridge. Polity Press.

Rawls, J. (1999a). *A Theory of Justice*. Cambridge/MA. Harvard University Press.

Rawls, J. (1999b). *The Law of Peoples*. Cambridge/MA. Harvard University Press.

Risse, M. (2006) "What to Say About the State". *Social Theory and Practice*. Vol. 32. No. 4. Pp. 671-98.

Sangiovanni, A. (2007). "Global Justice, Reciprocity, and the State". *Philosophy and Public Affairs*. Vol. 35. No. 1. Pp. 3-39.

Scheffler, S. (2003). "What Is Egalitarianism?" *Philosophy & Public Affair.* Vol. 31. No. 1. Pp.5-39.

On the Applicability of the Ideal of Equality of Opportunity at the Global Level

Sylvie Loriaux

Introduction

Recent contributions in the field of global justice have to a large extent been attempts to determine whether, in virtue of the profound changes that have occurred in the world over the last decades, John Rawls's difference principle should apply globally or not. Two specific and critical issues in this debate have been 1) to specify why Rawls views the basic structure of society as the primary subject of justice (normative issue) and 2) to establish whether a basic structure can be said to exist at the global level (empirical issue), the underlying assumption being that the scope of the difference principle is primarily a function of the scope of the basic structure (Abizadeh, 2007).

Surprisingly, however, comparatively little attention has been paid to another, particularly attractive global egalitarian principle: global equality of opportunity. In its most general form, this principle demands that equally talented and motivated persons should have a roughly equal chance of attaining social advantages, no matter the society to which they belong. When interpreted in a substantive way, it also requires that persons be given a fair chance of becoming talented and motivated, irrespective of the society to which they belong. As such, it may be expected to have significant implications for human development and global inequality; but insofar as it displays no special concern for the plight of the untalented or unmotivated, it may also be expected to authorize inequalities more than would some other global egalitarian principles (e.g., a global difference principle). The principle of global equality of opportunity has therefore the apparent advantage of being considerably demanding, but not too demanding. Yet, the few attempts made to defend it have been extremely cautious, sometimes even quite vague (Caney, 2001; Moellendorf, 2002; Pogge, 1994, pp. 196, 198, 221-222), and no conclusive counterarguments have been offered to defeat the criticisms of its most radical opponents (Boxill,1987; Brock, 2005; Miller, 2005).

Admittedly, the principle of global equality of opportunity can be attacked from various angles. Some criticisms can be directed to the ideal of equality of opportunity as such. It can, for instance, be objected that global equality of opportunity – just as its domestic counterpart – amounts to rewarding persons for characteristics that are to some degree attributable to brute luck (namely, their talents and motivation) and therefore morally arbitrary (Arneson, 1989; Cohen, 1989, pp. 916-917; Roemer, 1998). On this view, which is sometimes called "responsibility-sensitive egalitarianism" or "luck egalitarianism", it is morally unacceptable that agents be allowed to benefit from aspects of their person for which they cannot be held responsible.[1] Another worry concerns the implementation of a principle of (global) equality of opportunity: if equally talented and motivated persons are to have an equal chance of attaining given advantages, then it seems to follow that all factors that can affect the development of their talents and their willingness to make efforts must be equalized, including the transmission of an affective, cognitive, cultural or material heritage through the family, the nation, the state or else. (Charvet, 1969; Fishkin, 1983, pp. 44-82; Lloyd Thomas, 1977; Rawls, 1999, p. 64). This raises the question of whether equality of opportunity does not, by its very nature, jeopardize important personal and social commitments, and if yes, whether this is morally permissible. Other criticisms are specifically related to the global application of the ideal of equality of opportunity. So it can be argued that, insofar as persons are to some extent responsible for the political decisions made in their society as well as for the beliefs and values articulated in its public culture, their membership of a particular society cannot be seen as a morally arbitrary feature, but should be allowed to influence the nature and extent of their opportunities (Miller, 2005, pp. 67-70). Neutralizing the differential effects of these political decisions, beliefs and values on their opportunities would amount to undermining the principles of political responsibility and national self-determination. Finally, it can also be doubted whether the ideal of equality of opportunity can make sense in such a culturally diverse world as ours (Boxill, 1987; Miller, 2005, pp. 59-64; Walzer, 1983). The

1 Andrew Mason distinguishes between two views of "equality of opportunity": *1)* the traditional ideal of "advantages open to talent and motivation", which is the view that I will adopt in this paper, and *2)* what he calls the "new" view of equality of opportunity", which is a view supported by "responsibility-sensitive egalitarians" or "luck egalitarians" (Mason, 2001). The main difference between both is that the former is merit-based and holds that access to advantages must depend on some "relevant" attributes, whether or not people can be held responsible for them, while the latter is desert-based and holds that access to advantages must as far as possible depend on attributes for which people can be held responsible.

reason is that in order for opportunities to be equalized they must at least be comparable, and it might not be possible to compare them where people deeply disagree on the meaning and relative importance of particular social advantages.

My aim in this paper is not to develop a complete conception of global equality of opportunity. To be sure, I will propose a specific (competitive) principle of global equality of opportunity – that is, a principle whose agents, goal and obstacles are specified. However, my primary concern will be to show that some principle of global equality of opportunity is *called for* given the design of the existing global economic order, can *make sense* in a culturally diverse world, and can be *morally acceptable* if supplemented with some other moral principles. More specifically, I will defend the following three claims:

1) We should not abandon egalitarian commitments at the global level, for doing so would amount to leaving the potential unfairness of global market competitions unaddressed.

2a) A *"morally arbitrary feature of a person"* is not necessarily a *"feature for which a person cannot be held responsible"*, but is first and foremost a feature that is of no relevance given the nature of the goal of the stipulated opportunity. *2b)* Insofar as the goal under consideration is to benefit from the global economic order, it is reasonable to hold that agents' talents and motivation may, but that their membership of a particular society should not, be allowed to affect their chance of success.

3) When adequately specified, a principle of global equality of opportunity can (at least to a certain extent) avoid the charge that no standard can be found for comparing opportunities across cultures.

Claim 1 – We should not abandon egalitarian commitments at the global level, for doing so would amount to leaving the potential unfairness of global market competitions unaddressed.

In spite of its apparent simplicity, the standard definition of global equality of opportunity is too vague and indeterminate to be of any significant guidance. It holds that persons of similar talent and motivation should have a roughly equal chance of attaining social advantages, irrespective of the society to which they belong. Yet, it does not further specify the goal(s) to which it is directed (persons of similar talent and motivation should have a roughly equal chance of doing, having or being what?), nor does it tell us how the requirement of *equality* with regard to opportunity sets is exactly to be understood. As we will see in this section, this requirement might be taken to mean that all equally talented and motivated persons in the world should have *identical* opportunities, or that they should all have *equivalent* opportunities (Miller, 2005).

According to the first interpretation, global equality of opportunity demands that equally talented and motivated persons should have *exactly the same* opportunity sets – that is, an equal chance of attaining exactly the same bundle of advantages – no matter the society to which they belong. In this vein, Darrell Moellendorf tells us, for instance, that "If equality of opportunity were realized, a child growing up in rural Mozambique would be statistically as likely as the child of a senior executive at a Swiss bank to reach the position of the latter's parent" (Moellendorf, 2002, p. 49). If what he has in mind are identical opportunity sets, then he could just as well have claimed that "If equality of opportunity were realised, a child growing up in Switzerland would be statistically as likely as the child of a tribe's chief in rural Mozambique to reach the position of the latter's parent". For saying that equally talented and motivated members of different societies should have identical opportunity sets is another way for saying that they should have an equal chance of attaining exactly the same set of advantages, no matter how these advantages are valued within their own society.

This requirement, however, is too strong to be ever fulfilled: the fact that different societies endorse different values and scales of value makes it highly unlikely that all equally talented and motivated persons in the world could ever find it equally easy to attain the same bundle of advantages. A person's interests, aspirations and behaviour are to a large extent shaped by – and evaluated in the light of – the "ethos" of her society, that is, a specific range of customs, beliefs, understandings, shared experiences, etc. In order for her to be "successful", she will have to exhibit the skills and character traits that are most valued within her society. So, if different societies have a different "ethos", then they will also define different standards of success and so not all advantages valued and pursued in one society will be valued and pursued in another society. This is nicely illustrated by Bernard Boxill: "The bright girl in New York is inevitably going to have better prospects of becoming a business woman in New York than the equally bright boy in Hindu society; and he will have better prospects than she of becoming a priest in his society. This is only partly because the education needed to be a success in business in New York is different from, and probably incompatible with, the education needed to be a priest in Hindu society. Even if schools offering both educations existed in both societies, the ethos of each society would ensure that the inequality remained" (Boxill, 1987, pp. 148-149).

The second interpretation avoids this difficulty by somewhat relaxing the requirement of equality. Global equality of opportunity is now assumed to demand that persons of similar talent and motivation be given *equally valuable* opportunity sets – that is, an equal chance of attaining equally valuable (though different) bundles of advantages – whatever the society to which they belong. This is the option favoured by Simon Caney: "global equality of opportunity requires that people of equal talent have access to positions of an equal standard of living (...) equality of opportunity does not require equal opportunity to identical *tokens*; it can be met where people have equal opportunity to positions of the same *type*" (Caney, 2001, p. 121). More specifically, his strategy consists in reducing opportunities to a common denominator of "basic capabilities" – i.e., capacities to function in certain ways that are deemed to be valued in all cultures – and in specifying that equally talented and motivated persons enjoy equal opportunities when they have an equal chance of attaining positions enabling a similar achievement of basic human functionings (e.g., being well-fed, being free from avoidable disease, being educated, taking part in the life of the community). This allows him to avoid the difficulty raised by Boxill, since it is in principle possible for members of different societies – and in particular, societies embodying a different ethos – to enjoy an equivalent standard of living without their having an equal chance, or even a chance, of attaining the same particular advantages.

However, from the moment "equal" opportunities are understood as "equivalent" (instead of "identical") opportunities, the question must arise of how to assess and compare the value of different opportunity sets. Here again, the magnitude of cultural diversity found at the global level might be thought to represent a serious obstacle. It might indeed be wondered whether the fact that societies differ both with respect to the meaning and with respect to the relative importance they attach to particular basic human functionings does not prevent us from comparing and *a fortiori* equalizing opportunities globally (Miller, 2005, pp. 60-64; Walzer, 1995, pp. 292-293). What it means, for instance, to be "educated" will vary from one society to another: the one will put the emphasis on the development of intellectual skills, while the other will pay more attention to the provision of a religious instruction. Whether one society can be said to offer its members a better opportunity to achieve this basic human functioning than another will depend on which understanding of "being educated" is taken as the benchmark for comparison. The trouble is that, when applied to a setting in which there are no common understandings of this basic human functioning, equality of opportunity requires that a benchmark for comparison be chosen and this choice might amount to arbitrarily favouring the understandings shared in some societies over those shared in other societies. This difficulty is further accentuated when we broaden the scope of comparison from a single basic human functioning to a "standard of living" as a whole. For to the difficulty of finding a standard of comparison for each opportunity separately there must be added the difficulty of finding a standard of comparison for an entire set of opportunities, knowing that different societies also vary with respect to the hierarchy they establish among various basic human functionings.

In view of the difficulties faced by the usual interpretations of the principle of global equality of opportunity, some have argued that instead of trying to equalize opportunities globally, we should only see to it that some standard opportunities or capabilities are available to everyone. So, Gillian Brock has focused on the provision of a "decent set of opportunities", and more particularly, on the removal of "barriers to developing a range of skills and capacities that would be useful no matter what goals people set themselves" (Brock, 2005, p. 350). Similarly, David Miller has talked of the satisfaction of an "international decency standard" and has acknowledged an obligation to help people who cannot engage in the range of core human activities that we find recurring across culturally varied societies (Miller, 2004, pp. 130-131). What their approaches have in common is a scepticism about the very *meaning* of global equality of opportunity: equalizing opportunities makes sense only between agents who share enough cultural understandings with respect to the meaning and relative importance of particular social goods; yet, the requisite level of shared understandings is not to be found at the world level. Therefore, global equality op opportunity should give way to global decency.

Yet, the giving up of global egalitarian commitments has a price. Obviously, a world in which decency standards are satisfied for all can still be characterized by huge inequalities of resources. By themselves, such inequalities need not be objectionable, but they certainly become so if they translate into unfair (dis)advantages. As G.A. Cohen has pointed out, "a person's effective share depends on what he can do with what he has, and that depends not only on how much he has but on what others have and on how what others have is distributed" (Cohen, 1978, p. 252). Resources are power; when they are too unevenly distributed, they can call into question the fairness of institutional processes and arrangements. This is likely to happen in a globalized economy, where members of different societies are competing against one another for the same advantages: their chance of success will largely depend on the amount and kind of resources made available in their respective society. This is illustrated by the following two observations.

(1) As far as global economic negotiations are concerned, it can hardly be denied that gross inequalities of resources tend to translate into inequalities of bargaining power, which cause the interests of the stronger parties to be weighed much more heavily than those of weaker parties, thereby reinforcing initial inequalities (Beitz, 2001, pp. 107-108).

(2) Taking into consideration the kind and the level of educational resources available in western societies, members of these societies can be expected to enjoy a better opportunity to attain positions that require superior training and intellectual skills than members of developing societies. Yet, as remarked by the *Human Development Report 2005*, "[s]uccess in global markets depends increasingly on the development of industrial capabilities. In a knowledge-based global economy cheap labour and exports of primary commodities or simple assembled goods are insufficient to support rising living standards. Climbing the value chain depends on managing the processes of adapting and of improving new technologies" (United Nations Development Programme 2005, pp. 120-121).

What these observations suggest is that gross global inequalities of resources are likely to undermine the fairness of global market competitions: members of wealthy societies are likely to have a better opportunity to benefit from the global economic order than members of poor societies.

Now, the fairness of competitions is at the heart of what is called "competitive equality of opportunity". This type of equality of opportunity applies to existing competitions and makes their fairness conditional upon the satisfaction of the following two requirements: *(1)* success in the competition must be determined by qualification, in accordance with relevant criteria, and *(2)* all competitors must have had a fair chance of becoming so qualified. The first requirement is a requirement of *formal fairness:* it is concerned with the rules governing a competition and demands the removal of those legal or quasi-legal barriers which arbitrarily prevent some agents from succeeding in the competition. The second requirement, for its part, is a requirement of *substantive fairness:* it is concerned with competitors' starting positions and demands the redress of those background disadvantages which arbitrarily prevent them from acquiring the qualifications that predict success in the competition.

Now, nobody will deny that today global markets exist, which function as sites of competition for desirable social and economic advantages. It belongs to the very essence of economic globalization that transnational flows of goods, services, capital, technology and persons are facilitated in order to encourage global competition, and thereby increase economic growth and enhance human welfare. But as in any competition, there will be winners and losers: some will enjoy the advantages at stake, while others will either not enjoy them at all or only in a much more limited way than others. What is needed, therefore, is a procedure that tells us how to distribute the advantages and burdens of economic globalization in a way that is fair.

According to competitive equality of opportunity, the fairness of global market competitions is secured when no competitor is prevented from attaining the advantages at stake because of morally arbitrary factors. From a formal point of view, the main concern will be with the representativeness of global economic rules. Because international trade agreements are to a large extent based on the norm of strict reciprocity – according to which the concessions made by each party should be of roughly equal value –, those parties that have little to offer that is of interest to other parties are likely to be given relatively little voice in the negotiation process (and, for instance, not to obtain liberalisation in the sectors that are most important to them). The challenge will be to see to it that parties' capacity to influence and to benefit from the global economic rules is not impaired by a lack of wealth or power. In the first place, it will be important to strengthen the bargaining skills of the weaker parties – i.e., their capacity for understanding and analysing the negotiations taking place –, be it by facilitating their access to top level education or by providing them with qualified personnel, having expertise in international trade law and in multilateral trading systems. In the second place, it will also prove necessary to provide weaker parties with benefits that they cannot fully reciprocate and to constrain the freedom of action of the stronger parties accordingly. In this context, Ethan Kapstein has suggested that great powers might exchange the principle of "strict" reciprocity for that of "diffuse" reciprocity and renounce some specific advantages now (e.g., by effectively integrating weaker societies into the international trade regime) in order to obtain some more general advantages in the future (e.g., the guarantee that potentially dissatisfied societies do not try to destabilize the global economic order) (Kapstein, 2006, pp. 31-38). Whether or not stronger parties may be expected to adopt a principle of "diffuse" reciprocity is a controversial issue, but the important point is that something like this principle must be at work if formal fairness is to be achieved in the global economic order. From a substantive point of view, competitive equality of opportunity is concerned with competitors' capacity to acquire the relevant qualifications. As already suggested, inequalities in the capacity to use and to benefit from the global marketplace can persist because of initial inequalities in social and economic resources. The challenge will be to see to it that participants' capacity to develop and exercise the talents that predict success in the global economy is not impaired by a lack of such resources. This, of course, is likely to involve massive investment in human development, trade-related infrastructures and governance structures, social safety nets, trainings, etc.

Claim 2 – A "morally arbitrary feature of a person" is not necessarily a "feature for which a person cannot be held responsible", but is first and foremost a feature that is of no relevance given the nature of the goal of the stipulated opportunity. Insofar as the goal under consideration is to benefit from the global economic order, it is reasonable to hold that agents' talents may, but that their membership of a particular society should not, be allowed to affect their chance of success.

At the core of any ideal of equality of opportunity is the compelling intuition that access to social advantages should not be governed by morally arbitrary factors. Yet there is likely to be disagreement about how exactly the phrase "morally arbitrary factor" should be understood. More specifically, two (closely related) objections can be raised to the proposed principle of global equality of opportunity. On the one hand, it can be claimed that one's membership of a particular society is not a morally arbitrary factor and that persons should therefore not be compensated for the global competitive disadvantages they may suffer as a result of their being members of a particular society. On the other hand, it can be claimed that talents are undeserved and that they should therefore not be allowed to affect persons' access to advantages, including their success in the global economy.

My answer to these objections will proceed in two steps. In the first place, I will argue that, insofar as competitive equality of opportunity is concerned, whether an attribute of a person is to be considered morally arbitrary or not depends on the nature of the goal(s) at stake, and not on the person's responsibility for possessing this attribute. In the second place, I will argue that, insofar as the goal at stake is to benefit from the global economic order, it is reasonable to hold that persons' talents may, but that their membership of a particular society should not, be allowed to affect their chance of success.

a) Morally arbitrary features and undeserved features.

For global egalitarians like Caney and Moellendorf, the primary reason why a person's membership of a particular society is morally arbitrary and thus not allowed to affect her access to advantages is that it is *undeserved*. In keeping with the tradition of "responsibility-sensitive egalitarianism", they assume that persons should be compensated for all those circumstances for which they cannot be held responsible and which negatively affect their access to advantages. What they add, or at least presuppose, is that persons are not responsible for those aspects of their society which impede their attainment of various social and economic advantages.

But if this is their rationale for extending the ideal of equality of opportunity to the global level, why do they keep talking in terms of "equally talented and motivated persons"? Put another way: if a feature of a person is morally arbitrary whenever it is undeserved, why then should one's possession of talents, but not one's membership of a particular society, be allowed to affect one's access to advantages? If Caney and Moellendorf want to ground their principle of global equality of opportunity in the tenets of "responsibility-sensitive egalitarianism" they have no other alternative but to provide an argument to the effect that one's possession of talents, unlike one's membership of a particular society, is deserved. This may be done by arguing that the development and maintenance of talents most often presuppose a certain amount of voluntary choice and effort, and that therefore, the distribution of talents is not always or completely the result of a natural lottery (Green, 1989, p. 14). More particularly, it might be pointed out that in such a complex and highly specialized world economy as ours, it is very unlikely that competitors will owe their success only to their possession of natural endowments, without having taken some risks, made some sacrifices and spent a considerable amount of time and energy. And if the talents needed for success in the global economy must for a large part be voluntarily acquired, then the "winners" of economic globalization cannot be said to be benefiting on morally arbitrary grounds.

But there are several difficulties with this kind of argument. *First*, exactly the same line of reasoning can be used to support the opposite conclusion. So it might be said that talents are always to some degree the product of fortunate circumstances, and that therefore allowing them to affect the distribution of social and economic advantages amounts to rewarding people for features that are not due to any credit on their part. On this view, unequally talented persons could legitimately enjoy equal access to social and economic advantages.

Secondly, there might also be some sense in which persons are responsible for the opportunities that are available to them as a result of their belonging to a particular society. So Miller has argued that persons are to some degree responsible not only for the political decisions in which they have a voice, but also for the beliefs and values articulated in the public culture of their society; and that they should therefore also be held responsible for the impact of these political decisions, beliefs and values on their opportunities.

Third, and more fundamentally, it is questionable whether persons' "undeserved features" can so easily be equated with "morally arbitrary features". There are indeed many cases in which undeserved attributes like nationality, age or gender may legitimately be allowed to influence a person's chance of attaining some kinds of advantages. In order, for instance, to qualify for a post of obstetrician in a hospital with a high proportion of Muslim patients, applicants may be required to be female. The same holds for one's talents and membership of a particular society. So, having the requisite physical skills for being a professional football player can hardly be discounted as a good reason for being appointed in a national football team. Similarly, being a French citizen may be considered a necessary condition for qualifying for the presidency of France. And conversely, we might consider that a person's talents and membership of a particular society are on balance deserved, and still deny that they should always be allowed to affect her access to advantages. So we might acknowledge that a young pupil has developed, after a lot of training and renunciations, an exceptional talent for moving her ears, while at the same time denying that she should therefore gain higher marks in mathematics. Or we might believe that persons who have voluntarily acquired the Belgian nationality should not be treated differently in the Belgian electoral system than persons who did not choose to be born with the Belgian nationality.

This all suggests that whether some feature of a person should be considered a morally arbitrary feature and should thus not be allowed to affect her access to advantages depends on the nature of the advantages at stake. Or put another way: whether an agent's lack of talents or membership of a particular society should be considered an obstacle that "must" be removed depends on the nature of the goal of the stipulated opportunity. The next question is therefore: "Does the nature of the goal of the opportunity considered in this paper – namely, to benefit from the global economic order – justify that agents' chance of success be a function of their talents, but not of their membership of a particular society?"

b) Talents and membership of a particular society

1) Saying that the goal of the stipulated opportunity is *to benefit* from the global economic order is another way for saying that its agents must have a fair chance of "*actively* participating" in this order. The point is to ensure that all participants in the global economic order can contribute in a significant way to global economic exchanges and reap the benefits that flow from their contribution. Saying further that the goal of the stipulated opportunity is to benefit from *the global economic order* amounts to saying that its agents should have a fair chance of benefiting from a specific set of institutions, namely, existing global economic institutions. The focus is, on the one hand, on "global economic" institutions and, on the other hand, on the form that these institutions "currently" take. To be sure, the working of domestic and non-economic institutions is also of interest to the proposed principle of global equality of opportunity, but only indirectly, insofar as they are affected by global economic institutions and insofar as they have an impact on persons' effective participation in these institutions.

It is also worth emphasising that the proposed principle of global equality of opportunity makes sense only where global market competitions are taking place. It is because members of different societies are today encouraged to compete for the same social and economic advantages *and* because all participants in a competitive process have an equal standing as such participants, that egalitarian requirements of formal and substantive fairness are activated at the global level. That is to say, the applicability of the proposed principle of global equality of opportunity is intrinsically related to the current process of economic globalization.

Economic globalization is a specific way of organizing the world economy: at its heart is the willingness to remove barriers to the free movement of goods, services, persons and capital, and to thereby encourage global market competitions. It finds its *raison d'être* precisely in the gains that might result from the exploitation of relative differences in productive resources (that is, from the exploitation of comparative advantages) on a global scale. It belongs to its very nature that those who can support market pressures by being more productive than others or by differentiating themselves from others are also more likely to be appreciated by the global buying public and to carve for themselves a place within the global economy. It is therefore very unlikely that the possession of talents like a sense of entrepreneurship, good (oral and written) communication skills (especially in English), an innovative mind, mastery of modern technology, etc. might be ranged among factors not allowed to count in the determination of persons' success in global market competitions.

It is important to note that the proposed principle of global equality of opportunity applies to the existing global economic order and asks what must be done in order for this order – in the liberalized form it currently takes – to be fair, or at least fairer; but it does not question the fairness of the choice of such a liberalized economic order itself.[2] Put another way: it asks what must be done in order for global market competitions to be fair, but not whether it is fair that such competitions be promoted in the first place. Yet, success in competitions of this kind presupposes an array of complex skills (e.g., sophisticated literacy and mathematical skills, understanding of complex legal and economic rules, mastery of new technologies like the internet, computer programmes, etc.), which some persons may be unable to acquire, even if effective measures for improving the formal and substantive fairness of these competitions are implemented. The proposed principle of global equality of opportunity is thus no guarantee against exclusion: it is compatible with a considerable part of the world population being denied active participation in global economic exchanges. This matter of fact is all the more problematic that what determines a person's success in an economic order is not simply a function of her talents, but is more fundamentally a function of how her talents are

2 On the choice of a dominant cooperative scheme as an important question of justice, see: Allen Buchanan (1990).

valued within this order. In a complex knowledge-based world economy, individuals are excluded from active participation who might be included in a different economic setting.

It might therefore be wondered whether current global economic institutions – and in particular, the rules that define the current global economic game – should not themselves be modified so as to become more inclusive. Assuming that *all* persons who participate in the global economy are to be treated as *equal* participants: should a just global economic order not also aim at promoting and rewarding a "wider" range of talents, that is, talents that do not maximize the global output? And would this requirement still be part of the ideal of equality of opportunity or would it rather express independent moral considerations, like for instance a concern for persons' life prospects as human beings (instead of a concern for their chance of success in a given competition as competitors)?

2) The second issue that needs to be investigated is whether a person's membership of a particular society should be seen as a morally arbitrary feature. Should we not follow David Miller in admitting that persons are, to some extent, responsible for the political decisions made by their society as well as for the values and beliefs conveyed by its public culture, and that they should therefore not be compensated for the worse opportunities they might suffer as a result? On this account, trying to achieve global equality of opportunity would lead to undermining both the principle of political responsibility and the principle of national self-determination. Not only would domestic societies not have to bear the costs of their decisions (they would in fact be compensated for their "bad" choices), but they would also be denied any control over their own fate, since the differential effects of their policy decisions on the opportunities of their members would have to be systematically neutralized. So why, it might be asked, would it be objectionable that persons have an unequal opportunity to succeed in the global economy because of their being members of different societies?

A first thing to note is that Miller's line of argumentation, with its focus on (individual and political) responsibility, remains significantly within the framework of luck egalitarianism. Yet, as we have seen, this framework is problematic: as far as her membership of a particular society is concerned, there is always a certain extent to which a person can be held responsible and a certain extent to which she cannot. And even if she could, on balance, be held responsible for her membership of a particular society, this would still not entail that this fact has relevance in any context whatsoever.

In a globalized economy, the primary criteria of success include differentiation, efficiency, innovation, entrepreneurship, and so forth. While these talents can in principle be acquired by agents regardless of their nationality or citizenship, some societies may lack the resources necessary to foster their development. Yet, just as it is unfair to deny agents formal access to global market competitions on the ground that their society lacks bargaining power, so too is it unfair to deny them active participation in these competitions on the ground that their society lacks the resources needed to provide them with the necessary qualifications. If their society expresses the willingness to promote their inclusion in the global economy, then it should receive adequate assistance from other societies. If their society does not express this willingness, then it might be up to other societies to afford them the chance of acquiring the talents that predict success in the global economy (by facilitating access to their own educational system, for instance), a chance which they would remain free not to seize.

Claim 3 – When adequately specified, a principle of global equality of opportunity can (at least to a certain extent) avoid the charge that no standard can be found for comparing opportunities across cultures.

It is important to see how, in addition to addressing the potential unfairness of the global economic order, the principle of global equality of opportunity proposed in this paper can also escape (at least to a certain extent) the problem of cross-cultural metric raised by Brock and by Miller. As we have seen, Caney's interpretation of "equal opportunities" in terms of "an equivalent standard of living" is problematic – not because the concept of "standard of living" would be too subjective to allow any comparison (remember that he thinks of a person's "standard of living" in terms of her "basic capabilities", that is, in terms of her capacities to function in various ways deemed to be *objectively* valuable), but because, given the different meaning and importance given to a same basic human functioning in different societies, it might not be possible to decide whether the standards of living to which members of different societies have access are equivalent or not.

This "comparison" problem arises to a lesser extent with the proposed principle of global equality of opportunity. The first thing to note is that this principle is confined to one *single* opportunity. It is not concerned with persons' prospects for *success in life* as human beings, but only with their chance of success *in a given competition* as competitors. In particular, its goal is not, like in Caney, to attain an equivalent standard of living, but to benefit from the current process of economic globalisation. It is satisfied when all those who participate in the global economic order are equal with respect to this single opportunity, however unequal they may be with respect to other opportunities. The fact that different societies will rank opportunities differently may therefore not be an insurmountable obstacle to its implementation.

To be sure, the proposed principle of global equality of opportunity is not completely indifferent to persons' standards of living: the occasions created by economic globalization for those who sell their labour, buy goods and services, develop ideas and raise capital, are in the last instance occasions to advance their welfare. However, the fact that the attainment of the goal of a given opportunity is accompanied with an increase in welfare does not make this increase in welfare the goal of the opportunity. Saying that persons of similar talent and motivation must have an equal chance of winning the Roland Garros tennis tournament irrespective of their nationality is not equivalent to saying that persons of similar talent and motivation must have an equal chance of advancing their welfare irrespective of their nationality, even though the winning of this tournament is likely to be accompanied with an advance in welfare. The difference lies in the fact that the opportunity to win the Roland Garros tournament – just as the opportunity to benefit from the global economy – is but one element of the broader opportunity to advance one's welfare, and not even a necessary element as welfare might be increased in other ways too.

The second thing to note is that the proposed principle of global equality of opportunity is limited not simply to one single opportunity, but to one single *specified* opportunity. It has already been noted how problematic it is to compare and *a fortiori* to equalize an opportunity whose goal (e.g., "to be educated") means something different in different societies. But what about an opportunity whose goal is "to benefit from the global economic order"? Isn't it the case that it can also be understood in different ways and can therefore not be equalized at the global level? The principle of global equality of opportunity proposed here tends to avoid this difficult by fixing the meaning of the opportunity under consideration, and in particular, by giving a definite content to its goal. In doing so, it tends to establish a unique standard of comparison.

But of course, this poses several difficulties. A first difficulty concerns the legitimacy of the chosen understanding of the goal under consideration. By establishing what it means "to benefit from the global economic order", one runs the risk that other worthwhile understandings be overshadowed. A second difficulty concerns the desirability of the goal under consideration. Once global equality of opportunity is conceived of in terms of a single specified and thus identical opportunity, it is vulnerable to Boxill's objection that "the ethos of each society would ensure that the inequality remained". Even if there is an agreement on the content of its goal, there might still be broad disagreement on whether this goal is worth pursuing: some societies might praise and promote an active participation in economic globalization, while other societies might instil different, sometimes conflicting, aspirations in their members. If so, some persons might be prevented from succeeding in the global economy because of their belonging to a society, which inculcates them with "unfavourable" kinds of aspirations. The proposed principle of global equality of opportunity cannot but entail a homogenization of standards of success and ambitions.

By way of conclusion, it is worth emphasizing that the point of the proposed principle of global equality of opportunity is not to praise free trade, but to show that those who support free trade are by the same token bound to undertake significant global institutional reforms and redistributive measures. As such, this principle represents an important component of global justice. Yet, it does obviously not constitute the whole of global justice. As indicated, it suffers from two important limitations: not only does it permit certain forms of objectionable exclusion, but it also has difficulty accommodating cultural differences. The moral acceptability of its implementation will therefore be a function of the room it allows for the expression of independent moral considerations.

References

Abizadeh, A. (2007). "Cooperation, Pervasive Impact, and Coercion: On the Scope (not Site) of Distributive Justice". *Philosophy & Public Affairs*. Vol. 35. No. 4. Pp. 318-358.

Arneson, R. (1989). Equality and Equal Opportunity for Welfare". *Philosophical Studies*. Vol. 56. No. 1. Pp. 77-93.

Beitz, C. (2001). "Does Global Inequality Matter?". *Metaphilosophy*. Vol. 32. No. 1-2. Pp. 95-112.

Boxill, B (1987). "Global Equality of Opportunity and National Integrity". *Social Philosophy and Policy*. Vol. 5. No. 1. Pp. 143-168.

Brock, G. (2005). "The Difference Principle, Equality of Opportunity, and Cosmopolitan Justice". *The Journal of Moral Philosophy*. Vol. 2. No. 3. Pp. 333-351.

Buchanan, A. (1990). "Justice as Reciprocity versus Subject-Centered Justice". *Philosophy & Public Affairs*. Vol. 19. No. 3. Pp. 227-252.

Caney, S. (2001). "Cosmopolitan Justice and Equalizing Opportunities". *Metaphilosophy*. Vol. 32. No. 1-2. Pp. 113-134.

Charvet, J. (1969). "The Idea of Equality as a Substantive Principle of Society". *Political Studies*. Vol. 17. No. 1. Pp. 1-13.

Cohen, G. A. (1978). "Robert Nozick and Wilt Chamberlain: How Patterns Preserve Liberty". J. Arthur and W. Shaw (eds.) *Justice and Economic Distribution*. Englewood Cliffs/NJ. Prentice Hall. Pp. 246-262.

Cohen, G. A. (1989). "On the Currency of Egalitarian Justice". *Ethics*. Vol. 99. No. 4. Pp. 906-944.

Fishkin, J. S. (1983). *Justice, Equal Opportunity, and the Family*. New Haven & London. Yale University Press.

Green, S. J. D. (1989). "Competitive Equality of Opportunity: A Defense". *Ethics*. Vol. 100. No. 1. Pp. 5-32.

Kapstein, E. (2006). *Economic Justice in an Unfair World*. Princeton. Princeton University Press.

Lloyd Thomas, D. A. (1977). "Competitive Equality of Opportunity". *Mind*. New Series. Vol. 86. No. 343. Pp. 388-404.

Mason, A. (2001). "Equality of Opportunity, Old and New". *Ethics*. Vol. 111. No. 4. Pp 760-81.

Miller, D. (2004). "National Responsibility and International Justice". D. K. Chatterjee (ed.). *The Ethics of Assistance*. Cambridge. Cambridge University Press. Pp. 123-143.

Miller, D. (2005). "Against Global Egalitarianism". *The Journal of Ethics*. Vol. 9. No. 1-2. Pp. 55-79.

Moellendorf, D. (2002). *Cosmopolitan Justice*. Boulder/CO. Westview.

Pogge, T. (1994). "An Egalitarian Law of Peoples". *Philosophy & Public Affairs*. Vol. 23. No. 3. Pp. 195-224.

Rawls, J. (1999). *A Theory of Justice*. revised ed. Oxford. Oxford University Press.

Roemer, J. E. (1998). *Equality of Opportunity*. Cambridge. Harvard University Press.

United Nations Development Programme (UNDP) (2005). *Human Development Report 2005*. New York. United Nations.

Walzer, M. (1983). *Spheres of Justice*. New York. Basic Books.

Against Relational Views of Justice and Parental Duties[1]

Gianfranco Pellegrino

Introduction

In the realm of morality, several kinds of obligation and duty[2] are clearly limited in their scope. Professional duties of physicians, teachers, and soldiers are closely restricted to the agents playing these roles. Moreover, these duties are contingent on the agent's will to perform her role, and on the specific occasions in which she acts in her official capacity. Hippocratic oaths, for instance, may be considered as holding only intermittently. A surgeon in her holidays is not obliged to treat patients – even though she is obliged to treat a suddenly broken leg, at least if no other physician is around. Likewise, obligations created by promises bind promisers only. To give a promise is a morally relevant relation that not only does limit the addressees of the connected obligation, but also creates the obligation itself. Had no promise been made, no duty would have been

1 A (now) remote ancestor of this paper was commented by Michele Bocchiola, Eszter Kollàr, Michele Loi, Sebastiano Maffettone and Raffaele Marchetti. That paper was presented at the Workshop on Equal Respect held at the University of Genoa in December 2007 and to the 10th Symposium "Contemporary Philosophical Issues: Truth, Justice, and Beauty" at the University of Rieka. Elvio Baccarini, Boran Bercic, Ian Carter, Emanuela Ceva, Sergio Cremaschi, Elisabetta Galeotti, Valeria Ottonelli, and Mauro Piras raised very insightful and acute questions and suggestions. A later version was discussed in the Graduate and Faculty Seminar of the PhD Program in Political Theory (Luiss "Guido Carli" University of Rome), and I benefited from questions and suggestion from Marcello Di Paola, Volker Kaul, Domenico Melidoro, Aakash Singh, Daniele Santoro, and Ivana Trkulja. Finally, another version was presented at the conference "Global Justice and the Nation State", at the University of Lisbon, where I received helpful questions from Daniel Kofman, Margaret Moore, Rekha Nath and Kok Chor Tan. I am very grateful to all of them and deeply indebted to their suggestions. I also wish to thank Michele Bocchiola for substantial editing of this text and Gabriele De Angelis for many useful questions, comments and suggestions concerning the present version. Responsibility for the views expressed here is only mine, though.

2 From now onwards, "duty" and "obligation" will be used as synonymous.

established. Another instance of limited obligations are parental duties. It is uncontroversial that the duties of caring for children are limited to their parents only.

A common account of these duties and their limits relies on what we might call a *relational* analysis.[3] The general idea is that a) the limited scope of certain duties originates in the morally relevant relations that link the holders with their targets, and, hence, b) the duties themselves arise from these very relations (Scheffler, 1997, 2001, 2004). Thus, the caring relationship linking physicians and patients, parents and children is both the source of the special duties of medical practitioners and parents and what establishes their limits. Likewise, promising – regarded as a relation – both produces and limits the duty to keep the promise (Jeske, 2008, Ch. 4). To put it shortly, those obligations are *relational* or *associative* in kind.

In recent times, inspiration was taken from the general notion of associative obligation in order to establish and justify the limited scope of the duties of egalitarian justice. The main idea in the so-called *relational arguments for the limits of justice* is that the requirements of justice are to be considered as relational obligations: such requirements are connected with specific relations among members of a political community, and their limits coincide with the boundaries of the community. In particular, justice is viewed as connected with relations obtaining within the boundaries of states. Accordingly, the boundaries of states coincide with the limits of obligations of justice (Sangiovanni, 2007 provides a detailed description of this view). Nagel (2005) voiced this statist view of justice in the clearest way:

> Every state has the boundaries and population it has for all sorts of accidental and historical reasons; but given that it exercises sovereign power over its citizens and in their name, those citizens have a duty of justice toward one another through the legal, social and economic institutions that sovereign power makes possible. This duty is *sui generis*, and is not owed to everyone in the world, nor is an indirect consequence of any other duty that may be owed to everyone in the world, such as a duty of humanity. Justice is something we owe through our shared institutions only to those with whom we stand in a strong political relation. It is, in the standard terminology, an *associative* obligation. [...] It depends on positive rights that we do not have against all other persons or groups, rights that arise only because we are joined together with certain others in a political society under strong centralized control. It is only

3 The relational analysis is aimed also at showing that those obligations are objectively agent-relative ones, not reducible to, and with a ceteris paribus priority over, other kinds of obligations (Jeske, 2008, chaps. 2 and 3). Here, I will not focus on these features. However, to show that the relational analysis cannot account for the limits of those obligations might be the premise from which to argue that also other features of those duties are not accounted for by this analysis.

> from such a system, and from our fellow members through its institutions, that we can claim a right to democracy, equal citizenship, non-discrimination, equality of opportunity, and the amelioration through public policy of unfairness in the distribution of social and economic goods (pp. 121, 126).[4]

In different versions of relational arguments, justice has been viewed as connected with relations of *cooperation*, *coercion*, *common responsibility for*, or *joint authorship of*, a shared social and legal system, and *reciprocity* – the latter interpreted in various ways (Nagel, 2005; Tan, 2006; Julius, 2006; Sangiovanni, 2007; Abizadeh, 2007). Moreover, the different implications ensuing from the fact that the relevant relations may be voluntary or not, beneficial or not to the participants have been discussed (Julius, 2006; Tan, 2006). Typically, objections to these relational arguments have concerned the specific nature of the mentioned relations, and have attempted to show either that those specific relations obtain globally or that justice is not connected to those relations in a way able to set limits to our duties of justice.

Here, I take a partially different path. I am going to consider the general argumentative scheme that is common to several relational arguments for the limits of egalitarian justice. In other words, I shall focus on the relational analysis of the duties of justice, without considering specific issues about the nature of the relations that originate requirements of justice.

Moreover, I am going to raise a different kind of objection to the relational views of justice. I endorse both the premise (justice is somehow connected with certain relations) and the conclusion (our duties of justice are limited in scope) of the relational arguments. However, I shall show that both the premise and the conclusion might be true even if there is no correspondence between the limits of the duties of justice and the boundaries of the corresponding relations, and indeed in certain cases duties of justice hold even though the relevant relation does not obtain. Accordingly, the relational analysis is false, at least if considered as a claim about the limits of certain duties and their sources in certain relevant relations. If I am correct, the conclusion of this paper will be that justice and certain relations are connected in significant ways, and that in certain cases our duties of justice might be strengthened by our involvement in those relations. However, this does not mean that the limits of justice strictly coincide with the boundaries of those relations. There indeed are significant

4 Egalitarian justice has been viewed as an associative duty by several authors: among others, Tamir (1993), MacCormick (1982), Rawls (1999), Dworkin (2000), Blake (2001).

cases in which such relations subsist without entailing duties of justice, and vice versa. Therefore, the relational analysis cannot account for the limits of our duties of justice.

In some now historical versions of relational arguments for the limits of justice, justice is likened to parenthood. Edmund Burke advocated this view in its clearest form:

> Parents may not be consenting to their moral relation, but, consenting or not, they are bound to a long train of burdensome duties towards those with whom they have never made a convention of any sort. Children are not consenting to their relation: but their relation, without their actual consent, binds them to its duties. [...] So, without any stipulation on our own part, are we bound by that relation called our country. [...] The place that determines our duty to our country is a social, civil relation. [...] The place of every man determines his duty (quoted in Simmons, 1996, p. 247).

This analogy has been recently revived by Nagel (2005), who claimed that justice is contingent on the existence of co-citizenship relations just as certain parental obligations are contingent on relations of parenthood:

> Furthermore, though the obligations of justice arise as a result of a special relation, there is no obligation to enter into that relation with those to whom we do not yet have it, thereby acquiring those obligations toward them. If we find ourselves in such a relation, then we must accept the obligations, but we do not have to seek them out, and may even try to avoid incurring them, as with other contingent obligations of a more personal kind: one does not have to marry and have children, for example (p. 121).

Unfortunately, this analogy is far from reinforcing the relational views of justice, for even parental duties in some cases fail to behave as relational obligations. Accordingly, while possibly correct for some kinds of obligations – such as promise, friendship and professional duties –, the relational analysis fails to account for deeply entrenched intuitions concerning other sorts of obligation – such as parental duties and justice. Or at least this is what I claim here.

The Relational Analysis

The argumentative pattern that is common to many relational arguments for the limits of justice and parental duties might be spelled out in the following way. First, the following premises are posited:

A. *Morally valuable relations.* In normal lives, certain relations (such as those between parents and children and our relations to our co-nationals) bear a distinctive moral import.

B. *Morally valuable relations and connected obligations.* Part of the moral significance of certain relations might be realized in, and signified by, certain connected obligations. Part of the moral import of being a parent lies in parental duties of care. Likewise, part of the moral significance of being a member of a political community might lie in egalitarian obligations toward other members. On the other hand, an understanding of the moral significance and value of certain relations may be required in order to grasp the connected duties, or even in order to begin the specification of those duties that is requested in particular cases. No doubt, this happens in the case of promises. To grasp what a promise is amounts to understanding the obligations connected to promising. Likewise, to appreciate the duties of friendship is part and parcel of understanding what friendship is. Possibly, even to understand the point of parental duties, one should grasp the moral significance of parenthood. The same may hold for distributive justice and citizenship. Hence, justice and parenthood may share part of the explanatory and justificatory pattern of the kind of obligations involved in promising, or of the duties of friendship.

These premises might be assumed as a ground to deny any reductionist view of the moral point of the relations mentioned in them. Attempts to reduce situations such as promising and friendship to non-relational facts or premises (to wit, to facts or premises obtaining outside the relevant relation) misinterpret their very nature, and will possibly fail to properly guide our behaviour. For instance, someone who takes the point of friendship as *entirely* reducible to its instrumental value risks to be inauthentic to her friends, failing to behave as a friend when this conduct is no longer beneficial (Scanlon, 1998, pp. 88-90; Scheffler, 2001, chap. 6; Tan, 2006). These anti-reductionist claims hold also for co-citizenship and parenthood.

More positively, the above premises might be interpreted as leading to the following view about the connection between morally valuable relations and obligations:

C. *The source claim.* Certain morally valuable relations act as *sources* of the connected obligations, at least because their value is a source of reasons to act, or, to put it otherwise, valuing those relations is to have special reasons to act in a particular way, i.e., reasons to fulfil certain relational obligations (Scheffler, 2001, 2004).

The source claim is more than a positive counterpart of the anti-reductionist claims about morally valuable relations. Arguably, it might be the case that the significance and value of certain relations is a primitive factor, because it is not reducible to non-relational facts, even though those relations are not sources of reasons to comply with certain obligations. In other words, it might be that even though the moral value of certain relations is primitive, the connected obligations are rooted in non-relational facts. For instance, even though friendship cannot be reduced to the social benefit of the practice it realizes, the duties of friendship bring about social benefits and this might be the reason of their bindingness.

Be that as it may, the source claim makes a step further, and assumes that the premises **A.** and **B.** authorize to claim that the morally valuable relations act as sources of the connected obligations; accordingly, those obligations are *relational* ones, and hence they cannot be reduced to non-relational factors. The source claim allows to set limits to relational obligations only if it is interpreted in a specific way. In particular, it should be regarded as including the following claims:

C1. *Co-variation.* Morally valuable relations co-vary with the connected obligations: when the relation does not hold or disappears, then the connected obligation vanishes as well. The contrary also holds. When those obligations are in force, then the connected relations obtain.

C2. *Selected addressees.* Moreover, since these co-variant obligations are incumbent only upon the agents involved in the relevant relations, these relations appear to be able to select the specific addressees of the connected obligations. In some cases, the same obligation is incumbent on both sides (e.g., the duties of justice equally concern any citizen involved in the co-citizenship relation), in other cases only one side is obliged, even though the other side may be subject to a different but related obligation (parents only have parental duties, but sons and daughters have filial obligations).

From C1. and C2., the following conclusion on the limits of certain kinds of obligation descends:

D. *Limits of obligations.* Certain kinds of obligation connected in various ways with morally valuable relations are limited in their scope; in particular, the scope of the obligation co-extends with the scope of the relevant relation.

When the above scheme is applied to justice and parental obligations, a *relational* view of the obligations of justice and parenthood is obtained. According to this view, obligations of justice and parenthood have limits, since they are contingent on the existence of certain moral relations and addressed only to the people connected by those relations. If I am a parent, I have duties toward my children, not toward others' offspring. The limits of my parental relation – the fact that it embraces my children and me only – set the limits of my parental obligations. Duties of distributive justice between co-nationals behave in the same way. They do not exist independently of the relevant relation of co-citizenship, and they hold only among co-citizens. Accordingly, there is no such thing as global justice.

In what follows, I am not going to deny the premises **A.** and **B.**, or the conclusion **D.** To be true, I shall not reject even **C.**, the source claim. I merely argue that this claim is false, or exaggerated, *if applied* to justice and parental obligations. That it might turn out to be a suitable account of other kinds of obligation is not a possibility that will be considered in this paper.

Notice that rejecting the view of justice implied by the source claim does not necessarily produce full-fledged cosmopolitanism. Even those who argue for a double standard of justice (namely, global and social justice) grant the fact that there is some justice outside the State. Also the claim that we have milder duties of justice toward foreigners amounts to a denial that the limits of justice are set by state boundaries. Supporters of a statist conception of justice typically claim that we have *no duties of justice whatsoever* toward foreigners. Some of them (such as Nagel, 2005) allow that we have basic humanitarian duties. Thus, in arguing against this view of justice, I am providing support to a cluster of different positions, ranging from *absolute cosmopolitanism* (a single standard of justice, in the domestic as well as in the global arena) to *liberal theories of justice* (two or more standards of justice, varying according to the context). By contrast, I am denying a single specific view, namely *statism.*

Against the Source Claim: Parental Duties

The source claim might have an initial plausibility. After all, it seems that in several cases many morally important relations both co-vary with certain obligations and select the proper addressees of the latter. Plainly, there are parental duties when there are parents, and parents are the obvious holders of those obligations.

However, notice that the source view requires that co-variance between the source-relations and the connected obligations is without exception and bi-conditional. In other words, the derivation of the limits of certain duties from their roots in morally important relations is valid if and only if there are neither cases where the relevant relations obtain but the connected obligations do not hold, nor situations where the relational obligations hold but the alleged source-relations are not in place. Better, the relational analysis assumes that there are no cases of non-alignment where both the relations and the connected duties are clearly grasped and picked out. Accordingly, the best, and simplest, objection against any relational analysis of parental duties and the obligation of justice is to mention cases in which the required alignment of relations and obligations fails to occur. This is a general objection to the analysis, since it does not rely on any peculiar conception of the relevant relations. Moreover, it differs from usual the arguments, since it does not aim at showing either that the relations considered extend globally, and therefore certain duties have a global scope, or that these relations and their allegedly corresponding duties are systematically disconnected. There are connections between certain morally relevant relations and certain duties. Simply, those connections do not behave as the source claim would require.

I shall consider parental duties first. Their limits seem to mismatch parenthood in several important situations. For instance, there is no doubt that caring attention is due to children below their legal age of majority, but there are no settled views either on what this requires or on how this duty evolves after children have come of age. On the other hand, it is clearly felt that some boundaries are in place to delimit these obligations. It seems over-demanding to ask parents unlimited care towards their children, no matter their age. Plainly, there are limits on the self-sacrifice that the care for one's offspring might justify – especially for women. Now, those limits do not seem to be accounted for by the presence of the relation of parenthood. When they come in, there are no relevant changes in the background relation. In other words, when a point of hardship comes where it seems sensible that a mother is to be exempted from extreme sacrifices in favour of her child, it is not the case that her relation with the kid has changed in some way. That relation keeps its moral significance, even though it no longer issues moral demands. A mother who avoids extreme sacrifices in favour of her child does not lose or weaken her morally significant relation with that child. The natural regret (and even despair) that could follow the decision not to sacrifice herself signals that the relation is keeping its deep moral significance. Accordingly, the boundaries of the relation do not overlap with, and do not explain, the boundaries of the obligation.

Likewise, it seems that merely being in the age of majority does not relieve parents of any obligation to their offspring. Of course, it is not the case that the day after their eighteenth birthday, children lose any right to rely on their parents. However, parental obligations should not be assumed as eternally binding. There is a moment when a parent is rightly exempted from any further care towards her adult sons and daughters. Still, the moral significance of parenthood as a relation, and the relation itself, can be everlasting. Very old parents might plausibly keep on finding their relations with their adult sons and daughters morally significant and valuable. Obviously enough, then, at a given moment this moral significance and these relations are no longer sources of duty.

These remarks show that parenthood and parental obligations are not perfectly aligned, as the relational analysis assumed. Therefore, this analysis is inaccurate, at least with respect to parental obligations. Sometimes, parenthood as a morally significant relation co-occurs with parental obligations; but this is not always the case. Accordingly, we do not have decisive grounds to claim that parenthood as a relation constitutes the normative source of parental obligations.

Against the Source Claim: Duties of Justice

Some more complications should be faced if one tries to address the same line of refutation to the relational analysis of distributive justice – at least, if (as in Nagel, 2005) justice is identified with distributive equality or socio-economic fairness, as contrasted to mere beneficence or humanitarian duties. Applied to justice, the relational analysis takes co-citizenship as a relation that co-varies with the demands of distributive equality. Nagel supports this claim through a complex elaboration of the underlying assumptions of co-citizenship. Roughly, his idea is that each and every citizen is jointly author of, and subject to, the legal system imposed on her and her co-citizens. For this reason, each citizen is responsible towards her fellow citizens for any of the inequalities ensuing from this legal system. Therefore, the demands of justice (conceived of as requirements of equality) bind citizens, and only them, on account of their mutual relation as joint authors and subjects of the legal and political system they live in (Nagel, 2005, pp. 121, 128-130, 138, 140). It seems, then, that co-citizenship as a relation and the duties of distributive justice are perfectly aligned, unlike parenthood and parental obligations.

However, this view of justice can be questioned along the same lines I have followed in the case of parental obligations. Justice and co-citizenship can be shown to diverge in some cases. As Frankfurt (1987) famously argued, considerations concerning equality might be dismissed as irrelevant, and substituted by standards focusing on absolute levels of provisions. Frankfurt's main contention is that what is morally important, at least in the case of resources and their allocation, is not the relative level at which any individual is placed, but rather her being beyond a given level of subsistence, i.e., the level where individual basic interests and needs are aptly satisfied. Frankfurt calls this "the doctrine of sufficiency," and contrasts it with resource egalitarianism. In particular, Frankfurt maintains that, due to its focus on relative and comparative levels of provision, egalitarianism dangerously distracts our concern from the moral relevance of the absolute levels of satisfaction of people's needs and interests (as well as from the conceptual tools required to appreciate them), and this is harmfully "alienating", contributing as it does "to the moral disorientation and shallowness of our time" (*Ibid.*, pp. 22-24).

Frankfurt claims also that in several cases equal distributions fail to account for the moral relevance of certain thresholds of goods or assets in people's life and choices. In other words, certain goods or achievements become good, or morally relevant, beyond a given absolute threshold, and below the threshold no equal distribution is able to guarantee the moral value one could achieve by placing herself beyond that threshold. Indeed, equal distributions to people below the threshold can prevent some individuals from achieving the threshold, without benefiting anybody else. Accordingly, Frankfurt concludes, considerations about equality fail to track what is morally relevant in alternative choices among different options in which people could be placed below certain relevant thresholds of allocated goods. In those cases, Frankfurt claims, what is morally objectionable are not inequalities among individuals, but rather the fact that "those with less have *too little*" (*Ibid.*, p. 32).

In his argument, Frankfurt considers two egalitarian claims applied to the condition where everyone is below the threshold of sufficient provisions. He shows that these seemingly plausible claims are both mistaken, because egalitarian distributions may lead to various kinds of disasters. The claims are that "no one should have more than anyone else" and that "no one should have more than enough" (*Ibid.*, pp. 30-32). Frankfurt's general line of reasoning is that egalitarian distributions, when unable to raise each and every individual beyond the threshold, do not produce any improvement, but rather worsen the situation of some individuals (those placed at levels that are not too inferior to the threshold, who lose the resources apt to bring them beyond the threshold) without improving the status of others (those being so far from the threshold that any extra resource does not constitute an improvement of their state).

Moreover, when people are well beyond the threshold of sufficiency, inequalities are not morally objectionable. Differences in levels of resources, if placed very high over the level of sufficiency, are not registered as morally challenging in the common phenomenology; therefore, equality is not an independent, or absolute, moral factor:

> We tend to be quite unmoved, after all, by inequalities between the well-to-do and the rich; our awareness that the former are substantially worse off than the latter does not disturb us morally at all. And if we believe of some person that his life is richly fulfilling, that he himself is genuinely content with his economic situation, and that he suffers no resentments or sorrows which more money could assuage, we are not ordinarily much interested – from a moral point of view – in the question of how the amount of money he

> has compares with the amounts possessed by others. [...] The fact that some people have much less than others is morally undisturbing when it is clear that they have plenty (*Ibid.*, pp. 32-33).

Here, Frankfurt is attracting our attention to the fact that well beyond the threshold of sufficiency (however defined), equalizing moves seem not to be required, or at least not morally relevant. Accordingly, Frankfurt's view includes the following claims:

1. Below the threshold of an adequate living, equalizations are morally required insofar as they represent substantial improvements towards the sufficient level, and much more so if they permit to achieve sufficiency.

2. However, below the threshold, minor equalizations are not required, contrary to what egalitarians hold; indeed, they can also be mischievous, preventing individuals in close proximity to the threshold from achieving sufficiency.

3. Beyond the threshold, any equalization is morally insignificant.

Here, I shall not endorse Frankfurt's view completely. In particular, I would like to leave aside his controversial idea that, *below the threshold*, there are equalizations that are either unimportant or even pernicious from the moral point of view – i.e., claims **1.** and **2.** above. Indeed, it seems that these claims are independent from the less controversial point made in **3.**, about our intuitions concerning people placed well *beyond the threshold* of an adequate standard of living. In other words, I suggest that, even though equality has an independent moral value below the threshold of a decent living, and more so among people having just the resources for that living, it might be the case that it loses its relevance well beyond the threshold. I find unavoidable the intuition according to which, in a very rich society where abundance of each primary good is diffused across the whole citizenry, even if with different levels of possession, a strictly egalitarian policy is not morally required. It seems that many kinds of egalitarians – for instance, people supporting principles similar to Rawls' difference principle – can accept this without any protest. Notice that Nagel (2005) regards the "difference between rich and poor in a rich but unjust society" as "highly arbitrary" (p. 126). Here, I am not denying this. I am simply claiming that differences between *the rich and the less rich, but still well off citizens* in a rich but unjust society are not arbitrary in that way. Moreover, I contend that, if this is the case, then the relational view of justice falters.

To be true, three objections can be raised against this intuition. First, Frankfurt's argument concerns mainly equality of *resources*. What about equality of other goods, such as self-respect? It seems that in those cases our intuitions about the rich society are not so indifferent to equality. Second, it is not so clear that Rawlsian justice concerns the allocation of goods. For Rawls, justice is more plausibly depicted as a fair design and regulation of the system of basic institutions and norms that make allocation of goods – in its various forms (production, exchange, distribution) – take place. Third, what about the so-called positional goods? It seems that in this case equality has a more robust role than Frankfurt acknowledges.

To deal with these objections would require a very long discussion. For the present purposes, I have the following answers. First, if self-respect is one of the goods to be equalized, this raises a problem even for a relational view of justice. It does not seem that we can limit our respect to our fellow citizens only, and that we can root respect in the relation of co-citizenship. Human beings as such are worthy of respect. Moreover, respect from others is one of the main conditions for self-respect (as Rawls, 1999 p. 388 claimed). Accordingly, in limiting my discussion only to equality of resources, I am relying on an assumption that is shared also by the supporters of a relational analysis of socio-economic justice. It is plausible to say, then, that equality of resources is not strictly required at certain levels above the threshold, even though equality of respect could be still required. However, this does not amount to an objection to my argument, since I am considering only equality of resources, which is the focus of relational views of justice.

Second, the distinction between justice as a problem of allocation and justice as a requirement imposed on a basic structure does not seem to matter here. Frankfurt's contention is that there are situations where the moral significance of equality fades away, and at the end vanishes at all. This seems true for the two different conceptions of equality. Over a certain threshold, further adjustments of the institutional arrangement of the basic structure seem quite pointless.

Finally, in the case of positional goods whose enjoyment depends on our relative position as opposed to the position of others, some level of inequality, instead of strict equality, is required to make room for them. Accordingly, a policy where some inequalities are allowed, at least well beyond the threshold of a decent and comfortable life, seems to be a necessary step in acknowledging the role of positional goods. Claim 3. in Frankfurt's argument, then, cannot be challenged in the name of the relevance of positional goods; rather, its plausibility is reinforced if one wants to make room for those goods.

My interest here concerns the consequences of the vanishing value of equality beyond the threshold of sufficiency on a relational view of social justice. It seems that the citizens of a rich society, whose members are all beyond the level of sufficiency, are still involved in the relation of co-citizenship as mentioned by Nagel (2005). They are both authors of and subjects to a common legal system, and that system brings out certain inequalities among them. Nevertheless, the intuition expressed in Frankfurt's last claim (claim **3.** above) holds that equalization moves are not required at that level of provisions. Therefore, the power that the co-citizenship relation had to give rise to requirements of justice seems to vanish in this case. However, if so, a suspicion comes in – namely, that at those levels that were closer to the threshold requirements of justice have not been created by co-citizenship as a relation, since even at those levels where justice is not binding such a relation obtains and is unchanged. This is enough to cast doubts on the source claim. When perfect co-variance is not occurring, it seems that we have no decisive grounds to assume that co-citizenship as a relation is the source of the demands of socio-economic justice. Accordingly, also concerning social justice the relational analysis is inaccurate.

Conclusions: A Piece of Moral Geography

The moral geography we are facing is as follows. Justice and parental obligations have limits, but those limits do not overlap with the boundaries of co-citizenship and parenthood. In some cases those relations hold, but the obligations do not. Perhaps, even the reverse is true. A possible, but still not decisive, reason to believe that this is the case is that parenthood and co-citizenship can strengthen the responsibility for these duties, but in some cases responsibility is transferred to other moral agents without any connection with the relevant relations. In case of sudden death of both parents, for instance, the surviving children do not cease to be worthy of care. Simply, the responsibility of other agents towards them increases. Sometimes, the mere fact of being present, or nearby, may shift the responsibility on another agent. An uncle living nearby may be the holder of the most stringent duty to care for those children. Other relatives may have increasingly lower levels of responsibility, depending on their increasing distance – with respect to both degrees of kinship and purely geographical distance.

In this kind of cases, responsibility seems to increase independently of relations. Contrary to what it may appear, our judgments of responsibility do not behave in a purely relational way. True, we ascribe the greatest responsibility to parents, and this may lead to think that responsibility is connected to proximity and kinship. However, as previously said, sudden death of parents does not erase the duty; it simply shifts responsibility on relatives. Even in this case, it seems that nearness – which can be construed as a relation – triggers responsibility, since a relative nearby seems to be more responsible than a distant one. Nevertheless, if the relatives living nearby fail to comply with their duties, distance does not excuse other potential carers. Every available adult may be deemed responsible for needy children, no matter her geographical and biological stance. In this case, mere availability or possibility might shift responsibilities.

The same might hold for duties of general beneficence and justice. In condition of (even partial) compliance, responsibility may be graduated according to certain relations, such as co-citizenship. Therefore, it seems appropriate to held Italians more responsible for justice and beneficence in Italy, Americans in USA, and so on. Nevertheless, if a general failure to fulfil those duties on behalf of Italians obtains, other individuals abroad may see their levels of responsibility rapidly increased. This is our situation as Westerners with respect to justice and beneficence in the Third World. Therefore, the scope of parental obligations and duties of justice (i.e., their addressees) is influenced by certain relevant relations, but this influence is not linear. Even people not involved in the relevant relations might be addressees of these obligations in certain cases (and people involved might be free from any of those duties in other cases). Responsibility is as well influenced by relations, because these relations can strengthen it. Even in this case, however, this does not mean that certain relations can create responsibilities on their own. In cases involving orphans, asylum-seekers, and the like, mere nearness, and also non-compliance, might shift responsibilities in somewhat unexpected ways. The claim that parenthood and co-citizenship as relations are the only source of parental obligations and justice – i.e., the source claim that is embedded in the relational analysis of parental obligations and justice requirements – is not able to account for the above intuitions.

References

Abizadeh. A. (2007). "Cooperation, Pervasive Impact, and Coercion: On the Scope (not Site) of Distributive Justice". *Philosophy and Public Affairs*. Vol. 35. No. 4. Pp. 318-358.

Blake, M. (2001). "Distributive Justice, State Coercion, and Autonomy". *Philosophy and Public Affairs*. Vol. 30. No. 3. Pp. 257-296.

Dworkin, R. (2000). *Sovereign Virtue*. Cambridge. MA. Harvard University Press.

Frankfurt, H. (1987). "Equality as a Moral Ideal". *Ethics*. Vol. 98. No. 1. Pp. 21-43.

Jeske, D. (2008). *Rationality and Moral Theory. How Intimacy Generates Reasons*. New York. Routledge.

Julius, A. J. (2006). "Nagel's Atlas". *Philosophy and Public Affairs*. Vol. 34. No. 2. Pp. 176-192.

MacCormick, N. (1982). "Nation and Nationalism". *Legal Right and Social Democracy: Essays in Legal and Social Philosophy*. Oxford. Clarendon Press. Pp. 247-264.

Nagel, T. (2005). "The Problem of Global Justice". *Philosophy and Public Affairs*. Vol. 33. No. 2. Pp. 113-147.

Rawls, J. (1999). *A Theory of Justice*. Cambridge. MA. Harvard University Press.

Sangiovanni, A. (2007). "Global Justice, Reciprocity, and the State". *Philosophy and Public Affairs*.Vol. 35. No 1. Pp. 3-39.

Scheffler, S. (1997). "Relationships and Responsibilities". *Philosophy and Public Affairs*. Vol. 26. No. 3. Pp.189-209.

Scheffler, S. (2001). *Boundaries and Allegiances. Problems of Justice and Responsibilities in Liberal Thought*. Oxford. Oxford University Press.

Scheffler, S. (2004). "Projects, Relationships, and Reasons". Wallace, R., Pettit, P., Scheffler, S., & Smith, M. (eds.). *Reason and Value. Themes from the Moral Philosophy of Joseph Raz*. Oxford. Clarendon Press. Pp. 247-269.

Scanlon, T.M. (1998). *What We Owe to Each Other*. Cambridge. MA. Harvard University Press.

Simmons, J. (1996). Associative Political Obligations. *Ethics*. Vol. 106. No. 2. Pp. 247-273.

Tamir, Y. (2003). *Liberal Nationalism*. Princeton. Princeton University Press.

Tan, K. (2006). "The Boundary of Justice and the Justice of Boundaries: Defending Global Egalitarianism". *Canadian Journal of Law and Philosophy*. Vol. 19. No. 2. Pp. 319-344.

Cosmopolitanism, Sovereignty and Global Justice

Regina Queiroz[1]

Introduction

In "Cosmopolitanism and Sovereignty" (1992, pp. 48-75) Pogge sustains that a global order founded on sovereign states thwarts the equal right to justice of every citizen, independently of religious, linguistic, ethnic or historical differences, which are morally irrelevant in a cosmopolitan perspective (*Ibid.*, p. 68). Thus, it is necessary to *reallocate* the political authority, that is, to eliminate the prevalence of nation-states in the global order. This must be replaced by the equal moral consideration of individuals, by the abandonment of the concentration of governmental authority, and by the institutionalization of global justice

Despite the above mentioned theory of vertical dispersion of sovereignty Pogge does not abandon the idea of global institutions to realize economic justice at a global level – the unavoidable concretization of that justice results from the existence of those institutions – and to decide the conflicts between the different political units. Such dispersion does not exclude the idea of a global state. The idea of global institutions is not surprising, for states privilege the interests of their compatriots, and therefore they will not be able, contrarily to global institutions, to distribute economic goods among global citizens with fairness and impartiality. The idea of a world state is more unexpected, mainly because his theory of dispersion of sovereignty tries to overcome the Westphalian international order. In this order, among other characteristics, the world is divided into sovereign states, which do not recognize any superior authority. The process of legislation, the solving of disputes and the laws of coercion are largely in the hands of the states and recurring to force as a last resort solves the conflicts among states. International laws do not offer any minimal guarantee to eliminate the primacy of states in the international sphere.

---

1 The presentation that lies at the basis of the present paper was made possible by the Fundação Para a Ciência e a Tecnologia, Scholarship SFRH/BPD/2007.

However, although Pogge's argumentation aims to overcome the international order established by the Westphalia Treaty I sustain that his reflection, seems to misunderstand the principle of sovereignty, and that this misunderstanding can have devastating consequences similar to those of the Westphalian order that he rejects. Thus, I criticise his cosmopolitan theory of a vertical dispersion of sovereignty and then I compare it with Kant's cosmopolitan conception. Although Kant's cosmopolitanism is not related with the distributive issues of global justice, I will try to show that it seems more consistent than Pogges's.

Despite this criticism, I do not aim to give up the cosmopolitan ideal of global justice. The existence of transnational institutions and the creation of a global market do not allow us to ignore the distribution of economic goods, that is, the issues of global justice. However, the shift from a world order based on states to a global one reconfigures the nature of political institutions and requires the stipulation of political principles, different from political sovereignty in order to realize the global justice ideal.

1. Dispersion of sovereignty and war

Globalization, characterized by deterritorialization, interconnection and multidimensionality, moved our attention from domestic to global. If within the national arena we face not only different conceptions of domestic justice, but also its rejection by conservatives and libertarians, also global justice has several interpretations. Among them a cosmopolitan interpretation stands out, which claims global principles of justice – including human rights, and individual capabilities. Cosmopolitanism claims in particular a) individualism: the fundamental political units are not families, tribes, ethnicities, cultures, communities, nations or states, but individuals or persons; b) universality: the status of those units equally refers to every human being and not only to aristocrats, Aryans and whites; c) generality: this status has a global strength and it not only applies to compatriots or inhabitants of the same region (Pogge, 1992, pp. 48-9).

Even though some supporters of social domestic justice do not believe that primary goods must only be distributed by the state, they recognize its important role in that distribution (Cf. Rawls, 1971; Walzer, 1983). At a global level we do not have a consensus about the role of the state in the distribution of goods, not only because globalization has brought about a reconfiguration of state power, but also because cosmopolitans identify individuals as the main units of moral and political concern, and disagree about the importance of the state and its congenital quality, sovereignty, in achieving global justice (Beitz, 2005; Nussbaum, 2006; Pogge, 1992).

Grosso modo sovereignty is the power of the state to make decisions with ultimate authority and, as a last resort, to wage war (Thompson, 1995, p. 213). States are defined by the existence of an anonymous political apparatus organised on the basis of roles instead of being bound up with the person of the ruler, are furthermore characterised by supreme jurisdiction over their territory, by a monopoly of coercive power and control of means of violence, by the introduction of a steady army and by a non personal structure of power, with no regard to sources of legitimacy such as religion and privileged groups.

According to Pogge, sovereign states dispute natural resources among themselves, because to possess them affects the distribution of power in international bargaining (economic and political), and because the most powerful also try to interpose frontiers between them and the poorest in order to circumvent the duties of justice towards its compatriots (Pogge, 1992, pp. 70-1). So, the establishment of social policies at a global level imposes the reallocation of political authority (*Ibid.,* p. 62). This means the elimination of the predominance of nation-states in a global order and its replacement by individuals, as well as the abandonment of the concentration of governmental authority, and consequently the institutionalization of global justice.

The dispersion of sovereignty is followed by the stipulation of the principle of positive intervention in the case of the violation of human rights. Pogge accepts, in function of the principle of checks and balances, that if any unity is tyrannical and oppressive we will always have another which will protect the oppressed and publicize the abuses and if necessary fight against the oppressors (*Ibid.,* p. 63). However, the stipulation of the principle of positive intervention in the case of the violation of human rights eliminates one of the more relevant principles of modern sovereign state and *ipso facto* the principle monopoly of violence, broadening to political units. But, if the small political units above the state have power to intervene, to refute the non-divisibility and the absolute nature of their sovereignty does not impeach us from attributing them the state's power to make war.[2] Moreover, not only is the principle of territorial jurisdiction also associated with those units, but also the attribution of citizenship (*Ibid.*, pp. 69-70). Therefore, the vertical dispersion of sovereignty over political units that fight one another for the implementation of human rights, extends conflicts between states to further political units, and does

2 The dispersion of sovereignty into little units does not protect them from tyranny (Cabrera, 2005, p. 198).

not decrease the intensity of conflicts across frontiers. Such dispersion furthers the distrust among states, which is common in the Westphalian order. When Pogge sustains the right of political units to intervene in the internal affairs of other political units, that right destroys the recognition of political sovereignty, which, understood as the ultimate authority, can hardly be violated by the interference of other state(s) without unavoidably leading to an armed conflict. The right of political units to intervene leads to devastating consequences such as the Westphalian order that Pogge rejects.

Pogge's theory could possibly avoid this consequence if his reference point was not the Westphalian conception of international order (inspired by Grotius, as Nussbaum highlights). This establishes a society of states, any one of which respects some political principles and considers other states as equal moral and political actors.

Even though this conception admits the existence of trans-state moral principles and stipulates that states are obliged to follow a system of norms similar to those applied among individuals in a state of nature, it establishes that states and not persons are entitled to rights and duties in the international sphere. According to this principle, those states must give up fighting for resources and territories. So, if the reflection about global justice in light of the conception of the moral society of states allows us to conceive the existence of international political principles as compatible with the ideal of political sovereignty, it does not diminish the power of the states in its achievement. It is not easy to subsume that reflection by the cosmopolitan ideal and at the same time insure the impartiality of the distribution of goods at a global level.

2. World state and global injustice

Despite the fact that Pogge defends the dispersion of sovereignty his proposal:

a) Preserves states – they are reference measures of political units below the regions and the world and above the neighbourhood, city and province (*Ibid.*, p. 69);

b) Is compatible with the creation of centralized mechanisms meant to solve that problems that emerge between the local and global level such mechanisms do not exclude the participation of people in the process of decision making with regard to problems that affect everybody, such as ecology, and allows for solving conflicts between the different political units (*Ibid.*, p. 65);

c) Does not give up on global institutions to realize economic justice at a global level and to decide issues about the distribution of goods among different political units (*Ibid.,* p. 71). The existence of global problems that require the participation of every citizen for a solution to be found – would presuppose these institutions both in order to resolve conflicts among local units and in order to ensure the participation of every human being in a sole global institutional scheme. Even if we had no global institutions, the conflicts resulting from the fact that the local units had the right to intervene in case of violation of human rights and the divergences among local units about the global distribution of economic goods would require global sovereign institutions, which would then have the right to deliberate on these issues. Nevertheless, the vertical dispersion of sovereignty ought to be understood in analogy with the absolute and indivisible sovereignty of the states, for the global institutions still have the final authority to decide the issues of justice in different political units. Indeed, solving conflicts of social justice depends on those global institutions.

d) Finally, the vertical dispersion does not necessarily imply the refusal of the hypothesis of a world democratic state. Despite the critical arguments against a world state (it would not respect social and cultural diversity and allow for the coordination of political units at different levels of sovereignty) (*Ibid.,* p. 63) the hypothesis of dispersion of sovereignty seems to presuppose that the achievement of global justice does not exclude the existence of an impartial world state, which would have the final authority to solve conflicts concerning the distribution of economic goods among the political units. So, although Pogge refutes the hypothesis of a world state, whose emergence could only result in a revolution or global catastrophe (*Ibid.*, p. 63), his theory of dispersion of sovereignty does not eliminate that possibility, which is justified by the existence of global problems, such as ecological ones. In fact, when Pogge tries to justify the need of the dispersion of sovereignty and mentions ecological problems that transcend the national frontiers, he adds that people are not free to choose to live in an unpolluted environment and are therefore prevented from saying what they think about this question. In the current state-centric model the environment is unilaterally ruled upon by national governments through inter-governmental bargaining deeply influenced by huge economic and military differences. To address this issue Pogge sustains that ecology must be replaced by democracy, that is, by the right of people to an institutional order which is affected by political decisions and in which people have equal opportunity to take influence upon, either directly or through representatives or delegates (Pogge, 1992, pp. 63-64). The reference to the world state appears in this context when Pogge sustains that, if the right to political participation supports his model of institutional dispersion, it also supports a greater autonomy in local issues, as it happens in the majority of current states and could also happen in a democratic world state (*Ibid.*, p. 64). So, his theory of dispersion of sovereignty does not eliminate that possibility, which is justified by the existence of global problems and by the fact that all human beings live in a single and global institutional scheme. The latter implies nowadays the existence of institutions such as the territorial state, a system and international diplomacy, and a global market of capitals, goods and services (*Ibid.*, p. 51).[3] Although Pogge maintains the polemical idea that a global state is still a version of the Westphalian conception of the state (Pogge, 1992, p. 58) and denies in his proposal the sovereignty of states, he still safeguards its principle. Indeed, his suggestion forcibly leads to figuring out a world state, however democratic, for in case of conflicts with regard to the distribution of economic goods among the different sovereign levels the claims raised by the divided and relatively sovereignty entities would require a final authority. In other words, global institutions based on the checks and balances exercised by different political entities cannot impair the right of each institution to a final decision about political disputes. The defence of the dispersion of sovereignty falls then victim of the ideal of a final authority. It is not by chance that Kant, one of the greatest supporters of the cosmopolitan ideal, when conceiving an international right, hesitates in separating it from the sovereignty of states. When in *Zum ewigen Frieden. Ein philosophischer Entwurf* Kant ties up the idea of a free federation with the right of peoples to a contract among states stipulating coercive laws and a State of Peoples (*civitas gentium*) (Kant, 1796/96, B 35, 36), he also recognizes the states' power to reject the idea of a world republic (B, 37, 38). Kant's political realism leads to a peaceful federation of states, in which the sovereign states, without alienating their final authority, accept to participate in international federation, which allows them to go out from transcend the state of nature. Contrarily to the idea of a world republic, the peace federation does not locate the sovereignty in a supra-state institution, but in the multiplicity of sovereign states. The cosmopolitanism of Kant renounces to an ideal stipulation (which at is correct *in thesi* (*Ibid.*, B 37), that of a world republic, and defends a less wanted solution, that is more practical, the peaceful federation. This renunciation is based on the preliminary principles to perpetual peace

3 Even if we didn't have an institutional global scheme, the conflicts resulting from the right to intervene when we had the violation of human rights or divergences about the global distribution of economic goods claim for sovereign global institutions, with the right to deliberate about these issues reported above.

among the States, as is affirmed in such as the articles 2 and 4, which affirm, respectively: "No independent state (...) could be acquired by another through inheritance, exchange, purchase or donation" and "No State should intervene by force in the constitution and government of other State" (*Ibid.*, B, 6 e and B 11).

Kant's model of cosmopolitanism seems more consistent than Pogge's not only because it better evaluates the nature of the principle of sovereignty and the circumstances under which it can be relevant – i.e., in the context of a plurality of sovereign states – but also because it avoids the consequences of Pogges's model. In fact, in the frame of the theory of dispersion of sovereignty the hypotheses of a world state does not hinder the confrontation between the democratic state and the political units that it has to rule on. So, if such a dispersion admits the inevitability of political conflict by eliminating the supposition that the world state would be pacific – as Pogge explicitly suggests (*Ibid.,* p. 63) – the solution found implies dislocating the legitimacy of violence in a democratic world state, without eliminating the conflict among sovereign instances. If, in the name of human rights, the principle of intervention is established, then it seems difficult to avoid a spread of war and violence. It seems likewise difficult that global institutions may take on the functions of the sovereign state without any limitation of its coercive force. In this case, the existence of a world democratic state does not impede that the cosmopolitan conception of dispersed sovereignty perpetuate the situations that it tries, in fact, to eliminate, for the global order would tend to degenerate into a state of war.

If the world democratic state has no monopoly of violence, the fact that it doesn't exist another similar state transforms it into an absolute state.

I guess that Pogge highlights the importance of the participation of citizens in the deliberation of a global democratic state in order to suggest that the tyrannical character of a world state, already sustained by Kant (1793, A 278), could be overrun by the rational and moral deliberation of its citizens. The way Pogge depicts this state could be inspired by the Kantian idea of the kingdom of ends. In this kingdom the strength of reason could establish a pacific and democratic order. However, if this hypothesis supposes an immediate relationship between citizens, it will eliminate the need of any institution and give up the justification of any world state.

According to Pogge to hinder the violation of human rights requires coercion. This is maybe the reason why he envisages a world state by analogy with the Kantian kingdom of ends. But by conceding sovereignty to that world democratic state he upholds a contradictory historical and logical conception of it, contradictory because it presupposes recognition by the other states, thus implying the plurality of states. Therefore, the idea of a final authority acknowledges the plurality of state's authorities. Even though they can be in an eminent situation of war, does not imply the refusal recognition of the sovereign right, even if violated, of other states. In this case, the states bargain, fight, and establish contracts. This implies that there is also a dispersion of sovereignty not only in federal regimes but also among different states. But when Pogge defends that the distribution of economic goods is dependent on a global institution, which can reallocate the resources besides the irrelevant facts of religion, language, ethnicity, and history, Pogge excludes the requirement of inherent recognition of the principle of sovereignty (*Ibid.,* p. 68).

It is clear that in Pogge's reflection the multiplicity of sovereign units rules out the undivided and absolute sovereignty of a world state. Instead, there seems to exist reciprocal recognition of authority among these units and therefore an acknowledgement of the plurality of sovereign units. However, on the one hand this establishment violates the principle of equality among states, since such a kind of global institutional order does not instate equal units but different hierarchical levels of sovereignty. On the other hand, even though the global democratic state does not have the monopoly of violence, such a state would develop into an absolute state. This stands opposite to what happens in a Westphalian international order, in which states accept to negotiate their external sovereignty, fight and sign contracts. Therefore, I can affirm that, at least in theory, such a system also foresees a dispersion of sovereignty among the different states.

This world state, far from ensuring the concretization of global justice, can be dominated by particular interests, which instead of allowing the decrease of economic and political inequalities intensify oppression and global injustice. The management of some international institutions such as the IMF and the World Bank, exposed by the Nobel Prize, Stiglitz (2002), gives enough empirical evidence.

I assume that these consequences result from conceiving the global order in terms of a principle of sovereignty. Therefore, I also disagree with Beitz when, in questioning the democracy of global institutions, he affirms that the strength of cosmopolitanism consists in its ability to question the rationality of international and translational regimes responsible by criteria of political justice similar to those applied to the state institutions (Beitz, 2005, p. 25). Independently of whether or not democracy is an intrinsic quality of states, the transnational institutions cannot be understood by analogy to the state. Indeed, as Beitz recognizes, the global order is organised according to the same institutional structure of nation states, for the latter is characterised by coercive institutions with the capacity of taking political decisions that include the reorganisation of the decision making process and some constraints on the power to use legitimate violence to enforce political decisions. Contrary to that, the global institutional order is not endowed with an executive sovereign power, nor does it have any effective legal or political capacity (*Ibid.*, p. 24). Furthermore, transnational political institutions cannot be understood in analogy to the founding and constitutive political principle of the states, i.e., sovereignty. Were they endowed with a sovereignty thus far restricted to the states, these institutions would transform into sovereign, self-interested entities, which would therefore be unable to make decision on global problems with impartiality. In this respect I would draw attention to the arguments of Luís Cabrera in "The Cosmopolitan Imperative" (2005) in relation to the tensions between norms of sovereignty and the moral cosmopolitan approach. Cabrera recognizes that the particularistic ethic is foundational in a Westphalian system and in the system of moral sovereignty (*Ibid.*, pp. 183 and 189).

However, if for Pogge the democratic quality of a global State is granted by the deliberation of global citizens, then I can infer that citizens are supposed to find themselves under a veil of global ignorance, which eliminates every political particularism – including religion, language and nationality – with regard to the deliberations that govern global institutions. This is the condition for them to rule impartially such a world democratic state.

Nevertheless, this last supposition is very controversial, not only because it eliminates the consideration of the particularity of the states, peoples, nations, cultures as well as of every political difference, but also because it is based on the individualistic premises of his ethical-institutional cosmopolitanism. This superposes the right of individuals, organized in institutions, to the power of sovereign units, among which we can include the states. This also gives individuals, rather than institutions, central importance in deliberation. The first moral responsibility and the last political choice are based on individual persons (Pogge, 1992, p. 64).

To focus the political deliberation on people – which denotes a rupture with the impersonality of state institutions – seems to depend on the Kantian idea of the kingdom of ends. If the impersonality, in modern political thought, of the sovereign, artificial person, without any relationship to its personal biography is distinguished from the personality of power in the kingdom of the Middle Age, then thinking about the global community through the idea of a kingdom of ends can lead to two conclusions. On the one hand it seems to retake the personal character of the sovereign in medieval age, and on the other hand, contrary to Kant's idea, it mixes up ethical and political-juridical legislation. The first is internal and can be related to a non-institutional moral world, because its legislation is "intimate". On the contrary the second, related to an external legislation, is transformed in political institutions, and the performances of its officials requires impersonality and impartiality. The impartiality of the institutions that Pogge depicts is dependent on the judgements of the citizens. In other words, then he is not only superposing the internal legislation to the external, but also defending a popular model of global sovereignty. He furthermore determines the global order by the democratic liberal ideals. In *The Law of Peoples* Rawls presents categorical arguments about the ethical and political risks of the universalization of those ideals (Cf. Rawls, 1999).

Nevertheless, despite the fact that we do not have any further clarification of the institutional global structure, as is for example defended by David Held in his project of global democracy,[4] Pogge's reflection about the concept of sovereignty in the context of his claim of global justice does not eliminate the institutional dimension. His theory is developed within the frame of an ethical-political cosmopolitan perspective, in which he associates his political concern with the ethical one. If ethics is referred to a legislation, which, as Kant defended, obliges *foro interno*, without any need of institutionalisation, when we envisage a political perspective we need to include the institutional dimension in the reflection on global justice. However, if the reflection about global justice is reduced to the ethical interactionism or to pure cosmopolitanism, which attributes direct responsibility for the concretization of human rights to the others, individually or collectively (Pogge, 1992, p. 50), then such a cosmopolitan claim is reduced to a vote of *pietas*, without any political consistency[5]. Indeed, it lacks the institutions that are able to endorse and enforce the ethical principles of global justice. It is not by chance that Pogge's ethical-

4 The reformation of the Security Council of the United Nations (to give to the developed countries a meaningful voice and an effective decision capacity); the creation of a second chamber in the UN (in accordance with an international constitutional convention); to deepen political regionalization (EU and others); the usage of translational referendums; compulsive jurisdiction previous to International Court; creation of a new Court to Human Rights; foundation of a new economic coordination agency with a regional, local and global scope and establishment of an effective international military army (Cf. Held, 1995).

5 Beitz highlights that moral cosmopolitanism is agnostic about the content of political global justice because it is committed neither for nor against the proposition that it should have a global sovereign state. It has not an automatically interference of cosmopolitanism about the cosmopolitan justification about the institutions (Beitz, 2005, p. 18). This lack of commitment questions how we must answer this practical indetermination (*Ibid.*), and ignore that a global theory of justice must have as principal concern the definition of the basic structure of international society (*Ibid.*, p. 24).

institutional reflection on global justice focuses on the principle of sovereignty. Thus, the fact that to move from an international to a global order affects immediately the founding principle of modern states. This shows that Pogges's reflection on global justice is right in associating the issues of global justice to the political conditions of global institutions.

Nevertheless, his cosmopolitan theory of sovereignty, preserved in the frame of its separation of power among political units, implies an inconsistent conception of sovereignty and compromises Pogge's aim. This inconsistency is not a particular characteristic of his sovereignty's theory, but it expresses a deeper tension between this principle and individualistic cosmopolitanism – the congenital particularism of sovereignty is not compatible with the universalism of moral and institutional cosmopolitanism. It is this incompatible principle that renders Pogge's theory difficult to accept, and leads to the impossibility of realizing the claim of global justice.

Pogge's reflection shows the limits of a conception of a global and impartial institution for the distribution of economic goods, but suffers at the same time from the limits of a cosmopolitan conception of sovereignty contrary, for example, to the Kantian one. Even though Kant does not include in his reflection questions of global justice, he sustains a cosmopolitan ideal that does not alienate the principle of state sovereignty (Kant, 1795/96, B 37, 38, 1793, A, 278).

Conclusion

Even though Pogge's theory of individualistic cosmopolitanism highly problematic as far as sovereignty is concerned, this does not mean that we must give up the ideal of global justice. Firstly, I agree with Pogge that we already have a sole global institutional scheme, due to the existence of transnational institutions such as the IFM, WTO, WB, UN and a world market. And, secondly, the current world financial crisis claims for global solutions.

However, if we abandon the international state order, the conceptualization of this ideal presupposes the stipulation of a political principle different from political sovereignty. Although the progressive erosion of every country's internal and external sovereignty does not allow us to decide if we have a candidate to replace it or if the end of the state-centred order will be founded on a single principle, its design must be done in the ethical-institutional sphere. If in the tradition of Wolff and Vatell, some thin-

thinkers defend a moral society of states[6], whose political organization should integrate the concern with the global order and in which sovereignty is not only limited to the domestic sphere, but also related to the sphere of international relations. These suggestions do not eliminate the pre-eminence of the interest of the citizens. In such a way they do not run the risk of transforming the ideal of global justice into a utopia, which is impoverished, oppressive and unfair from an economic and political standpoint.

References

Beitz, C. (2005): "Cosmopolitanism and Global Justice". *Current Debates in Global Justice.* Brock. Gillian and Darrel Moellendorf (eds.). Berlin. Springer. Pp. 11-27.

Cabrera, L. (2005). "The Cosmopolitan Imperative: Global Justice through Accountable Integration". *Current Debates in Global Justice.* Brock, Gillian and Darrel Moellendorf (eds.) Berlin. Springer. Pp. 171-199.

Held, D. (1995). *Democracy and the Global Order. From the Modern State to Cosmopolitan Governance.* Cambridge. Polity.

Kant, I. ([1793] 1968.) "Über der Gemeinspruch. Das mag in der Theorie richtig sein, taugt aber nicht für die Praxis". "Immanuel Kant Schriften zur Antropologie, Geschichtsphilosophie, Politik und Pädagogik". Vol. 1. *Immanuel Kant Werkausgabe* Band XI. Wilhelm Weischedel (ed.). Frankfurt am Main. Suhrkamp. Pp. 127-172.

Kant, I. ([1795] 1968). "Zum ewigen Frieden. Ein philosophischer Entwurf". "Immanuel Kant Schriften zur Antropologie, Geschichtsphilosophie, Politik und Pädagogik". Vol. 1. *Immanuel Kant Werkausgabe* Band XI. Wilhelm Weischedel (ed.). Frankfurt am Main. Suhrkamp. Pp. 195-251.

Nussbaum, M. C. (2006). *Frontiers of Justice: Disability, Nationality, Species Membership.* Cambridge. MA. Belknap Press of Harvard University Press.

Pogge, T. (1992). "Cosmopolitanism and Sovereignty". *Ethics.* Vol. 103. No. 1. Pp. 48-75.

Rawls, J. (1971). *A Theory of Justice.* Oxford. Oxford University Press.

Rawls, J. (1999). *The Law of Peoples.* Cambridge. MA. Harvard University Press.

Stiglitz, J. E. (2002). *Globalisation and its Discontents.* New York. W. W. Norton & Company. Inc.

6 According to Beitz the main ideal of a moral society of states: states and not persons are the privileged of rights and duties; the states are obliged to follow a normative system analogous to that applied between the individual in the state of nature; the equality value is expressed in a principle which requires that the other states treat the others as equal moral persons. (Beitz, 2005, p. 16).

Thompson, J. (1995). "State Sovereignty in International relations: Bridging the Gap Between Theory and Empirical Research". *International Studies Quarterly.* Vol. 39. No. 2. Pp. 213-233.

Walzer, M. (1983). *Spheres of Justice. A Defence of Pluralism & Equality*, Oxford. Blackwell.

III. On Kant & Rawls

On Kant's Aesthetics and his Progressing Treatment of Peace

James Garrison

Introduction

Many readers fixate on Kant's ([1795] 1910) intriguingly titled work *Towards Perpetual Peace* and take it to be his definitive statement on geopolitical theory. However, in that essay and his later work, *The Metaphysics of Morals* ([1797] 1910), Kant offers two related, though substantively different geopolitical ideas of peace. Both works include a notion of agreement, which hearkens back to Kant's notion of taste and its role in bridging the gap between subjective intuition and objective ideals. The vocabulary of taste and beauty that Kant develops in his *Critique of Judgment* ([1790] 1910) sheds light on his ethical and aesthetic ideas of peace, both in their points of convergence and divergence. Specifically, Kant's aesthetic philosophy relates to peace through its discussion of whether beautiful objects necessarily relate to human taste (as a matter of reality) or if the connection is merely contingent (and thus ideal). For Kant only the latter option coheres with taste, for it maintains that the subject's reflection on the artwork is free and undetermined by causal structures. By the same token, the nature of beauty cannot be determined and presumed real for all rational agents prior to experience. Hence, matters of taste come down to agreement and not formal demonstration. This schema allows free autonomous subjects to converge ever indeterminately on a question with objective force – what should other rational agents find beautiful?

With this in mind, it appears strange that Kant's later treatment of similar issues of agreement, subjective opinion, and objective claims in *Towards Perpetual Peace* argues contrarily that peace is a real end of nature's will. I believe that, on some level, Kant tries to rectify this awkward position by amending it two years later in his *Metaphysics of Morals*. There he argues for a rational idea of peace while avoiding any claim about empirically deducing its purposiveness. My position is that these two discussions should not be seen as complimentary remarks on peace by Kant, but rather as a first attempt and a subsequent revision of his theory of peace.

From this perspective, I shall analyze the results of this shift in Kant's thinking by looking at how an ideal purposiveness of peace forces him to subsequently deemphasize the possibility of peace being genuinely perpetual. As a result, it will be shown that Kant's work on peace relates very strongly to his aesthetics and that perhaps Kantian geopolitics should be read on those terms, if his revisions are to be taken seriously. This will also give a basis for evaluating contemporary post-Kantian political philosophies in terms of how they variously incorporate Kant's aesthetics and theory in judgments in their different theories of peace and international right.

Quarreling Over the Beautiful

Judging beauty has both subjective and objective aspects. It is subjective insofar as common experience shows that people can differ wildly in their opinions of whether a given thing is beautiful. On the other hand, everyday experience not only shows that there are some things that many humans judge as beautiful, but that there are things that one *should* find beautiful, giving a normative, pseudo-objective force to claims about beauty.

Kant explains this apparent contradiction through his notion of taste. For him, aesthetic experience, like experience in general, starts with sensation. These sensations are by necessity subjective, for they are the subject's immediate sensory information of the object in question. Thus, the subject exists in special, private relation to the sensory impressions and any subsequent intuitions. This subjectivity, however, is mitigated by the fact that aesthetic judgments rest on an idea or archetype of beauty.

Here ideas properly refer to rational concepts (Kant [1790] 1910, p. 232) arising from the objective conditions of experience. Ideas thus have objective validity even though they lack objects. More precisely, they are effects of reason conditioned neither by the sensible world's causality, nor by the form of understanding. As such, these ideas escape determinate cognition, for they lack an appropriately determined object. However, ideas (*Ideen*) can still be thought indeterminately in terms of ideals (*Ideale*), which only approximate the missing object of cognition (*Ibid.*, p. 232).

Consequently, beauty is an ideal and refers to an unreachable maximum state of sensible intuition (idea) presented to the subject (*Ibid.*, p. 232). Judgment of beauty therefore bridges subjectivity and objectivity by considering subjective thoughts in terms of an objectively real, though indeterminate concept. As a result there exists a basis for common discourse and disagreement about matters of beauty.

Judgment of beauty thus pairs objectivity with indeterminacy, all while not minimizing the importance of subjective experience. The objective component of judgment explains why aesthetics involves a normative component. There exists a real, yet indeterminate concept of reason belonging to all humans, which grounds aesthetic experience and gives warrant to the view that one *ought* to find a given artwork beautiful. However, in the indeterminacy of the imaginative ideal, there also exists the free space in thinking that allows for two rational people to hold two different opinions of an object's beauty.

Thus, the "should" in aesthetics, while weakly objective, is not the "should" of physical science, which says that Occurrence B absolutely should follow Occurrence A (all things being equal). Nor is the "should" in question the "should" of morality, for judgments in that sphere involve the practical faculty and not the imaginative. For Kant, both of these are matters of "dispute [*disputieren*]" (*Ibid.*, p. 338), which reasonable people can settle by demonstrative proofs. However, aesthetic judgment is similar to claims from these spheres in that there is a *claim* of objective validity. Judgments of beauty thus may be thought of as intersubjective, since they transmute private impressions into claims that can and should have an objective hold on all rational subjects.

This more or less is Kant's notion of taste, about which humans can quarrel (*streiten*)[1] due to beauty's indeterminacy and the objective hold of the ideal on imagination. Taste thus includes with it the possibility of communication and the possibility of resolving authentic disagreements on matters that involve a community of subjects. If one abstracts these aspects of taste and judgement away from particular application in the sphere of beauty and art, it is quite easy to see how they have social and political implications. Furthermore, if one takes up these political connotations in the widest possible context, it is easy to see how they can lead to a theory of international relations. I believe that Kant does exactly this in constructing his notion of peace, thereby giving his political thinking an aesthetic flourish.

However, before moving to consider Kant's notion of peace vis-à-vis his work on aesthetics it is worth thinking through the relation of humanity to beauty in terms of purpose. Doing so will yield a vocabulary with which to assess the progress of peaceful relations and investigate Kant's view on the inevitability of world peace. This will show that Kant's geopo-

1 Here quarreling (streiten) is meant in distinction to holding proof-driven disputes (disputieren) over matters of science or morality.

litical ideal is related to his ideal of beauty and that his progressing work on peace can be read as an attempt to strengthen the analogy between the two ideals in their formal characteristics.

The Purposiveness of Taste

To understand how purpose works with taste and beauty, Kant looks at whether or not the objective nature of taste concerns some real purpose extant in nature or if its purposiveness (*Zweckmäßigkeit*) is ideal in a way that has no necessary bearing on the causal structure of the sensible world. This debate relates to an issue in the *Critique of Pure Reason* and its finding (Kant [1787] 1910, p. 366) that there are two aspects of causality, one which determines sequences in nature and one which orders thought for free, rational beings. Considering beauty through the first viewpoint yields the notion that nature has an actual purpose aligned with human judgment (Kant [1790] 1910, p. 347). Meanwhile, looking at it in terms of the latter leads to the thesis that judgments of beauty are freely related to objects in nature, which only concern one's reflection on the object in terms of the imaginative ideal.

According to the first perspective, the natural patterns such as the mathematical precision of crystalline structures (*Ibid.*, p. 348) or the arabesque-like intricacy of a pheasants' plumage which people deem beautiful would be a matter of design (*Ibid.*, p. 347). As a result, the fact that phenomena like these appeal to human taste would be completely natural. The subject's thoughts would thereby relate to apprehensions of beauty necessarily, and not contingently.

Kant, therefore, dismisses the first option that would reduce aesthetic judgment down to the level of occurrences in nature and the empirical laws of cause and effect. Such laws are determinate in character and deny the sort of genuine quarrel that Kant sees as crucial for aesthetic experience. If this perspective were valid, it would be possible to have a science, in the proper meaning of the term, of beauty, since objects could be classified as determinately with regard to a concept, and not an ideal, of beauty. This would make it so that one could prove an object's beauty by showing that it bears the identifying marks of the concept (Kant [1787][1]1910, p. 477). For Kant, beauty cannot annihilate the freedom of the subject, since doing so would also determinately confine the imagination in a way antithetical to its autonomous nature. Beyond this, the realist belief in peace's purposiveness ends up uncomfortably near in spirit to a physico-theological proof of God (*Ibid.*, p. 414), which Kant dismisses as impossible (*Ibid.*, p. 419). As a result, the absurdity of insisting on a real purpose in nature as regards taste shows rather that its purpose must be ideal in nature.

Towards Perpetual Peace sees Kant consider a theory of international relations that heavily trades upon the views advanced in his *Critique of Judgment*. *Towards Perpetual Peace* most notably borrows from his aesthetics in its attempt to reconcile competing claims in a community of moral agents (here nation-states) all of whom are subject to an objective notion of peace that humanity will certainly achieve. However, the symmetry between the two works is lacking in certain aspects. Accordingly, the less bold tone and formal revision of peace in Kant's later work *The Metaphysics of Morals* can be read as an attempt to remedy this lack of symmetry. Thus, Kant shifts his geopolitics to be in alignment with his aesthetic theory.

A Kantian Framework for International Relations

Towards Perpetual Peace begins by laying out a loosely-utopian framework for international relations and free trade. Its precepts include a respect for national sovereignty (Kant [1795] 1910 §1.1 and §1.5) described with a legal stricture (*Ibid.*, p. 347) that seems linked to respect for rational agents as a matter of duty (Kant [1785] 1910, p. 428 & pp. 462-3); [1788]1910, p. 76). The type of sovereign nation that interests Kant is a republican one, which separates legislative power from executive (Kant [1795] 1910, p. 352), because this subjects citizens to law in accordance with the principles of freedom (*Ibid.*, pp. 349-50) that follow from "the pure source of the concept of right" (*Ibid.*, p. 351). One reason for his endorsement of republicanism with respect to peace is that shared interest and consent of a citizenry tends to curb impulses (*Ibid.*, p. 351) toward what Kant (*Ibid.*, p. 348), echoing Hobbes, deems to be the natural state of war.

International relations, however, are not like those that occur within sovereign republics. Inside the context of a nation, legal authority determines citizen action with respect to the pure concept of right, thereby making the nation-state the context for moral reasoning. For Kant (*Ibid.*, p. 354), extending this to the international would contradictorily make "a nation consisting of nations" and require a uniform moral/legal structure for all of humanity. Rather, Kant (*Ibid.*, p. 354) holds that international relations are best carried out via a federalism of nations subject to plural authorities opposed to martial inclinations.

This suggests three conclusions. Firstly, international relations, since they lack a republican form like sovereign nations, do not similarly follow solely from the pure concept of right, if at all. Secondly, international relations concern parties whose quarrels (*streiten*) may be mediated and not parties whose disputes are determined by a single legal source (*disputieren*). Thirdly and finally, this federalism, like beauty, is a merely "adequate" ideal (*Ideal*) (Kant [1790][1]1910, p. 232), insofar as Kant believes it to be a negative surrogate to the positive idea (*Idee*) of an all-encompassing nation (Kant [1795][1]1910, p. 357).[2] At first glance this vocabulary links very directly with the notion of taste that Kant lays out in his earlier *Critique of Judgment.*

The Ideal of Perpetual Peace

The similarity to, and eventual departure from, the tenets of taste introduced in *The Critique of Judgment* become all the more striking as Kant transitions into explaining the actual idea of perpetual peace. Peace is an idea (*Idea*) of practical reason, which does not exist in the sensible world and its causal structure, but is rather a matter of autonomous reason (Kant [1788][1]1910, p. 43). The rational idea of peace conceptualizes nature as an archetype that is subject to practical reason's moral law rather than physical causality (*Ibid.*, p. 43). Thus the idea of peace furnishes a determining ground for the will (*Ibid.*, p. 43), which all rational agents share as a formal ectype (*Ibid.*, p. 43), and which refers to an imagined world totally shaped by good will.

The ideal correspondent to the idea of perpetual peace is one of public/international right, which, while not conforming to the idea of international peace, does address the rights of sovereign nation states with complex histories rooted in the phenomenal world. According to Kant this ideal should direct international relations towards a federal structure as discussed earlier. It is worth asking though, what is the nature of this progress toward diplomacy? What, if anything, would drive humanity towards a state of peace, especially if its starting point is a Hobbesian state of nature? Would such progress be borne of ideas and rational autonomy or instead does a drive toward a state of peace really exist as a necessary end of the natural world?

This line of questioning coincides with the dilemma that Kant confronts in his *Critique of Judgment* concerning the purposiveness of beauty. There Kant puts forward that beauty's purposiveness is not to be found in

2 It is important to note that Kant views the idea of such a worldwide nation as possible if approached through measured (non revolutionary) action (Kant, [1795] 1910, p. 357).

the empirical world, as if nature were designed so as to arouse human sentiments. Rather, beauty's purposiveness resides in an idea of the imagination and the free play of unconditioned thinking. Thus, if international right is like beauty in its relation of private interest to public quarrel, it too should be indeterminate in its purposiveness.

However, *Towards Perpetual Peace* leads to an opposite conclusion. (Kant [1790] 1910, p. 360) identifies peace as something guaranteed by nature's will, "whose mechanical course illuminates purposiveness [*Zweckmäßigkeit*]," which is directed toward global harmony. Kant, (*Ibid.*, pp. 362-3), in a long footnote, distances this perspective from a belief in Providence as predetermination, which would make unwarranted assumptions about God's will. In a footnote Kant (*Ibid.*, p. 363) makes it clear that appeals to the will of nature are effective only in grounding human striving toward the good, and not as part of any explanatory schema. In any case, this footnote shows that Kant (*Ibid.*, p. 363) believes that a teleology of peace is a genuine component of nature, which highlights a major difference between the ideals of beauty and of international right.

For Kant (*Ibid.*, pp. 365-6) the progress of humanity from a general state of war to one of peace is guaranteed by nature because proximity to others and a natural inclination to self-preservation bid humanity to establish legal relations and engage in free trade, independent of moral reasoning. Rather than the dictates of pure morality leading to peace, Kant (*Ibid.*, pp. 366-7) believes that it is nature which nullifies opposing drives and necessarily leads to a concept of international right prevailing over time.

However, nature does keep humanity apart in ways that preclude one nation from adjudicating for all, like a one-world government. Kant believes that the main *differentiae* are language and religion. However, in a footnote he denies (quite troublingly) that the differentiation of religions is anything other than historical accident, since they all are religions to the degree that they have the form of his transcendental theology (*Ibid.*, p. 367). Moreover, he implies that linguistic barriers can be overcome by the spread of culture and mutual understanding (*Ibid.*, p. 367). However, borders between peoples are ultimately necessary for Kant due to his postulate that states of limited size are needed so that laws can be enforced (*Ibid.*, p. 367).

Hence, in *Towards Perpetual Peace* Kant takes it as an operating premise that such natural separation is the condition of having meaningful laws. As a means to overcoming what could be a world made of fractured national interests, Kant (*Ibid.*, p. 367) argues on behalf of a federative union, not unlike the United Nations in form, and with it a legal framework for free trade mildly similar to the World Trade Organization, as a means to guard against conflict. The notion of a federative union is connected to a rational idea of peace. The legal structure for trade meanwhile follows from nature's guarantee that the ideal will come to pass through its power to resolve competing interests (*Ibid.*, p. 368). In fact, Kant (*Ibid.*, p. 368) unabashedly puts forward that the spirit for free trade "sooner or later dominates every people" and that its progress and its abatement of bellicose impulses owes nothing to reason, but rather to the will of nature. Therefore, even though international right is an ideal of reason, Kant's *Towards Perpetual Peace* maintains that peace is actually a necessary effect of the order of the natural world.

International relations are thus like judgments of beauty insofar as both transmute private concerns (national interest and sense data respectively) into objective ones in terms of an ideal (peace in the first case and beauty in the second), as the means for mediating genuine quarrels. However, *Towards Perpetual Peace* cheerfully holds that international disagreement will be resolved eternally because of nature's intention, which seems to make international right something involving disputation and its determinate form, thereby separating it from aesthetic concerns.

When considered in terms of the language of purpose, the contrast between the eponymous ideal of *Towards Perpetual Peace* and the ideal of beauty becomes even starker. For Kant, the ideal of beauty cannot belong to the empirical chain of cause and effect as an object, but rather must belong to the autonomy of reason. Hence a gulf exists between the ideals of beauty and international right in their formal moments, the result of which leads Kant to an exceedingly optimistic theory of international relations.

Peace in The Metaphysics of Morals

Whether to soften the incautious optimism of his earlier work on the subject or to more closely match it to his ideal of beauty, *The Metaphysics of Morals*' argument for peace sees Kant reverse course and adopt a somber outlook that is more consistent with his thinking in general. Here, instead of coloring his language of peace with lofty words like "perpetual", Kant is less bold, employing words like "unachievable" and "approximation". He thus throws cold water on the hypothesis of *Towards Perpetual Peace* that a federation of all nations will come to pass. Specifically, Kant holds (without, it is worth noting, clear justification) that an association of states necessarily implodes if it extends too far (Kant [1797] 1910, p. 350), as though international associations require bounds for consensus to occur just as nations need borders to focus laws so that they might have meaningful sanction. Also, he argues that plural super-state organizations would merely lead to the same discord and eventual war (Kant *Ibid.*, p. 350). Kant therefore claims that international right requires a congress of states, thereby departing from his optimistic advocacy of an international federation. Even though he describes it as "permanent" (*Ibid.*, p. 350), the congress of states described in his later work is arbitrary and as capable of being dissolved at any time (*Ibid.*, p. 351). Thus, he concludes that, while the idea of perpetual peace may be practically impossible, its principles (the idea approximated by reason, as an ideal) let humanity at least strive to approximate it (*Ibid.*, p. 350).

Kant more strongly repudiates his earlier view of the idea of peace as perpetual in his later *Metaphysics of Morals*, where he writes:

> [If complete establishment of perpetual peace and ending war] also always should remain a pious wish, we certainly do not thus lie to ourselves with adoption of the maxim to work unceasingly towards it; for this is duty (*Ibid.*, pp. 354-5).

Kant (*Ibid.*, p. 355) goes on to say that even if this impulse were deceptive, it is far better to take it up than "to see its basic principles [as] thrown in with the other animal species to the same mechanism of nature." This language strongly rejects, using similar terms, the faith in nature that Kant displays in *Toward Perpetual Peace,* in which he does in fact regard peace, not only as being thrown into nature's arrangements, but in fact as its necessary end. Thus it is clear that Kant's thinking on peace changes as he moves to champion peace as an effect of reason's autonomy in imagining ideas and to disavow its purpose as real in the sensible, natural world.

Kant's rejection of the inevitability of perpetual peace further aligns with the notion that peace's purposiveness is ideal in character, where he continues:

> [This very idea alone of an *a priori* ideal of a legal association of humans under public laws] "if...attempted and accomplished through measured reform according to a steady constitution, can lead into continual approximation to the highest political good, to perpetual peace" (*Ibid.*, p. 355).

Here peace is not a determined end of nature, but rather its ideal of international right is purposive only in accord with the autonomy of reason. The political good is something that can be reached only through approximation (much like the objective ideal of taste, through which communication about beauty is possible, only adequately represents beauty). It is not something that will occur, absolutely. Thus, the ideal espoused in *The Metaphysics of Morals* has no connection to any end of nature, in clear repudiation of that from *Towards Perpetual Peace.*

Harry van der Linden's reading of duty and international right shows that by aiming at mirroring, rather than determinately replicating, the ideal of peace, Kant is able to coherently offer a program for peace that accounts for imperfect legislators (van der Linden, 1995, p. 75).[3] Van der Linden (*Ibid.*) goes on to say that the mirroring approach from *The Metaphysics of Morals* is beneficial, since it allows for political intervention and is not burdened with the problem of giving full respect to the autonomy of imperfect agents. Thus, the aesthetic turn helps Kant's theory of peace better deal with political scenarios where it is difficult to absolutely respect national autonomy, like in response to genocide or global warming.

Furthermore, the ideal of international right from *The Metaphysics of Morals*, is much more like that of beauty than that from *Towards Perpetual Peace*, since the later Kant holds that peace's purposive aspect is thought *a priori* and that it is not encountered as a real object of the empirical world. This later work thus closes the gap between Kant's view of international frameworks for right and intersubjective agreement about beauty.

Kant, the World-Observer

Careful attention to the ideal of international right as Kant develops it in his later works shows a deep connection to his ideal of beauty. The case for viewing the two in the same light is twofold. Firstly, the ideals of beauty and international right are alike in that they function as an objective ground for individual parties to communicate about their private interests. Secondly, the transition between the geopolitical ideal as developed in *Towards Perpetual Peace* and *The Metaphysics of Morals* respectively indicates an attempt, whether conscious or unconscious, to make that ideal correspond to the ideal of beauty in terms of approximation and imperfect purposiveness. This second point of argument vindicates the first, since it shows that the similarity in their community mediating function is not superficial, but rather something that Kant appreciates more and more with the passage of time.

The transition which leads Kant to a geopolitical ideal that harmonizes with his ideal of the beautiful begets many interesting questions. Is Kant's more cautious language in *The Metaphysics of Morals* due to perceived theoretical shortcomings? Was he merely trying to inject some fallibilism into his theory? Was Kant intentionally trying to make his international

3 Van der Linden (1995, p. 75) flirts with the idea there are two distinct approaches to peace, though he ultimately collapses the distinction assessed here. This leads him to declare dissatisfaction with Kant's approach to intervention (Ibid., p. 77). I believe that evaluating Kant in terms of earlier and later approaches to peace would help assuage some of van der Linden's concern.

relations look more like his aesthetics? Was his regret, if any, specifically keyed to his sunny tone in *Perpetual Peace* or rather its inconsistency with regard to teleology? Or was his shift in tone the result of political changes in the real world, like the trials and tribulations of the French revolution, which shook all of late eighteenth century Europe, including Kant?

In Hannah Arendt's view, even after undergoing a great deal of introspection during French revolution, Kant still consistently applies precepts from his theory of judgment, chiefly the primacy of the judging observer over the observed in settling questions of right. Regarding its Hume-like effect on his political philosophy, Arendt writes that the revolution "awaked [Kant], so to speak, from his political slumber" (1982, p. 17). Though Kant's thoughts on the revolution are complex, Arendt discerns two clear and enduring opinions, viz. a high regard for the "grandeur" of the revolution as well as a condemnation of the participants (*Ibid.*, p. 45). This apparent contradiction stems from his endorsement of struggles against demonstrably wrong despotic regimes, on the one hand, and a similar rejection of rebellion, on the other (I., p. 49). For Kant ([1795] 1910, p. 382), it can likewise be demonstrated, within the framework of the categorical imperative, that the maxims upon which rebels act cannot be publicly avowed without defeating their formal purpose of serving as maxims for good will. That, for Kant, publicity and political right share a basic link indicates how judgment and aesthetic language function in terms of ideals of peace – the social/political life is a spectacle and is open to *observation.*

For Kant, right, by its very nature, its communicable maxim-form, is public in scope. And so there is a transcendental formulation of public right, curiously phrased in the negative – that actions relating to the rights of others are wrong, if they cannot bear publicity (*Ibid.*, p. 381). This public right, which in Kant's view forbids insurrection and revolution on the basis of the unspeakable treacheries involved (*Ibid.*, p. 382), nevertheless grounds international right with publicity as the basis for common will (*Ibid.*, p. 383). This of course creates any number of problems concerning despotism, international right, and intervention familiar to Kantian scholars and, sadly, to followers of world affairs.[4]

Arendt sees Kant operating on the basis of corollary premises, namely that malicious intent must exist in private and that the good will is always

4 In a footnote Kant ([1788] 1910, p. 373) explicitly calls public right (das öffentliche Recht) an ideal (Ideal). The related term "right of peoples" (das Völkerrecht, translated often as "international right") refers later to such a free association, though without the terminology of an ideal per se (Ibid., p. 383). Despite the lack of obvious terminological clues, I believe that public/international right is related to perpetual peace as an idea to an ideal.

at least potentially public. She states that for Kant "publicness is already the criterion of rightness in his moral philosophy" (1982, p. 18) with morality being "the coincidence of the private and the public" (*Ibid.*, p. 49). Moreover, if right is to be public, then its progress, like that of peace, ought to be observable in the world at large. For Arendt, Kantian judgment relies on two key ideas, the commonality of judgments to humanity (the possibility of genuine quarrel), and the idea of purposiveness in objects in the world, both in artistic approximation and natural phenomena (*Ibid.*, p. 76). When the object becomes the human spectacle itself, the ideal striven for and purpose of public/international right is peace. This is to say that in Kant's thinking there is an implicit link among the nature of right, its publicity, and the possibility of observing (and judging) human progress toward peace.

Arendt (*Ibid.*, p. 61) keenly observes that for Kant judgment must be explained in terms of the observer and not the object. This means that the world-observer, and not the observed human spectacle, is the prime factor in progress. To understand Arendt's well-honed appropriation of Kant's political/aesthetic sensibility, consider Dana Richard Villa's disjunctive formulation (1996, p. 102):

> What Nietzsche specifically holds *against* Kant – namely, that he, "like all philosophers, instead of envisaging the aesthetic problem from the point of view of the artist (the creator) considered art and the beautiful purely from the point of view of the spectator" (GM III, 6 [1887] 1998, III, §6]) – is the primary reason that Arendt holds that his aesthetic theory has political relevance.

Just as Kant subordinates spirited genius to intellectual taste, Arendt (1982, pp. 61-62) believes that he similarly diminishes the spectacle of human progress and promotes the observer's perspective. Hence, the observation of human progress in deeds and acts of particular self-legislators is where the ideal of peace functions. This preserves the aesthetic schema whereby the ideal of beauty and its guidance of the taste of observing subjects is primary and the relation to the moment of genius is secondary, if not incidental. This notion that the observing perspective is paramount may be the reason for believing in the progress of the human species and the possibility of peace, even if its reality cannot be proven. Arendt puts her own gloss on this "world-as-stage" idea where she writes that "the alternatives for Kant are either regress, which would produce despair, or eternal sameness, which would bore us to death" (*Ibid.*, p. 51). It is as though a condition of the possibility of observing human affairs is the belief in progress, for to do otherwise would be contrary to the observer's relationship to the object spectacle. If the world is a stage, and humanity is the spectacle, then it worth asking whether human affairs, like artworks, are all subject to the sort of non-demonstrable, quarrelsome mode of judgment that rests solely in the eye of the beholder.

Questions of Kantian Legacy

This inquiry thus boils down to the question as to what degree should Kant's political thinking be read as aesthetic. The issue filters down to the present day. In fact, Larry Krasnoff (1995, pp. 62-4) claims that the schism in Kantian constructivism between Rawls and Habermas on the topic of justice can be understood respectively in terms familiar to readers of the *Critique of Judgment* – namely, as a division between argumentation (*disputieren*) from the premises of a Rawlsian original position and the mode of discussion (*streiten*) underlying the communicative rationality of Habermas.

Rawls distinguishes between what he terms "the law of peoples," which exists on the basis of liberal societies affirming similar modes of government, and international law, which is incomplete and without the sanction of law in the domestic sphere (1993, p. 43). This leads him to claim that the former serves as content to the form of the latter. Hence, even though he states a willingness to deal with the law of peoples in ways that do not presume a global original position, Rawls still takes the original position in its domestic guise as that which gives content to the murky form of international law (*Ibid.*, pp. 42-43). In this regard, there is license to claim that Rawls' notion of international law still relies on argumentation to secure goods and rights for people whose circumstances are cloaked by a veil of ignorance. If the only content to Rawlsian international right comes from the original position, then it follows that it is a system of situation-independent principles, which, as Alessandro Ferrara notes (*Ibid.*, p. 395), sets formal or external limits to the will of peoples.

By contrast, Habermas' idea of communicative rationality fits much more closely with the notion of discussion advanced by Kant in his work on aesthetics. Most crucial here is Habermas' denial that the veil of ignorance can bring about impartial judgement on the part of legislators, as intersubjective arbiters of something akin to Kant's categorical imperative (1995, p. 116). In Habermas' view the common perspective presumed by Rawls' original position comes at the price of diminishing particularity to the point of uniformity. Indeed for Habermas, Rawls "imposes" this common perspective. Habermas, meanwhile sees his own discourse ethics as a mode of discussion which enlarges individual perspectives to arrive at universality (*Ibid.*, p. 117). This mode of discussion, which takes subjective claims seriously as a foundation for working towards objective agreement, has strong resonances with Kant's understanding of how judgements of beauty operate in aesthetic discourse. Therefore, if weight is given to Kant's later treatment of peace and its increasing concord with his notion of aesthetic quarrel, it would lend credence to Habermas' particular appropriation of Kantian thought and his heavy emphasis on intersubjective agreement in the mode of *streiten*.

However, many people sympathetic to Habermas' project and its merger of Kantian aesthetic and political philosophies point out that it too is lacking. For example, Villa (1996, pp. 70-1) takes issue with Habermas' notion of discourse ethics, particularly as the commonality of discourse flattens all action and turns it into "speech" and allows for a hegemonic preference that the "right" kind of discourse prevail. He lauds Arendt over Habermas for giving serious attention to the performative aspect of political action, which goes over and above discourse in search of agreement. Villa writes, "Arendt hopes to preserve the political dimensions of performance *and* persuasion, deliberation *and* initiation, agonism *and* agreement" (*Ibid.*, p. 71). This line of thought is at work where Arendt holds the opinion that understanding Kant's thought on peace requires taking seriously the role judgment plays in synthesizing the observations of the world citizen and the actions of the individual subject (1982, p. 54).

When Habermas collapses the distinction between political agency and political discourse, he turns his attention away from the detached world-observer perspective so integral to Kant's account of progress and Arendt's account of hope and imagination. In fact, by drawing personal agency and discourse so close together Habermas imagination no longer works as it does in Kant's schema, as means of overcoming the gap between private judgement and public reason, for the gap simply does not exist. Imagination ceases to draw together the concerns of the individual human and the concerns of sociable human communities in the providential quest of progress for the entire species. Hence, though there may be reason to claim, per Krasnoff, that Kant's emphasis on quarrel over dispute in matters international right supports Habermasian rather than Rawlsian interpretations of Kant, this does not give any warrant to assert that Habermas corners the market on insights into the aesthetic underpinnings of Kantian political philosophy. Setting aside what is likely to be a futile attempt to legitimate intellectual legacy, it is clear that there is a genuine similarity between Kant's aesthetics and his geopolitics and that this connection only grows stronger as he revises his thinking on peace. Moreover, it is certain that contemporary thinkers must contend with this convergence between aesthetic and political concerns in working through thoroughly Kantian notions of autonomy and intersubjectivity in prosecuting the question of international right.

As the work of other post-Kantians like Ferrara shows, Habermas' appropriation of Kantian political theory and aesthetic philosophy may not only commit the petty crime of diverging from Kant's own approach to these topics, but it may lead to its unsettling consequences, including a non-pluralistic (Ferrara 2003, p. 399) and perhaps hegemonic discourse on right (Villa 1996, p. 71) arising from an insensitivity to what is actionable in context for the involved parties (Ferrara 2003, pp. 397-8). The work of Ferrara on judgment, which wrestles with some of the limits of Habermas' thinking, is instructive here. While adopting a view that he identifies as akin to Habermas as regards the publicity of right, Ferrara ameliorates it by not reacting with the conventional skepticism about cross-cultural meaning ever since Wittgenstein's insights into the diversity amongst languages and their "games". Instead of promoting the idea of a context-free normative discourse of right, which might seem natural post-Wittgenstein, he sees the need for public reason to be transcontextual (1998, p. 39) in a manner which goes above dealing with a plurality of free-floating acontextual Rawlsian or a plurality of diverse subjects in a singular Habermasian discourse. Ferrara prefers to take on the diversity of cultures, histories, and interests that abound in the world in terms of a transcontextuality which finds truth and basis for right in the coherence of judgements (1998, p. x). This coherence would bind together the widest possible range of subjects in the world; each freely relating to ideals, like that of international right, in a myriad of different ways; each authentic with regard to contexts like culture and not subservient to the truth values of any single overarching discourse or set of rational principles.

For Ferrara, it makes sense to "ground justice no longer on principles of right but on judgment or, more specifically, on 'oriented reflective judgment'" (2003, p. 393). This means abandoning the notion that international right contains principles independent of human events in favor "the situated cogency" (*Ibid.*, p. 393) of a "normative idea of humanity," in which the "eudaemonistic self-reflection of the actor [would be] conducted in postmetaphysical terms" (*Ibid.*, p. 403). Such a normative idea of humanity, open to ongoing revision, would not flatten human difference and reduce the variety of human plights down to one archetype with one set of rights (*Ibid.*, p. 405), nor even to the contemporary scope of agency and action (*Ibid.*, p. 407). Ferrara (*Ibid.*, p. 406) believes that this is of benefit, since "when considering international or global justice, the judgment perspective offers the advantage of not forcing us to choose, like both Rawls's and Habermas's perspectives do, one particular unit of analysis ("individuals" or "peoples") as the ideal addressee of justice". Even discourses on international right could not be contained, as Habermas would have it, within the formal principles of any one paradigm of discursive rationality, in Ferrara's estimation. Rather international right and its ideals would be the topic of an array of, presumably coherent, context-sensitive discourses. Justice (and presumably the ideal of peace of international right) would then bear a sort of exemplary validity for humanity, with parties free to approximate the exemplar ideal, not in terms of some universally demonstrable form, but in terms of imagination (*Ibid.*, p. 401).

This coherence notion of truth, clearly and by its own admission, rejects preoccupation with metaphysics and embraces the doubt and relativism about language so characteristic of philosophy in the wake of Wittgenstein (Ferrara, 1998, p. 39). And so by dispensing with the basic notion that logical principles exist beyond the coherence of judgments, Ferrara's project is at odds with many of the most basic tenets of Kantianism, adopting only selectively Kant's insights into judgement, agreement, and intersubjectivity. Beyond his subversion of Kantian orthodoxy, further, much deeper problems exist. Ferrara's plural discourse paradigm still relies on a single "standpoint of humanity," (2003, p. 409) and as Axel Honneth points out (2004, pp. 13-4), it fails to deal with the dangerous possibility that these transcontextual discourses would not lapse into hegemony (which would be much like the discourse of communicative rationality championed by Habermas). Even though Ferrara voices his opposition to this (2003, p. 409), he does not actually guard against exemplar ideals falling under majority control in such a way that "[...] minority cultures possess no more chance to bring their own practices and convictions to public representation". (Honneth 2004, p. 14). This is to say nothing of the broader problems with such a view, well-identified by Charles Larmore (2004, p. 8) occurring where Ferrara (1) rejects any universal precepts, (2) rejects any notion of autonomy which would operate according to such precepts, and (3) identifies wholly intersubjective authenticity as an all-encompassing ideals in an unnatural manner which does not "express when we are just being ourselves". Along much the same lines, Axel Honneth (2004, p. 15) says that rather than concentrating solely on intersubjective authenticity he would "like rather to start from a profound tension between demands of autonomy and claims for authenticity – a tension that cannot be mediated in the framework of our cultural aims."

Conclusion

While the topic of *streiten* vs. *disputieren* in Kant's thinking on political right might support the Habermasian platform communicative rationality over Rawls and his notion of justice proceeding from the original position along a demonstrable course, other concerns exist. Perhaps more than casting dispute and quarrel as an either/or proposition, the best way is to accept both. With that the issue becomes figuring out what to do with the firm dictates accompanying principled autonomous personhood *and* the diversity of authentic judging world-observers who comprise the human community. Just as quarrel and dispute deepen understanding, so do autonomy and authenticity broaden experience, even if the implications of these facets of humanity are vexingly contradictory. The contradictions of autonomous self and the intersubjective judging self are nonetheless productive, impelling imagination in its approximation of ideals which lack any determinate object, like the of peace.

I believe that Honneth and Larmore are right in their similar appraisal of Ferrara's work and in each pointing to genuine, and perhaps ineradicable, tensions between autonomy and intersubjective authenticity. With the principles of autonomy being given to determinable dispute and the judgments of authenticity being quarrels of taste, incommensurability is only natural, providing a further level of quarrel and deepening the affinities between aesthetic and political modes of judgment. I also believe that with these views they each recognize something very clearly seen by Arendt as Kant's major insight. Simply put, there is a distance between the judging world-observer and the autonomous self-legislator which imagination works continuously (and unsuccessfully) to bridge. Kant's statements on international right in the *Metaphysics of Morals* point to such a tension. Beyond fidelity to Kantianism though, there is something, I believe, to the notion that imagination bridges gaps between reason and representation, subject and object, self and other, in a way that brings a wholeness to experience. When it comes to international right, I applaud Arendt for not shying away from the paradox between the a-temporal dignity of autonomous beings and temporal progress of human communities and the attendant implication that such progress might go on for ages always only approximating its goal (Arendt 1982, p. 77). Though he perhaps errs in focusing too much on intersubjective judgment at the expense of other facets of cognition like autonomous rationality, maybe Ferrara (1998, p. 43) is right in claiming after Gadamer that Kant puts too much stress on the world-observing judge and not enough on the capacity for genius which might give purpose to the human spectacle. This and similar points are debatable, and may also contribute to post-Kantian discussions of international right. In any case, to bring about human progress we would do well to follow the various suggestions of Arendt, Honneth, and Larmore to investigate the tension between autonomy and authenticity, especially as it plays out in imagination and human endeavors which strain toward ideals such as peace.

References

Arendt, H. (1982). *Lectures on Kant's Political Philosophy*. Chicago. University of Chicago Press.

Ferrara, A. (1998). *Reflective Authenticity: Rethinking the Project of Modernity*. New York. Routledge.

Ferrara, A. (2003). "Two Notions of Humanity and the Judgment Argument for Human Rights". *Political Theory* Vol. 31. No. 3. Pp. 392-420.

Habermas, J. (1993). "Reconciliation Through the Public Use of Reason: Remarks on John Rawls's Political Liberalism". Trans. Ciaran Cronin. *The Journal of Philosophy*. Vol. 92. No. 3. Pp. 109-131.

Honneth, A. (2004). Considerations on Alessandro Ferrara's Reflective Authenticity. *Philosophy & Social Criticism*. Vol. 30. No. 1. Pp. 11-15.

Kant, I. ([1775] 1910). *Von der verschiedenen Racen der Menschen* [*On the Varying Races of Human Beings*]. *Gesammelte Schriften* [*Collected Writings*]. Vol. 2. Berlin. Reimer. Pp. 427-444.

Kant, I. ([1785] 1910). *Grundlegung zur Metaphysik der Sitten* [*Groundwork of the Metaphysics of Morals*]. *Gesammelte Schriften* [*Collected Writings*]. Vol. 4. Berlin. Reimer. Pp. 385-463.

Kant, I. ([1788] 1910). *Kritik der praktischen Vernunft* [*Critique of Practical Reason*]. *Gesammelte Schriften* [*Collected Writings*]. Vol. 5. Berlin. Reimer. Pp. 1-164.

Kant, I. ([1787] 1910). *Kritik der reinen Vernunft: zweite Auflage* [*Critique of Pure Reason: Second Edition*]. *Gesammelte Schriften* [*Collected Writings*]. Vol. 3. Berlin. Reimer. Pp. 2-552.

Kant, I. ([1790] 1910). *Kritik der Urtheilskraft* [*Critique of Judgment*]. *Gesammelte Schriften* [*Collected Writings*]. Vol. 5. Berlin. Reimer. Pp. 165-484.

Kant, I. ([1793] 1910). *Religion innerhalb der Grenzen der bloßen Vernunft* [*Religion Within the Limits of Mere Reason*]. *Gesammelte Schriften* [*Collected Writings*]. Vol. 6. Berlin. Reimer. Pp. 1-203.

Kant, I. ([1795] 1910). *Zum Ewigen Frieden* [*Towards Perpetual Peace*]. *Gesammelte Schriften* [*Collected Writings*]. Vol. 8. Berlin. Reimer. Pp. 341-386.

Kant, I. ([1797] 1910). *Metaphysik der Sitten* [*Metaphysics of Morals*]. *Gesammelte Schriften* [*Collected Writings*]. Vol. 6. Berlin. Reimer. Pp. 203-493.

Krasnoff, L. (1995). "Formal Liberalism and the Justice of Publicity". *Proceedings of the Eighth International Kant Congress*. Milwaukee. Marquette University Press. Vol. 2. Pp. 61-70.

Larmore, C. (2004). Alessandro Ferrara's Theory of Authenticity. *Philosophy & Social Criticism*. Vol 30. No. 1. Pp. 5-9.

Linden, H. Van der (1995). "Kant. The Duty to Promote International Peace". *Proceedings of the Eighth International Kant Congress*. Milwaukee. Marquette University Press. Vol. 2. Pp. 71-79.

Nietzsche, F. ([1887]1998). *On the Genealogy of Morality*. Trans. Maudemarie Clark and Alan J. Swensen (eds.). Indianapolis. Hackett.

Rawls, J. (1993). "The Law of Peoples". *Critical Inquiry*. Vol. 20. No. 1. Pp. 36-68.

Villa, D. (1996). *Arendt and Heidegger: The Fate of the Political*. Princeton, NJ. Princeton University Press.

Rawls' *via media*: Between Realism and Utopianism

Paulo Tunhas[1]

I begin with a very general remark on the topic of relations, from a metaphysical point of view. Its significance to what I intend to say will be, I hope, clear in a moment. According to the Australian philosopher David Malet Armstrong, "Two or more particulars are *externally* related if and only if there are no properties of the particulars which logically necessitate that the relation, or any relation which is part of the relation, holds"; and "Two or more particulars are *internally* related if and only if there exist properties of the particulars which logically necessitate that the relation holds"; Armstrong also speaks of "mixed relations", "partially internal and partially external" (Armstrong, 1980, II, p. 85; see also Tunhas, 2009).

When reading textbooks on international relations, such as *Contending Theories of International Relations*, by Dougherty and Pfaltzgraff (Dougherty and Pfaltzgraff Jr., 2001), it is easy to see that the problem of contingency and the modalities of the integration of contingency in a stable system lie at the heart of international relations theory.

Irrespective of the schools of thought – realist, neorealist, utopian, neoliberal (see Keohane, 1986; Baldwin, 1993; Spegele, 1996) –, the main concern seems to be double: to determine the most relevant factors of instability; and to find the best way of eradicating them, by their integration in a comprehensive order. In other words, to prevent the transformation of contingency into risk and of risk into disorder, by adopting the most efficient stabilizing mechanism.

Stability also means equilibrium. And it is not difficult to find here, in a different context, certain ideas that belong to Talcott Parsons's structural functionalism (Parsons, 1991) and to Niklas Luhmann's systemic approach to societies (Luhmann, 1995).

Realism, namely in Morgenthau's version (Morgenthau, [1948] 1973), postulating, as Hobbes had done, anarchy at the foundation of international relations, sees in the balance of power the process of obtaining a precarious but reasonably effective stability. The organizing principle

1 This investigation was supported by a scholarship granted by the Fundação para a Ciência e a Tecnologia.

seems to be here a principle of *accommodation* of contingency. This principle draws its legitimacy from the assumption of the externality reigning in the relations between the individuals, the unities, that states are, and from the power relations established among them. Various particulars are *externally* related; there are no properties of the particulars which logically necessitate that an internal relation holds between those particulars. This doctrine lies at the core of the scepticism Charles R. Beitz determined as essential to classical realism of Morgenthau's or Keenan's type (Beitz, [1979] 1999, pp. 185 ff).

Utopianism – "the legalistic-moralistic approach", to use George Keenan's phrase (Kennan, [1951] 1984, p. 95) –, in its turn, shares the same assumption of a reigning externality between the states, but the moral here is different: such externality would be something *contra natura*. The organizing device suggested by utopianism obeys a principle of *surmounting* contingency. This principle supposes that relations amongst the individuals, the states, should be conceived as internal relations, as relations between parts of a whole which is posited, at least ideally, from the beginning. Various particulars are *internally* related: there are properties of the particulars which logically necessitate that the relation holds. And this holding must absolutely come to light. It is a definite characteristic of utopias to conclude, from the imagined perfection, to the necessity of its realization. As in the ontological argument.

Neorealism and neoclassical realism, but also neo-liberalism, seem to point, although in different ways, to an intermediary position, defined by Armstrong's "mixed relations", "partially internal and partially external". Such position may be characterized by a conjunction of the accommodation and surmounting principles, its basis being a relational model differing both from the perfect externality defended by the realists – all relations are contingent – and the extreme internality posited by the utopians – all relations are logically necessitated by the nature of the particulars. A lot of the pessimism and scepticism specific to classical realism is rejected, and the role of international institutions in the cooperation between the states is not explained away. The kind of external/internal relations, which belongs properly to this model, seems to be the one that best succeeds in integrating contingency.

Let us take Kenneth E. Waltz's *Theory of International Politics* (Waltz, 1979) as an example of this approach. Anarchy, the major sign of relational externality, remains, according to the systemic approach, something not quite surmounted, but the systemic, or structural, level – as distinct from that of the interaction amongst simple unities – partially absorbs, so to say, this very same externality or, to put it another way, makes sense out of it.

The 'balance of power' – which exists whenever two, and only two, requisites prevail: anarchical order and the existence of unities who strive to survive – is the frame of such sense. The active unities, the States, the "unitary actors", as Waltz calls them, cease to be the only agents and also – Hegel would certainly approve of this development – are no longer thought as possessors of a self-conscious and transparent intentionality: their actions are loose, disordered. Contingency is conceived through this blending of externality – states exist as basic particulars, with no properties logically necessitating that the relation holds – and internality – there are properties of the states which, at the systemic level, logically necessitate that the relation holds –, which distinguishes international relations from foreign policy.

At another level, John Rawls's "law of peoples" seems equally to point to a middle way between externality and internality. (Thomas Nagel's position (see Nagel, 1991, Chapter XV) is, in many aspects, similar to Rawls's.) Before discussing *The Law of Peoples* (Rawls, 2002) and the previous 1993 article with the same title (Rawls, 2001, Chapter XXIV), some remarks seem, notwithstanding, to be appropriate.

As it is well known, the Third Part of *A Theory of Justice* (Rawls, (1971] 1989) deals with the question of the conditions under which justice as fairness can be realized. Rawls shows that justice as fairness – being itself a stable conception of justice, generating a great sense of justice, obtained through reflexive equilibrium (*Ibid.*, pp. 48 ff) – is capable of guaranteeing a greater social stability than its rival conceptions. (It is important that social stability should be distinguished from the simple regulation of conflicting situations, which would be merely a *modus vivendi* contingent upon circumstances (Rawls, 2005, p. 157). A decisive function of the veil of ignorance in the original position is nullifying the effects of the knowledge of individual contingencies (Rawls, [1971] 1989, p. 136)).

The very possibility of realization of justice as fairness (a problem which is linked to the frailty of political institutions and of the remedies to this frailty) gains a greater importance in Rawls' later work, from his 1985 article "Justice as Fairness: Political, not Metaphysical" (Rawls, 2001, Chapter XVIII) onwards, leading to the views of *Political Liberalism* (Rawls, 2005). In the search for an overlapping consensus – which is a precondition for stability – Rawls discards any comprehensive conception of justice. Coherently, Rawls' Kantianism becomes more mitigated – or, if you prefer, it becomes analogical – and the original universalism is partially substituted by the consideration of local particularities: it is for our societies, for the liberal democratic societies, that justice as fairness serves as a model. It seems fair to say that the negative action of contingency is more easily tamed if its existence is accepted from the very beginning.

It is in the context of this evolution – and supported by some ideas already expressed in paragraph 58 of *A Theory of Justice* (Rawls, [1971] 1989, pp. 377 ff) – that Rawls turns to the *ius gentium*, the law of peoples, as something distinct from international law. The law of peoples – which, by its very nature, supposes some kind of internality of relations – "provides the basis for judging the conduct of any existing regime, liberal as well as non-liberal" (Rawls, 2001, p. 562).

This immediately begs the question as to whether the device of the original position and the fiction of the contract also apply in this case. The answer – I will omit the details – is: yes. With an important difference: the representatives, hypothetically assembled, don't represent individuals anymore, but peoples. There is an objection – which has been put forward by Peter Singer (2002), Thomas Pogge (1990) and Charles Beitz ([1979] 1999), among others – according to which the law of peoples should begin with representatives of individuals, and not with representatives of peoples with their traditional attributes of sovereignty (an objection which clearly is formulated against the externality principle, from the standpoint of radical internalism). Rawls' answer to this objection proceeds in a number of steps: First, the represented peoples must obey certain conditions, some of them restrictive of their sovereignty as habitually understood (Rawls, 2002, pp. 26-27; 2001, pp. 534-535) (It is maybe useful to recall that one of the greatest proponents of a restrictive conception of sovereignty was Leibniz, who, both in the *Caesarinus Fürstenerius* (1677) and in the Preface to the *Codex Iuris Gentium* (1693), defended – against Bodin and Hobbes – that sovereignty implied only a high degree of independence and internal supremacy, not absolute independence and absolute internal supremacy) (Riley, 1972, pp. 111 ff and 165 ff). Secondly, it would be to take utopianism too far to suppose the non-existence of peoples as they exist nowadays (Rawls, 2001, p. 536) – the utopia must be realistic (Rawls, 2002, p. 11 ff). In third place, following Kant, Rawls points to the fact that the law of peoples should not, in any case, lead us toward a Universal State (*Ibid.*, p. 36; Rawls, 2001, p. 539). Finally, the existence of frontiers favours the individual responsibilities concerning what appears to the state's citizens somehow as their own property (in ecological matters, for example) (*Ibid.*, pp. 8, 38-39; Rawls, 2001, p. 541). (A similar argument can be found in Roger Scruton (2002, pp. 24-25).) Rawls' answer combines elements of internality (the first step) and externality (the three other steps, namely the defence of the existence of frontiers).

Rawls begins, accordingly, with a "family of societies". This "family of societies" doesn't include, however, only the liberal societies, but also the kind of societies Rawls calls "hierarchical societies" (I will return to them later). From this fact it follows that "liberal and hierarchical societies can agree on the same law of peoples, and thus this law does not depend on aspects peculiar to the Western tradition" (Rawls, 2001, p. 534), it is not "ethnocentric" (Rawls, 2002, pp. 121-122). It doesn't depend, for example, on the exclusivity of a "political conception of the person rooted in the public culture of a liberal society" (Rawls, 2001, p. 549). As with justice as fairness in the interior of each society, the law of peoples supposes no comprehensive doctrine, be it of a religious, philosophical or moral kind. An agreement concerning the law of peoples, which guarantees the respect of human rights is not an agreement that can only be accepted by liberal societies.

General conditions for the extension of liberal ideas to the law of peoples are less demanding than those, discussed in *A Theory of Justice*, which are required for particular societies. They include some basic rights, freedoms and opportunities; a high priority concerning basic freedoms; and some measures that can ensure citizens the necessary means to the actual practice of those freedoms.

The extension of justice as fairness to the law of peoples includes two stages – "ideal theory" (Rawls, 2002, Parts I and II) and "non-ideal theory" (*Ibid.*, Part III) –, each of them being composed of two steps.

Let us begin with "ideal, or strict compliance, theory". In accordance with it, all the participants (liberal, as well as hierarchical societies) respect the basic requirements for the application of the law of peoples. The two steps consist in the elucidation of those questions related to the general organisation, first, of liberal societies, and, secondly, of hierarchical societies, "societies which are well-ordered and just, often religious in nature and not characterized by the separation of church and state" (Rawls, 2001, p. 537). In the original position, under the veil of ignorance, "the representatives of well-ordered hierarchical societies would adopt the same law of peoples that the representatives of liberal societies do" (*Ibid.*, p. 544; cp. Rawls, 2002, p. 63).

The society of democratic peoples must obey the good stability aforementioned, it must be stable in what concerns justice – and it should be noted once again that such stability is not identical to a mere equilibrium resulting from the balance of power (a pure externalist device). Concerning war, for example, Rawls underlines the frequently mentioned fact that liberal societies rarely go to war with one another, a fact that is "as close as anything we know to a simple empirical regularity in relations among societies" (*Ibid.*, pp. 52-53; cp. Rawls, 2002, pp. 8, 16, 44 ff; Rawls, 2001, p. 543).

Turning now to hierarchical societies. What is it that makes them well-ordered societies, what is it that qualifies them for the law of peoples? First, they must be peaceful societies, relating to other societies by diplomacy and trade, and they must not be guided by some sort of religious expansionism; they must practice religious toleration. Secondly, they must be societies where a legal system, guided by a common conception of justice, prevails and that system must be put in practice by judges and other officials. Even if the persons living in hierarchical societies are not – in comparison with those living in liberal societies – citizens, they must be responsible members of such societies. In the third place, the members of these societies must have certain minimum rights to means of subsistence and security, to freedom and private property, and to some formal equality; that is, hierarchical societies must respect basic human rights (Rawls, 2002, Part II; Rawls, 2001, pp. 544 ff).

The problem of human rights, "a special class of rights" (*Ibid.*, p. 560; Rawls, 2002, p. 78 ff), and an internalizing factor, so to say, is obviously a fundamental problem, dealt with extensively, amongst many others, by R. J. Vincent, who, in *Human Rights and International Relations* (Vincent, 1986), insisted on the primacy of subsistence rights. According to the law of peoples, "these rights do not depend on any particular comprehensive moral doctrine or philosophical conception of human nature" (Rawls, 2002, p. 68; Rawls, 2001, p. 551), they express "a minimum standard of well-ordered political institutions for all people who belong, as members in good standing, to a just political society of peoples", they are "politically neutral" (Rawls, 2001, p. 552) (political neutrality, excluding ideological confrontation, is a sign of internalization). They represent "the outer boundary of admissible domestic law of societies in good standing in a just society of peoples" (*Ibid.*, p. 554). Their respect defines the legitimacy of a regime, and excludes any right to internal intervention by other states (in the form of economic sanctions or by military force); they establish a limit to pluralism amongst peoples, in the sense that they determine (in conjunction with the non-expansionism and a legal system which enjoys legitimacy in the eyes of its own people) "the limits of toleration in a reasonable society of peoples" (*Ibid.*, p. 561). Concern for human rights "should be a fixed part of the foreign policy of liberal and hierarchical societies" (*Ibid.*, p. 562). Ideal theory is reasonably internalist in its stance. The "outer boundary of admissible domestic law of societies in good standing in a just society of peoples" (*Ibid.*, p. 554) defines the space where peoples are internally related in view of a common end.

Let us now move to the second stage, which will confront us, at least partially, with the opposite view. The second stage – the "nonideal theory" – deals with a different situation; it deals with "the highly non-ideal conditions of our world" (*Ibid.*, p. 555) and with the possibility of the achievement of the ideal theory. The first step – the noncompliance theory – regards the relation between just societies (liberal or hierarchical) with states that "refuse to comply with a reasonable law of peoples" (Rawls, 2001, p. 537), the "outlaw regimes" (*Ibid.*, p. 555). The second step poses the problem of "unfavourable conditions" (poverty, poor technological development, etc.) which prevent certain peoples of attaining a situation where fair institutions (liberal or hierarchical) could be established.

As to outlaw regimes, everything that liberal and hierarchical societies can do is to establish with them a *modus vivendi* founded on the balance of power – an externalist device –, because the relation between just societies and outlaw regimes "exist in a state of nature" (*Ibid.*, p. 556). The legitimacy of war against such regimes is limited: limited to self-defence, and, "in grave cases, of innocent persons subject to outlaw regimes and the protection of their human rights" (*Ibid.*, p. 556). (Rawls seems to share some of Michael Walzer's assumptions in *Just and Unjust Wars* (Walzer, 1977).) We are no longer – as we were in ideal theory – in a space where individuals are internally related: the brute fact of basic externality defines the context of nonideal theory. At the same time, democratic and hierarchical societies share the obligation, through external policy and with help from political wisdom and good luck, of promoting the integration of other societies in the law of peoples. Theirs must be an "existential utopianism", to use Robert Nozick's phrase, not an "imperialist" one (Nozick, [1974] 2006, pp. 319-320). For such project, the creation of a "federative centre", representing "the alliance of well-ordered peoples" (Rawls, 2001, p. 557), is possibly a helpful device, and its effect could be of greater consequences than usually believed, as even outlaw regimes are not immune to a certain type of arguments. (These two points are already evident in Kant) The very idea of a federative centre (as opposed to the proposal of a universal state) joins internal and external relations.

The case of peoples living under unfavourable conditions is substantially different from the one of outlaw regimes. The main reasons for those unfavourable conditions lie in the political traditions and in a certain number of connected factors which should be altered "before a reasonable law of peoples can be accepted and supported" (*Ibid.*, p. 557). In the process of changing unfavourable conditions it is impossible to ask for immediate transformations concerning the adoption of principles of distributive justice (which are *sine qua non* conditions for the existence of liberal societies). The main point lies in the fact that unfavourable conditions reside, as said before, in the peculiar political traditions of those societies and very rarely, if at all, in the effective absence of natural resources. Symmetrically, the main wealth of well-ordered societies lies in their political and cultural traditions and, coherently, the efforts of the community of well-ordered societies must consist in trying to put an end to "oppressive government" and "corrupt elites". The emphasis on human rights is once again instrumental.

Two short comments and a conclusion. First, the law of peoples according to Rawls – even more than the revised version of justice as fairness, political liberalism – gives pride of place to contingency. Both at the level of ideal theory (we deal with dissimilar societies, liberal and hierarchical) and at the level of non-ideal theory (we are confronted, from the beginning, with outlaw states and with societies which, on the account of their political and cultural traditions, live under unfavourable conditions). There is no immediate decisional mechanism which determines us to action – whatever that action may consist of, economical sanctions or the use of military force – in a situation of crisis. Decisions, ideally resulting from the common will of well-ordered societies united through a federative centre, are heavily dependent upon the situation and will of different peoples.

Secondly, the very structure of the *ius gentium* proposed by Rawls is, under many aspects, similar to the point of convergence of neorealism and neoliberalism I mentioned in the beginning. Rawls' "realist utopia", as he calls it, significantly joining the two key-words, also looks for a conjunction of the accommodation and surmounting principles, based on a relational model which is neither one of perfect realist externality nor one of extreme utopian internality. Peoples accommodate each other: the law of peoples does not impose moral, or philosophical, or religious visions of a comprehensive kind. Each people has a right to its own individuality. But, at the same time, a global political consensus is looked for, something akin to a mitigated conquest of plurality, fundamentally exhibited in the respect for human rights, which would count as the frontier of toleration accepted by well-ordered societies. From the point of view of the law of peoples, a prudent blending of realist externality and utopian internality seems to be the best of solutions.

I do not pretend, of course, that the metaphysical distinction between internal and external relations is capable of rendering justice to all the subtleties and intricacies of international relations theory nor of Rawls's *law of peoples*. My aim was only to underline its descriptive potential. What I have called the accommodation principle at the core of the realist position can only be understood, I suppose, by reference to the externality of relations and, correspondingly, the surmounting principle proper to utopianism is only conceivable through the supposition of some kind of necessitation of an organic – that is, internal – relation between peoples (or, in its more radical formulation, through an absolute internalization which would dismiss the states as illegitimate entities). Finally, the integration of contingency – the proper aim of any theory of international relations – depends, I suggest, upon a mixture of internal and external relations, a mixture that would be able to deal with what Kant called the "unsocial sociability" of mankind (Kant, 1973, p. 9)– or, perhaps, to coin a new phrase, the unrelational relationality of peoples.

References

Armstrong, D. M. (1980). *Universals and Scientific Realism*. 2 vols. Cambridge. Cambridge University Press.

Baldwin, D. A. (ed.) (1993). *Neorealism and Neoliberalism. The Contemporary Debate*. New York. Columbia University Press.

Beitz, C. R. ([1979] 1999). *Political Theory and International Relations*. Princeton. Princeton University Press.

Dougherty, J. E, and Pfaltzgraff Jr., R. L. (2001). *Contending Theories of International Relations*, Harlow. Addison Wesley Longman.

Kant, I. (1973). *Kleinere Schriften zur Geschichtsphilosophie, Ethik und Politik*. Hamburg. Felix Meiner Verlag.

Keenan, G. F. ([1951] 1984). *American Diplomacy. 1900-1950*. Chicago. The University of Chicago Press.

Keohane, R. O. (ed.). (1986). *Neorealism and Its Critics*. New York. Columbia University Press.

Luhmann, N. (1995). *Social Systems*. Stanford. Stanford University Press.

Morgenthau, H. ([1948] 1973). *Politics Among Nations*. New York. Knopf.

Nagel, E. (1991). *Equality and Partiality*. Oxford. Oxford University Press.

Nozick, R. ([1974] 2006). *Anarchy, State and Utopia*. Oxford. Blackwell.

Parsons, T. (1991). *The Social System* (1951). London. Routledge.

Pogge, Th. (1990). *Realizing Rawls*. Ithaca. N. Y. Cornell University Press.

Rawls, J. ([1971] 1989). *A Theory of Justice*. Oxford. Oxford University Press.

Rawls, J. (2001). *Collected Papers* (1999). Cambridge. MA. Harvard University Press.

Rawls, J. (2002). *The Law of Peoples* (1999). Cambridge. MA. Harvard University Press.

Rawls, J. (2005). *Political Liberalism* (1993). New York. Columbia University Press.

Riley, P (1972). (ed.) *The Political Writings of Leibniz*. Cambridge. Cambridge University Press.

Scruton, R. (2006). *A Political Philosophy*. London. Continuum.

Singer, P. (2002). *One World: The Ethics of Globalization*. Yale. Yale University Press.

Spegele, R. D. (1996). *Political Realism in International Theory*. Cambridge. Cambridge University Press.

Tunhas, P. (2009). "Belief Relations". *Antropológicas*. Vol. 11. Pp. 205-223.

Vincent, R. J. (1986). *Human Rights and International Relations*. Cambridge. Cambridge University Press.

Waltz, K. N. (1979). *Theory of International Politics*. New York. McGraw-Hill.

Walzer, M. (1977). *Just and Unjust Wars*. New York. Basic Books.

Rawls's *The Law of Peoples* as a Guideline for the World as We Know It

Milica Trifunovic

Introduction

John Rawls opens *The Law of Peoples* with the claim that his theory is to be seen as "realistically utopian" (Rawls, 2002). Being the servant of two masters, the idealistic and realistic one, the idea of a "realistic utopia" has raised several criticisms. Rawls's concept of international law is considered either as too idealistic or as too realistic. Those who consider it to be too idealistic lament that it does not take into account current problematic political issues, such as poverty and the fair global distribution of resources; those who consider it to be too realistic claim that it tends to be too accommodating with illiberal societies, narrowing the list of human rights to be protected (Buchanan, 2006). In this paper I will try to demonstrate that these criticisms miss Rawls's point.

I will first of all explain Rawls's key term *peoples*. Then I will briefly explain how Rawls constructs his theory of international relations. I will point out the weaknesses of this project by analyzing some well known objections, namely the ones advanced by Thomas Pogge. Finally, I shall present my reinterpretation of Rawls's argument. If I succeed in defending Rawls from those objections, it should become apparent how his project might support a theory of global justice.

The Idea of 'Peoples'

The term *people* stands for two different kinds of domestic societies: liberal democracies as we know them from *Political Liberalism* and *decent* peoples, which Rawls also calls "decent consultation hierarchies", exemplified by the imaginary Kazanistan.

Liberal peoples are – institutionally speaking – constitutional democracies, organized around a political conception of justice as a "free-standing view", specified by the two principles of justice: The first sais that each person is to have an equal right to the most extensive scheme of equal basic liberties compatible with a similar scheme of liberties for others and the second deals with social and economic inequalities. These are to be arranged so that:

a) *offices and positions must be open to everyone under conditions of* fair equality of opportunity

b) they are to be of the greatest benefit to the least-advantaged members of society *(the difference principle)* (Rawls, 1971, p. 303).

The two principles are chosen among many other options by representatives of the individuals in the "original position" from behind a "veil of ignorance".

A political conception of justice allows comprehensive doctrines to play a role only in non-political spheres. Only those issues fall under the domain of "the political", and are therefore to be considered in public debates, that are neutral with regard to comprehensive doctrines.

Liberal democracies are also supposed to have a certain common culture, due to the shared history, common language and tradition. This should be expressed through the citizens' "common sympathies" for each other, which are to be developed while building and living together in a political system as a historical entity. Co-citizens are to respect the culture of one another and to work together to support the political system that they share. The moral character of peoples has its roots in the moral character of its citizens, who treat their co-citizens reasonably, i.e., with respect for their rational interests that may be different from one's own. The same reasonable conduct is expected from the peoples when they enter the international arena, just as reasonable pluralism within domestic society allows the coexistence of diversity among co-citizens. Now, not until liberal democracies become foreign policy-actors does Rawls use for liberal democracies the term *peoples*. Why?

One answer is that Rawls wants to distance his theory from principles of *Realpolitik*, which advocate that nation-states pursue their rational interests at any cost. This confines foreign policy to a *modus vivendi*. Rawls, on the contrary, wants a stable, durable peace and peace for the right reasons. Thus, Rawlsian peoples differ from the classical concept of state because they lack the traditional sovereignty, which consists in the right to declare war in pursuit of state policies and the right to an absolute autonomy in dealing with the state's citizens. Reasonable peoples fight wars just for self-defense or in the name of human rights.

Further guarantee of peace for the right reasons is the fact that liberal democratic regimes are administrated by perfectly reasonable statesmen. The idea of a politician who is at the service of the people and "selfless in judging his society's needs" (Rawls, 2002, p. 97) deepens the gap between factual states and the idea of peoples.

Consequently, Rawls's *peoples* are an idealized version of modern multinational states.

Decent Hierarchical Peoples

Decent hierarchical peoples are not liberal. Their internal structure was not modified through the first original position. Their legal and cultural systems are shaped by a certain comprehensive religious doctrine in which they all believe and that provides a common good. They are not aggressive. They respect *basic* human rights. However, members of these societies are viewed in public life not as individuals but as members of groups. Rawls calls this society *associationist.* Each group should be further represented in a hierarchical legal system. In this kind of society there is no such a thing as a Western public sphere in which people can practice what Rawls calls *public reason.* However, there are forms of *consultation* in which members of social groups discuss their common aims. In this context individuals are allowed to oppose to, or to depart from, the official opinion, and judges and other officials must address the objections.

The political body that makes the final decisions – the rulers of a decent hierarchical society – are to weigh views and claims of each of the consulted groups and, in that way, consult the opinion of the whole people. Thus, societies like Kazanistan are also entitled to be called peoples, idealized non-liberal cast-like societies.

To conclude, "peoples", both liberal and hierarchical, do not exist as real world political entities. Instead, they are normative ideas, guidelines for our world. As such, the peoples' primary interest is to take reasonable care of their co-citizens' conception of justice and the good.

Second Original Position

The second original position builds on an analogy with the domestic case. It deals first of all with decent liberal peoples, and then with decent hierarchical peoples.

In the case of decent liberal peoples the parties are representatives whose interest is to make sure that their citizens can keep their comprehensive doctrines, acknowledging at the same time the political conception of justice as an internal order of society. In other words, their interest is to ensure security and safety of their citizens and to preserve their free political institutions. Furthermore, each people will want to preserve self-respect and would want others to respect them, their culture and territorial integrity. Peoples need to find a "public basis of justification" (Rawls 2002, p. 32) for their interests in terms of law of peoples.

Now, for a law among peoples to be fair, the parties are going to be put behind a veil of ignorance. They do not know "the size of their territory, or the population or relative strength of the people whose fundamental interest they represent" (Rawls 2002, p. 32). Under such conditions Rawls states the eight principles of the "law of peoples" while reflecting on history and usages of international law and practice, without suggesting any alternative, whereas in the domestic case the parties in the original position were offered numerous alternative principles of justice from which they were to choose.

This list of eight principles is not by any means complete and its implementation may take different forms. Rawls mentions institutions that would be similar to GATT rounds, World Bank or United Nations, European Union or Soviet Union. However, a more detailed description of their institutional interpretation is absent.

The second part of the second original positions deals with decent hierarchical societies. The procedure is the same, but since the internal organization of liberal and hierarchical peoples differs and the model of representation requires equality of the representatives, the peoples have to be represented in two separate original positions.

Both decent and liberal peoples agree on the following eight Principles:

1. "Peoples are free and independent, and their freedom and independence is to be respected by other peoples.
2. Peoples are to observe treaties and undertakings.
3. Peoples are equal and are parties to the agreements that bind them.
4. Peoples are to observe a duty of non-intervention.
5. Peoples have the right of self-defense but no right to instigate war for reasons other than self-defense.
6. Peoples are to honor human rights.
7. Peoples are to observe specified restrictions in the conduct of war.
8. Peoples have a duty to assist other peoples living under unfavorable conditions that prevent their having a just or decent political and social regime" (Rawls 2002, p. 37).

The most disputable points are 6. and 8. Rawls (2002 §10) explains that in the law of peoples a special class of urgent human rights is expressed, such as freedom from slavery and serfdom, liberty (but not equal liberty) of conscience, and security of ethnic groups from mass murder and genocide. The enumerated rights are compatible with those from Article 3 through Article 18 of the Universal Declaration of Human Rights. The violation of this class of rights is equally condemned by liberal and decent peoples. The principle of assistance is meant to help burdened societies to become decent and then they are on their own.

Lacking a fully adequate scheme of human rights and a globalized version of the difference principle, the law of peoples seems not to be analogous to the domestic order. However, Rawls notices that it is very important on this stage that we, the citizens of current liberal societies, defend the principles and judgments of the law of peoples. It is important for Rawls that his theory is realistic as well as utopian and in that sense his reasoning has to be confirmed by the real people living in the reality of current international relations.

Pogge's Objections

As stated in the introduction, I intend to focus on the objections presented by Thomas Pogge (2006). Pogge deals with the rejection of normative individualism in Rawls's view of international relations, with the asymmetries between Rawls's domestic and international theory of justice, with the definition of the term *peoples*, and with Rawls's advocating "explanatory nationalism", the notion according to which each state has sole responsibility for its level of development.

Pogge's biggest concern is about the fact that Rawls doesn't have a global difference principle, as it would be the case if the law of people were analogous to the domestic order. Pogge ascribes to Rawls two theories of justice: one that applies to the domestic case and another that applies to the international arena. Pogge criticizes this second theory for neglecting the needs of hierarchical societies and rejecting normative individualism. In particular Pogge raises the following objections:

1. Rawls accommodates the opponents of liberalism in his theory of international relations by tolerating other non-liberal, but reasonable ways of ordering society, but he does not accept the same principle of toleration in his domestic theory. This needs to be explained.
2. Rawls is too accommodating with non-liberal societies, as he requires no concessions from decent hierarchical societies.
3. By not envisioning more liberal global arrangements, Rawls assumes that the accommodation of decent hierarchical societies is needed forever. This also needs to be justified. However, as Pogge suggests, it is uncertain whether a well-ordered hierarchical society such as Kazanistan

could ever exist. Should this be not the case, this accommodation could actually end up accommodating no living person at all (Pogge, 2006, pp. 208-209).

In addition, Pogge criticizes the vagueness of the notion of peoples. In Pogge's view, it is not clear which groups are to be counted as peoples, and whether "peoples" are any groups who live on a certain territory or nations that transcend state borders. It is also not clear how these peoples are to be identified: by their passports, culture, descent, choice, or combination of those (Rawls, 2002, p. 211).

Furthermore, Pogge finds structural asymmetries in the two theories. Domestic theory takes into account parties who choose the two principles of justice and then apply them to the basic structures in such a way that the principles can fit any empirical context. In the international case, the parties are presented with the basic structure and the endorsement of eight principles of the law of peoples does not foresee corrective measures for any possible misfortunate empirical case: bad negotiations of former generations or unluckily natural conditions are of no interest for this theory. The global economic order of Rawls's utopia is shaped by "free bargaining" without any principles that could prevent stronger societies from shaping the terms of international interaction in their favor. Here Pogge's notion of "explanatory nationalism" comes into play.

Pogge vehemently argues that the well-being of a country cannot have only local causes. Rich countries and the global institutional arrangements they design and impose are contributing to poor countries' deprivation. Rich countries do not shy away from negotiating trade agreements with unlawful rulers or even from encouraging civil wars or opportunistic military interventions. According to Pogge, the global order is gravely unjust and "those who cooperate in its imposition are harming those whose human rights avoidably remain unfulfilled" (Pogge, 2006, p. 217). Pogge sees no reason why the parties in the original position would not consider an alternative to the Rawlsian law of peoples that would do without "explanatory nationalism" and support some kind of global difference principle instead of the *principle of assistance.*

The Reinterpretation

There are indeed in Rawls's *The Laws of People* two theories of justice operating at different levels of abstraction. Although intertwined, those levels should be held apart in order to avoid confusion.

We start again with distinguishing two theories: a theory of justice for the domestic society and the law of peoples for the international arena. Both theories have to be taken as guidelines, the former for a just domestic society and the latter for the just international society. Accordingly, both theories could be interpreted as *descriptive ideal theories* (Burg, 1997, pp. 89-99), i.e., as theories that should give us a detailed elaboration of a particular ideal. In other words, Rawls's two principles describe a domestic society, whereas Rawls's eight principles describe the international society.

The process of coming to life of any descriptive theory parallels the process of formulating an ideal. Ideals are motivated by the dissatisfaction with the real world (Burg, 1997, pp. 23-24), e.g., in the domestic case, with social injustice. The tool we use to mediate between ideal and real world is reflective equilibrium. In the case of domestic society it is *Rawls, you and me* who use it. We are the citizens of a non-ideal world who are going back and forth between the principles and considered judgments, deciding on a fair strategy that should lead to the full description of an ideal.

Rawls, You and I create the original position as a means of representing an ideal situation, and we use the method of reflective equilibrium to affirm its fairness. The same method is then used by the parties in the original position to affirm the principles of justice and is constantly in use by the citizens of the well-ordered society that we envision. When reflective equilibrium is reached the theory is considered as justified, though not for ever. Reflection is constantly in action. Considered judgments as well as the principles of justice are equally subject to revision. A good example of that is Rawls's shift from advocating a comprehensive theory in *A Theory of Justice* to the political free-standing view of *Political Liberalism*.

However, at the domestic level Rawls goes beyond the descriptive theory and introduces a *normative ideal theory,* which tells us which particular principles should guide our political action in that ideal context, e.g., Rawls's elaboration of the institutions of the basic structure or his emphasis on the importance of public reason.

Now, in *The Laws of People* we find a *descriptive ideal theory*. The theory describes preconditions for peoples' coexistence and their cooperation. However, it says little about the institutional arrangement that should support the law of peoples, that is, there is no *normative ideal theory.* Rawls' theory of international relations starts already from a descriptive ideal theory of domestic affairs. In the latter we, *Rawls, you and me*, were creating the hypothetical subjects of the original position, those who will become the citizens of liberal peoples once the veil of ignorance is lifted. In the second original position the parties are either the citizens of a well-ordered society that we hypothesize or completely new entities who do not owe their existence to the first original position.

In order not to cut the law of peoples completely out of reality, Rawls, as a member of a real world, is presenting a list of principles to the parties of the original position. They are to serve as an ideal for the theory of international relations and originate in our reflection and our dissatisfaction: "These familiar and largely traditional principles I take from history and usage of international law and practice" (Rawls, 2002, p. 41). Such principles are by no means conclusive. In the light of new events they may change, but for the time being they are accepted as reasonable by the citizens of real world liberal and some non-liberal countries.

The problem starts when the eight principles are to be interpreted, implemented and supported by institutions. To do so, we need a normative ideal theory for the international arena. However, from a real-world perspective it would be too demanding to formulate a normative ideal theory, although Rawls briefly mentions what kind of institutions he was imagining: "Suppose there are three such organizations: one framed to ensure fair trade among peoples; another to allow peoples to borrow from a cooperative banking system; and third an organization with a role similar to that of the United Nation, which I would now refer to as Confederation of Peoples (not States)" (Rawls, 2002, p. 42).

Two questions should be considered here:

Why doesn't Rawls use individuals as the parties in the second original position, the same ones he used in the first original position in order to tackle the above mentioned problem?

Can a descriptive ideal theory of international relations be of any use as a normative real-world theory?

For the second original position to be enacted by individuals Rawls would need to completely give up his theory of justice for a domestic society, since the country borders would play no role at all. It would make even bigger idealistic claims on the real world than Rawls's *descriptive ideal theory* for the global arena, which, though ideal, has a realistic touch. Rawls hypothesizes a possible future ideal society of peoples, and in order to do so he relies on his considered judgments, in which nation states, as central actors of the current international arena, still play an important role.

Therefore, the question as to whether a descriptive ideal theory of international relations can be of any use for a normative theory of real world is to be answered affirmatively. Rawls claims that political philosophy has four distinctive roles, one of which is orientation. Using our reason we should find our bearings in the conceptual space of all possible ends: individual, associational, political, social (Rawls, 2003, p. 3).

Hence, descriptive ideal theory is to have an orientational role in advancing a political culture and developing political conscience is a long process:

> [...] the grounds of constitutional democracy and the basis of its rights and duties need to be continually discussed in all the many associations of civil society as part of citizens' understanding and education prior to taking part in political life. These matters need to be part of the political culture; they should not dominate day-to-day contents of ordinary politics, but must be presupposed and operating in a background (Rawls, 2002, p. 102).

Answer to Pogge

Pogge's argument about how the law of peoples allows rich countries to misuse global institutions, or even the objection about Rawls's neglect of individualism, fails at the level of a *descriptive ideal theory.* If Rawls had been more precise about how the global institutions were to work, then Pogge's objection would stand. Pogge's complains about global inequality, etc., are imply criticisms of politicians and politics of nowadays, and require normative theory for justification.

As to Pogge's question as to why we have to come to terms with theories that oppose to liberalism in the international arena, I would answer that Rawls's approach is not at all accommodating with any non-liberal theories, but only decent theories, which we can include in our reflective equilibrium. without immediately rejecting them. The conclusions that we draw as a consequence of our reflection modify what we have established in the domestic case, which does not mean that such conclusions cannot be modified again in order to favour liberalism completely. This would be an ultimate wish of Rawls's.

The objection that hierarchical societies do not make any concession is also incorrect. Hierarchical societies start a dialogue with societies that do not share their comprehensive doctrines.

Finally, do we have to accept non-liberal societies indefinitely? Since Rawls's main goal is peace – established on reasonable grounds –, then I do not see why our acceptance of non-liberal societies should not last for ever, provided that such an arrangement brings peace and stability, and decent peoples behave as described in Kazanistan.

Furthermore, while criticizing the vagueness of the term *peoples,* Pogge states that Rawls makes no effort to show that his concept of people reflects "general and entrenched facts in the contemporary world" (Rawls, 2002, p. 210). In my view, the term *peoples* does mirror the state of our world's affairs inasmuch as peoples are an idealized version of really existing societies. We get to such an idealised conception as a reaction to the dissatisfaction that we feel regarding our world, and the idea of *peoples* is therefore a guideline for the further development of the state-entities that populate the world that we live in.

However, by letting the idealised versions of the states interact with one another on a virtual international arena will not help solve the specific problems of the real world, at least not in the pragmatic and strictly empirical sense that Pogge expects. Pogge is mixing two different levels of argumentation. The same is true for Pogge's concerns with Rawls's "explanatory nationalism". Complains about "explanatory nationalism" are all part of our considered judgments: Pogge's dissatisfaction with current global organisations and trade agreements, his statistical data about the world poverty and need for its alleviation, etc., need to find their place in normative theory, not in descriptive ideal theory.

Pogge's ideas for a global theory of justice takes place at the level of our considered judgments about the current state of our world's affairs. Thus, Pogge looks for principles that would have a normative relevance for a global theory of justice that be able to have an impact on the peoples' conditions of existence. In so doing, Pogge fails to see that Rawls's theory is of a larger scope. Pogge's dilemma is how to prevent the existing, and obviously unreasonable, affluent countries from exploiting global institutions in order to further their interests, whereas Rawls asks "how would a world of well-ordered societies look like?" Rawls goes beyond the limits of what is possible here and now and in that way is realistically utopian.

Conclusion

If we bear in mind the distinction between normative and descriptive parts of ideal theories we become able to organize our thoughts about the problems of the real world and the possibilities for its development. Otherwise, instead of expanding the "limits of practical political possibility" we run the risk of looking for answers in the wrong conceptual domain. In my view, this is exactly what Pogge does. Without questioning his objections to the current state of the world – objections that I hold to be completely right –, my point is that he fails to see that Rawls is giving a guideline for a possible, though in near-term maybe not achievable society of peoples. Rather than a text-book on international law, Rawls is giving us a philosophical account of global justice.

References

Buchanan, A. (2006). "Taking the Human out of Human Rights". *Rawls's Law of Peoples. A Realistic Utopia?* Rex Martin and David A. Reidy (eds). New York. Blackwell. Pp. 150-159.

Burg, W. van der (1997). "The Importance of Ideals". *Journal of Value Inquiry*. Vol. 31. No. 1. Pp. 23-37.

Pogge, T. (2006). "Do Rawls's Two theories of 'Justice Fir Together?". *Rawls's Law of Peoples. A Realistic Utopia?* Rex Martin and David A. Reidy. (eds). New York. Blackwell. Pp. 206-225.

Rawls, J. (2002). *The Law of Peoples*. Cambridge MA. Harvard University Press.Burg, W. van der (1998). "Ideal and Ideal Theory". *Reflective Equilibrium. Essays in Honour of Robert Haager*. Wirben van der Burg und Theo van Willigenburg (eds.). Berlin. Heidelberg. Springer-Verlag. Pp. 89-99.

Rawls, J. (2003). *Justice as Fairness*. Cambridge MA. Harvard University Press.

IV. Economic Justice

Towards Fair Terms of Economic Cooperation

Heiner Michel

Introduction

Taking into account the dramatic progress in productive technology and the considerable increase of global trade, one might expect that humankind is living in something close to an economic paradise. In fact, we are a very far cry from it. Far too many people are living in profound misery, largely excluded from the benefits of economic progress, and even rich countries are subject to severe economic constraints. There is no doubt that the current financial and economic crisis has severely aggravated economic shortcomings, but the situation was not rosy before. Apparently, economic progress does not translate directly into human development.

There are many reasons why economic progress falls short of its potential. This paper concentrates on two issues of fairness in trade: first, the unfair distribution of burdens due to systematic shortcomings of free trade, and, second, unfair shares of global economic cooperation. With respect to (un)fair shares, the paper suggests a basic principle: everyone who contributes to the increasingly global division of labour should derive a fair return from it. The concern of the paper, justice within the economic sphere, is not a substitute for, but a complement to other approaches to global justice. In the terminology of Philippe Van Parijs the scope of the paper falls within the realm of peripheral global justice (Van Parijs, 2007).

An examination of fairness in trade cannot do without some economics. Because the particular view of economics which provides the background of this paper differs from the liberal view, which will be familiar to most from public debates and economic textbooks, some remarks might be helpful by way of clarification. The paper adopts the approach of old-style institutional economics, which holds that, if you want to know what the economy is, you have to take a close look at its institutions, from the oldest market regulation to the most recent Financial Services Act.

Institutional economics is a thoroughly normative approach: it is not concerned with *functioning* economic institutions alone, but also with *fair* economic institutions. Institutional economics tries to overcome the current problematic division of labour between economics, which is exclusively concerned with an efficient economy, and philosophy, which is exclusively concerned with issues of fairness and justice. Institutional economics considers economic institutions as means which allow society to influence and to steer economic affairs. It belongs to the larger family of political economic approaches, which regard economics as a technique or an art of steering the economy. Liberal or mainstream economics, by contrast, depicts the economic sphere as governed by eternal economic laws, similar to laws of nature, and it never tires of warning against interfering with these economic laws.

The paper works with a wide notion of liberal or mainstream economics, encompassing various classical and contemporary schools of economic thought. It considers as liberal any approach in economics, which embraces four basic presuppositions:

(1) *Methodological individualism*: every economic phenomenon is explained as the result of the rational behaviour of individual economic agents.

(2) *Superior efficiency of free markets*: the spontaneous self-organisation of markets is assumed to ensure superior efficiency.

(3) *Scientism*: liberal economics considers itself to be a branch of social science in search of economic laws, which are considered as analogous to the laws of nature.

(4) *Value-freedom*: liberal economics operates with a fact-value dichotomy and depicts itself as being exclusively concerned with facts.

The four presuppositions are spelled out for reasons of clarification and by way of contrast with institutional economics. We will encounter and challenge only the first and the second presupposition directly – namely, methodological individualism and the superior efficiency of free markets.

I. Towards Fairness in Trade

Liberal economics claims to have a cure for the insufficient translation of economic progress into human development. For most readers, the suggested solution will come as no surprise: it is free trade. Whatever problems there may be with economic globalisation, free trade is not to blame. When confronted with the patent discontent with economic globalisation, liberal economics rushes to accuse factors other than free trade, such as incompetent and corrupt governments, the lack of local infrastructure, armed conflicts, global monopolies, the persistence of trade barriers, and so on.

There is no doubt that liberal economics is right to emphasise these causes of global poverty and insufficient human development. In particular, it is right to blame the persistence of trade barriers. Tariffs, quotas, and subsidies hamper trade and its possible benefits. Even worse, rich countries managed to rig the rules of trade in their favour. There are numerous examples of this: rich countries subsidise agricultural products for export heavily, thus ruining markets on which developing countries would otherwise be competitive. What is more, some of their taxation policies are perverse: rich countries place higher tariffs on products from poor countries than on those from their fellow rich countries, with peak tariffs on manufactured goods where poor countries could profit most (Stiglitz, 2006, p. 18; UNDP, 2005, Ch. 4).

Having acknowledged that liberal economics is right to blame these causes of global poverty, one key problem remains to be mentioned, namely the free trade doctrine itself. Free trade does not work. It is not enough to remove trade barriers. Fair terms of global economic cooperation call for more. The paper challenges three major arguments commonly presented in favour of free trade – the *economies of scale argument*, the *superior efficiency argument* and the *comparative advantage argument* – and draws attention to four drawbacks of free trade: insufficient protection for infant industries, externalities, unemployment, and unfair shares.

I.1. The Economies of Scale Argument

The *economies of scale argument* holds that the production of a commodity becomes more efficient as the amount of the commodity produced increases. Extending supply beyond the boundaries of the domestic market would allow for even larger scales of production, so that production on a global scale would be even more efficient.

The economies of scale argument is sound for many commodities, in particular industrial commodities. However, in a context of economic development the economies of scale argument becomes problematic. In certain cases, economies of scale even turn into an argument *against* free trade. To reach the scales necessary for global competitiveness, productive enterprises may require some initial protection from foreign competition (Stiglitz & Charlton, 2005, p. 27). This is a version of the infant industry argument, which holds that new industries require a temporary period of trade protection in order to become established (Krugman & Wells, 2006, p. 424). Of course, the policy of protecting new industries has to be weighed against its costs, for example against the welfare losses of domestic consumers who have to pay higher prices for products of possibly inferior quality.

Nevertheless, it is an argument for 'asymmetric' liberalisation, where the asymmetry, of course, has to be the exact reverse of the actual configuration. Today, liberalisation is regularly forced upon developing countries, while developed countries uphold their trade barriers (Stiglitz, 2006, p. 20).

I.2. The Superior Efficiency of Free Markets-Argument

Since Adam Smith, liberal economics has been keen to stress the superior efficiency of free markets. According to the liberal view, free markets provide a maximally efficient mechanism for the coordination of economic activity. Competition on free markets forces producers to offer best quality at best prices. Only those who are innovative as regards the product or the process of production are able to offer best products at best prices and will have market success. In other words, free markets exercise an imperative to innovation: "Innovate or perish!" (Van Parijs, 1995, p. 189).

Unfortunately, the argument of the superior efficiency of free markets is sound only in part. Apart from innovation there is a second, dark route to market success, which is well known in economics but is frequently ignored in public debates. The dark route to market success leads through externalisation. Producers who shift the costs of production onto others, onto workers, onto the community or onto the environment, are also able to sell at the lowest prices. Even worse, in order to keep up, competing producers are often forced to pursue the same route of externalisation. As a consequence, externalisation is a notorious plague of free markets.

Within the domestic economic context of developed economies, unwanted externalities – work for a pittance, early industrial working conditions, child labour, the destruction of the environment, and so on – have been more or less effectively bridled by appropriate institutions, such as labour legislation, collective bargaining rights, environmental legislation, a social welfare system, and innumerable others. Today, the race to the bottom has been triggered anew, only this time on a global scale. Unbridled free trade is eroding formerly effective political-economic institutions, and it is preventing the founding of new effective institutions. Globalisation in the mode of free trade forces developing countries in particular to increase economic competitiveness by tolerating externalities.

There are two reasons for demanding a ban on externalisations, a moral one and a political-economic one. First, there are well known moral reasons for banning child labour, for protecting the health of workers, the environment, the safety of consumers, and so on. Second, there is the political-economic norm underlying the reasonableness of price information and therefore the reasonableness of markets themselves: prices should reflect the real costs of production, otherwise the price information is distorted and the distortion undermines the reasonableness of price signals. Both reasons call for a ban on externalisation and for restricting competition to the realm of innovation. Best prices and best quality should be reached by innovation only and never by externalizing costs on the environment, on the workforce, or on society as a whole. The task today is to design political-economic institutions, blocking externalisation in economically developed countries and, most urgently, in economically developing countries.

I.3. The Comparative Advantage-Argument

David Ricardo is credited with formulating the argument of comparative advantage, which remains to this day a major tool of economic thought. Applied to trade it states that international trade is mutually beneficial provided that every country specializes in producing those goods which it produces *comparatively* the best. International trade would even be beneficial for economically less efficient countries, because trade enables each country to transfer its domestic productive resources into comparatively more efficient sectors of the economy and to draw other goods from abroad. Thus, international trade enhances global economic efficiency, enlarges the global economic cake and realises welfare gains even for non-competitive countries.

An example already used by Ricardo may serve as an illustration. There are two countries, England and Portugal, both of which produce the same two goods, wine and cloth (Ricardo, 1973, Ch. 7):

(A) *Production before international trade* (if not stated otherwise, numbers signify production costs. Ricardo's unit is manpower per year: e.g., in order to produce 100 bales of cloth, Portugal has to employ 90 workers):

	Portugal	*England*	*Total production*
100 bales of cloth	90	100	200 bales
100 barrels of wine	80	120	200 barrels

Note that England is less efficient at producing both goods. Nevertheless, concentration on domestic comparative advantage will prove advantageous.

(B) *Production after trade and domestic specialisation on sectors of comparative advantage, according to the free trade ideal:*

	Portugal	*England*	*Total production*	*Increase*
Cloth	x	220	220 bales	10%
Wine	170	x	212,5 barrels	6.25%

As can easily be seen, the model of comparative advantage predicts significant welfare gains due to international trade. What is less easy to see is that there are some problematic assumptions and blind spots in this model, two of which shall be discussed in this paper: unemployment and, in the following section, unfair shares.

II. Unemployment

What, if for some reason demand does not keep up with the increase of efficiency? Should, for example, total demand remain on the pre-trade level, the result would be unemployment. As we all know, unemployment is an all too real situation in contemporary economies and especially so in the developing world. Stagnating demand has considerable negative effects on employment in internationally less competitive countries. To show this, I will take up Ricardo's example once again. When demand is stagnating on the pre-trade level, the producer which is more efficient in absolute terms, Portugal, cannot redeploy its entire labour force to the sector in which it is comparatively more efficient. Portuguese workers remaining in the comparatively less efficient sector are in competition with the English workforce and, since they are producing absolutely more efficiently, drive a certain percentage of English workers out of their jobs.

(C) *Production after trade and domestic specialisation: real world economics with stagnating demand (numbers rounded):*

	Portugal	*England*	*Total production*
Cloth	10	189	200 bales
Wine	160	x	200 barrels
Unemployment	x	31 (14 %)	8 % unemployment

There are two obvious consequences for unemployment caused by insufficient demand: first, in contrast to liberal predictions, there will be no welfare gains in internationally non-competitive economies, but instead an increase in unemployment and, therefore, welfare losses. The liberal argument of comparative advantage presupposes that demand keeps pace with the increase in productivity. Based on the firm belief in the optimal spontaneous self-regulation of markets, liberals presuppose full employment, a condition rarely met within the real world. On the contrary, persistently high rates of unemployment plague developing countries. Instead of an efficiency-increasing redeployment of their domestic workforce, they are in need of more employment in the first place (Stiglitz & Charlton, 2005, p. 25). Second, in the real world more then one country is plagued by unemployment. Each country stricken by unemployment will look for relief. An apparently easy way to overcome domestic unemployment is to opt for a strategy of export in an attempt to compensate for the lack of local demand by attracting foreign demand. Unfortunately, the export strategy has two serious repercussions:

(a) Since unemployment is pervasive, other countries will adopt the same strategy, thereby triggering fierce global competition. Thus, the existence of unemployment exacerbates the problems of protectionism and of externalization mentioned above.

(b) Even when one country manages to be on the winning side with its export strategy, this will merely displace the burden of unemployment onto others. On a global scale, the problem of unemployment remains and there will be no welfare gains.

A brief aside on Keynes for the economically minded reader: Keynes had a clear view of the repercussions which unemployment is bound to have on free trade. We can therefore reject the claim that his theory is outdated since it would not – or even could not – take account of economic globalisation. In his clear and resolute language Keynes emphasizes the malign effects of unemployment, which perverts free trade into "a desperate expedient to maintain employment at home by forcing sales on foreign markets ... , which, if successful, will merely shift the problem of unemployment to the neighbour which is worsted in the struggle" (Keynes, 1953, pp. 382, 383).

The ideological strength of liberal orthodoxy has blocked Keynesian policies thus far, though the ferocity of the current financial and economic crisis appears to have caused some rifts in the firm belief in the superior self-regulatory capacity of markets, and it has compelled governments to fall back on demand management by deficit spending, an economic policy commonly, though perhaps not altogether correctly (Pfeffer, 2007, pp. 67-68), associated with the name of Keynes.

For the time being we are left with a non-ideal world plagued by mass unemployment. What to do? If the Keynesian insight is correct and the true cause of unemployment is macro-economic maladjustment, it makes no sense to blame individual economic actors. That is to say, economic analysis prevents us from making inappropriate ascriptions of responsibilities.

A tentative solution for a world plagued by persistent mass unemployment appeals to a principle of fair distribution of the burdens of trade-derived unemployment. Unemployment should be borne in solidarity, which means that strong shoulders should carry more weight. Since pervasive unemployment aggravates the global race to the bottom, additional agreements on trade rules have to be reached which block externalisation by defining minimal environmental, labour and wage standards.

III. A Fair Share of the Global Cooperative Product

III. 1. Problematic Notions of Productivity

Apart from externalisation and unemployment, there is another major problem with free trade: what if there are unfair shares of trade? Some economists appear to entertain the suspicion that there might indeed be something like unfair shares of trade, although they frame the problem in somewhat different terms. Acknowledging that many developing countries derive only tiny revenues from trade, they advise countries to climb the value-added ladder (Stiglitz & Charlton, 2005, p. 307; Stiglitz, 2006, p. 18). Developing countries should concentrate on more profitable production, not on agricultural products but on manufactured products.

The economic advice reveals a decidedly affirmative view of market prices and wages. In the liberal view wages reflect the true productivity of labour and prices reflect the true economic value of a commodity. But is the productivity view of wages tenable? Two countervailing examples might give rise to first doubts.

If market wages were to reflect the true value of labour, we would have to conclude that the labour of an educator caring for children or the work of a nurse caring for the ill is rather worthless by comparison with playing football in the national league. To be sure, liberal economics offers explanations of the huge wage differences we observe, for example, by referring to differences in distributional infrastructures. But an economic explanation is not a moral justification. There are considerable doubts that playing football in the national league is so many times more important than educating children or caring for the ill. Judged from a normative point of view, the reverse is surely the case. The labour of educators and of nurses is more valuable than playing football. That wages do not reflect the real importance of labour raises doubts about the productivity view prevalent in liberal economics.

The second example: a Congolese physician immigrating to New York, where she finds employment as a taxi driver. In her new occupation she earns more than before when she worked as a physician in Congo. Should we conclude from this that driving New Yorkers around the city is more productive and more valuable than saving the lives of Congolese? Many economists are prepared to bite the bullet and maintain exactly that. They conclude from the observed wage increase that a productive redeployment of labour must have occurred. They might lend their conclusion a veneer of plausibility by appealing to the higher human capital of New Yorkers in general and the lower human capital of Congolese in general. But most people would arrive at precisely the opposite conclusion. Saving life is more important than driving people around. In matters of life and death it is simply immoral to take considerations of assumed individual productivity into account. Thus, these two examples suggest that the notion that wages reflect the productivity of labour is problematic. To be fair, they do not constitute decisive arguments against the wage productivity thesis; however, they do cast considerable doubt upon it. The next section tries to sketch the fundamentals of a more systematic account of fair economic returns.

III. 2. The Global Division of Labour

In developed economies, the production of commodities is organized as a large-scale division of labour. As a result of the process of economic globalisation, the initially societal division of labour is increasingly being transformed into a global division of labour. The large-scale division of labour has important taxonomic and normative consequences.

a. *The myth of individual productivity*: When a large-scale division of labour is in place, individual contributions cannot be easily ascribed and assessed. To elucidate the difficulty, I want to distinguish between two different kinds of contributions to the economic whole. The first kind is immediate and relates to a specific product. The production of a bicycle provides a good example: one worker designs the bike, another welds the frame, a third assembles the gears, and so on. When thinking about economic cooperation, what first comes to mind is undoubtedly immediate contributions to specific products. But there is a more indirect kind of contribution. The bicycle producers just mentioned rely on the production of innumerable other workers. They need steel and aluminium for the bike, bread and bananas to satisfy their hunger, a roof over their head, medical care in times of illness, legal advice to enforce their contracts, and so on. Because of this complexity, when a large-scale division of labour is in place, any attempt to ascribe and assess individual contributions to the value of specific products turns out to be a hopeless endeavour. It is impossible to determine how much of the value of the bicycle has been contributed by the welder, how much by the assembly line worker, how much by the lawyer enforcing their contracts, how much by the teachers who have taught them their metier, and how much by the baker baking the bread for them all (Schmoller, 1923, p. 426; Feinberg, 1973, pp. 115f.; Shaw, 1982, pp. 55-6).

b. *The issue of fair shares has to be discussed at the level of the economic whole* and not at the level of individuals, companies or nations. It is an issue of how to distribute the product of the social – and increasingly global – cooperation.

Discussing the issue of fair shares merely at the level of the company neglects the fact that companies might have drawn unfair shares. The revenues of cleaning contractors, for example, are dwarfed by the revenues of international investment banks, and it is by no means clear that each company got its fair share. Discussing fair shares at the level of companies fails to take account of the fact that economic cooperation entails more than immediate contributions to a specific product. The same holds for restricting discussions of fair shares to the national level. There is no guarantee that the national share is a fair share. Some countries might reap unfair gains from global economic cooperation while others lose out.

Together with the division of labour, the scope of the principles underlying economic cooperation now exceeds national boundaries. It would be simply arbitrary to maintain that principles of fair economic cooperation should be confined to the nation-state while the cooperation has transcended it.

c. *The economic reciprocity demand*: A demand of reciprocity underlies economic cooperation. Everyone who contributes to the social and increasingly global product should receive a fair return for their contribution. Giving and taking should stand in a reciprocal relation to each other.

The economic reciprocity demand needs to be fleshed out. We need criteria in terms of which fair returns can be determined. The following section aims to clarify the reciprocity demand by employing a pluralist approach. It presents three principles as promising candidates for explicating economic reciprocity. Note that the three principles establish a normative bottom line for fair returns, while leaving ample room for the free play of supply and demand above this line.

III. 3. What is a Fair Return for One's Labour?

When discussing the issue of a fair return for one's contributions, the proposed argument concentrates on a particular kind of economic contribution, namely the contribution of labour. In other words, the argument raises the old and thorny issue of just wages. It leaves unsettled the question of whether there are other kinds of productive contribution, most prominently the supply of capital.

a. The Aristotelian Principle: A Living Wage for All

In the *Nicomachean Ethics* Aristotle voices a fundamental political-economic principle. He maintains that commodities have to be exchanged in a proportion which supports the reproduction of the economy as a whole and, in particular, provides producers with an adequate material status (Aristotle, 1133a7 f.). To put it differently, in a well-organized economy everyone's economic contribution should be rewarded sufficiently for them to live well. Adam Smith takes up the Aristotelian demand in his *Wealth of Nations* and elaborates upon it further:

> A man must always live by his work, and his wages must at least be sufficient to maintain him. ... . No society can surely be flourishing and happy, of which the far greater part of the members [the workers] are poor and miserable. It is but equity, besides, that they who feed, cloath and lodge the whole body of the people, should have such a share of the produce of their own labour as to be themselves tolerably well fed, cloathed and lodged (Smith, 1991, pp. 72, 83).

Granted, the first part of the quote can also be read in merely functional terms. The sustainable reproduction of labour power calls for a living wage. The second part is explicitly normative, however, and echoes the Aristotelian and Scholastic legacy of a just wage. The quote appeals to two norms, in particular: first, labour, in Smith's view the only productive economic factor, is entitled to a fair share of its product; second, the measure of a fair share is the material basis of a decent and even flourishing human life. Real wages below this bottom line are unjust. They are nothing more than work for a pittance.

b. The Smithian Principle: To Each According to Their Toil and Trouble

"The real price of every thing, what every thing really costs the man who wants to acquire it, is the toil and trouble of acquiring it." (Smith, 1991, p. 36).

This quotation is taken from a chapter of the *Wealth of Nations* in which Smith develops an argument in support of what economists call the labour theory of value. Leaving technical details of the labour theory of value aside, the quote can also be given a normative reading. If toil and trouble are the real costs of production, reciprocity demands that everyone should be compensated for their real costs. Everyone should receive compensation for the *objective hardships* of their work.

The principle focuses on the 'input side' of economic contributions. It refers to those characteristics of a task which are hazardous, harsh or just dull and boring for everyone. Liberal economics presents compensation for the hardships of labour as a key factor in explaining actual wage differences. In the liberal view, only the amenities of money induce people to endure the hardships of labour. In order to explain the huge wages of certain economic positions, liberal economics refers to the special hardships of prolonged periods of education and the extraordinary burdens of great responsibilities.

Here liberal economics is informed by a normatively sound insight – the hardships of labour should be recompensed. However, when it comes to assessing the real hardships of labour, the assumption of liberal economics is mistaken. Passing off prolonged periods of education or special responsibility as the real hardships of work is misleading. The education of talent is largely self-rewarding and responsibility is not a mere burden but also a valuable opportunity to shape human affairs.

Often, the real economic world does not conform to the principle of compensation. Skilled labour generally benefits from a double advantage – satisfying tasks and high remuneration – whereas unskilled labour generally suffers from a double disadvantage – low pay for dull and unpleasant labour, especially so in the sweat shops of the developing world. Apart from the normative principle of compensation, there is a political-economic reason which supports the compensation of the hardships of labour. Compensating hardships increases the rationality of prices by making the real costs of production visible. Today, the toil and trouble of sweatshop labour are disguised by low prices.

c. To Each What They Deserve

"*To each what she deserves*: Tendency of those who are comfortably off to believe that this is what is actually happening." (Shaw, 1982, p. 60).

The principle of desert refers mainly to the output side of economic contributions and elucidates an important dimension of economic reciprocity. There is a vast array of literature dealing with the principle of desert (Pojman & MacLeod, 1999). For the purposes of this paper, I would suggest that desert has a twofold basis. Everyone who demonstrates outstanding *commitment* or special *achievement* in their work is owed a due reward. Examples of special achievements are contributions to the advancement of human well-being, such as the discovery of new remedies for diseases plaguing humankind, the development of new macro-economic devices which enable us to eradicate the evil of underemployment, or the creation of new forms of musical and poetical expression.

With respect to the *commitment* with which a task is performed, desert becomes democratic. Everyone is capable of acquiring desert as a result of special commitment. The dedicated teacher who always has an open ear for the problems of her students and successfully encourages them to elaborate their skills, deserves a reward for her efforts. The same holds for the conscientious street sweeper who does not use every opportunity to dodge work. There appears to be a connection between the commitment basis of desert and the economic interdependence which arises from the large-scale division of labour. If everyone relies on the contributions of innumerable others, everyone relies on a certain level of performance. This constitutes a political-economic reason for providing incentives for a certain level of commitment and performance.

There is a puzzle concerning the basis of desert. On the one hand, outstanding contributions to the welfare of others – in other words, to their subjective utility – appear to constitute a suitable basis of desert and reciprocity. People appear to deserve economic rewards 'for the contribution they make to the welfare of others by providing goods and services that others want' (Miller, 1999, p. 184). On the other hand, there are certain problems with this view. Apart from the taxonomic problem of assessing who has contributed how much to the utility of a product, the yardstick of subjective utility is inherently problematic. Grappling with the issue of just prices, Thomas Aquinas already pointed out that opting for the metric of subjective utility entails unwelcome consequences. It would legitimise taking advantage of people who are destitute. A seller, for example, would be allowed to sell a bottle of water to a person who is parched in the desert for an absurdly high sum. And according to the yardstick of subjective utility, a pharmacist would be justified in charging fantasy prices for cheaply produced, but life-saving antibiotics. Because of these unwelcome consequences, Thomas dismisses the yardstick of subjective utility altogether. On a closer examination, he puts forward a general principle for his rejection: people should not charge others for something they have not brought about themselves. Since sellers do not bring about the advantage of buyers, they are not justified to charge them for their subjective utility (Thomas Aquinas, 2.2, q. 77, art. 1).

Thomas is right to reject taking advantage of the unfortunate circumstances of others. Desperate exchanges have to be blocked (Walzer, 1983, p. 102). His argument also successfully refutes subjective utility as a yardstick of fair returns. It would be absurd to demand rewarding pharmacists or physicians exactly according to the subjective utility of their goods and services. Nevertheless, there are strong intuitions which suggest that subjective utility should be reflected to a certain extent in remuneration. Those who contribute to the welfare of others, however welfare is to be understood, deserve some reward. This suggests a tentative conclusion: fair returns should reflect exceptional contributions to the welfare and, more broadly, to the flourishing life of others to a certain extent.

III. 4. The Unemployment Objection of Liberal Economics

There is a host of objections against fair shares. This section aims to fend off just the most prominent objection levelled against fair returns, namely the unemployment-objection of liberal economics. For liberal economists, any realisation of fair returns constitutes a textbook example of well-meaning but ill-conceived economic 'interventionism'. According to liberal economics, fair wages serve only to increase unemployment and to decrease the total economic cake. Downward wage-flexibility is seen as an indispensable measure for clearing the labour market (Stigler, 1946). However, we should refrain from embracing the liberal unemployment objection too rashly. A brief consideration of the real economic world inspires initial doubts concerning the alleged causal connection between the fluidity of wages and employment. Despite allowing for lowest wages and even work for a pittance, developing countries are commonly plagued by persistently high rates of unemployment. But if low wages advance employment, how come that their rates of unemployment are so persistently high?

Without doubt, unemployment exerts pressure on wages. According to economic orthodoxy, this is a blessing because wages fall until the market-clearing price for labour is reached. How is this supposed to occur? It is assumed that a single employer would employ more workers, if wages were falling. However, she will employ more workers only under one condition, namely if she expects that demand for her goods will be stimulated by reduced prices, which she is able to offer because of her reduced labour costs. In order to sell more goods at reduced prices, aggregate or macroeconomic demand has to remain at least constant. But if we go beyond the narrow perspective of the microeconomic level and take account of the wider perspective of the macro-economic level, we must acknowledge that what holds on the micro-level of a single employer does not hold for the macro-level of all employers. If all workers have to put up with lower wages, aggregate demand cannot be assumed to remain constant. Rather it is going to shrink and the desired positive effect on employment will fail to materialise. Keynes raises this objection against a core assumption of liberal economics:

> The argument simply is that a reduction in money-wages will *cet. par.* stimulate demand by diminishing the price of the finished product, and will therefore increase output and employment up to the point where the reduction which labour agreed to accept in its money-wages is just offset by the diminishing marginal efficiency of labour as output (from a given equipment) is increased. [...] If this is the groundwork of the argument (and if it is not, I do not know what it is), surely it is fallacious. It is invalid [...] to transfer the argument to industry as a whole unless we also transfer our assumption that the aggregate effective demand is fixed (Keynes, 1953, pp. 257, 259).

On account of the direct repercussions of wages on aggregate demand, the wage level *cannot* function as a market-clearing price for labour. The result of falling wages is deflation, not an eradication of unemployment. Only by putting on microeconomic blinkers can the unemployment objection of liberal economics be sustained.

Should the Keynesian argument hold, the realisation of the normative ideal of giving a fair slice of the global economic cake to everyone – in particular, to those at the lower and the lowest end of the wage scale – does not result in increased unemployment. Instead, the prices of commodities would incorporate the needs, the toil and trouble, and the desert of producers. Readers who are reluctant to embrace Keynes's argument on the spot might be more easily convinced by a second, empirical argument. In general, the wages of workers in the developing world amount to merely a tiny fraction of the retail price of products in rich countries. Even multiplying wages would result in only small increases in the final prices and, therefore, in negligible effects on consumer behaviour; but it would significantly improve the living conditions of workers and boost the export revenues of poor countries.

IV. A Political-Economic Outlook

We have discovered four major systematic shortcomings of free trade. Free trade provides no protection for infant industries in developing countries, it does not block externalities, it entails the risk of merely increasing unemployment, and it does not guarantee fair shares. With respect to the remaining shortcomings, the final section dismisses an individualist approach which bets on the morality of consumers and argues for fair and effective economic institutions.

a. The Moral Saint Approach

Theorists close to liberal economics and grassroots activists suggest that consumers should exert their economic power and buy ethically. This strategy has one major disadvantage: consumers do not bother. At the cash point, consumers behave as liberal economics predicts, namely like rational egoists. Their only concern is the lowest price. There is ample empirical evidence of this. The global share of fair trade is negligible, just 0.01 per cent of trade. The average German, thrifty as ever, currently spends about 1.70 Euro per year on fair trade products; the average American, hardly more generous, spends about 2.50 Euro. While the average Briton spends at least around 12 Euro, they are all put to shame by the average Swiss who consumes fair trade products worth almost 21 Euro per year. In Germany, the market share of one of the best-known fair trade products, coffee, which is readily available in major supermarkets, is about 1.5 percent (all data from 2007; see Max Havelaar-Stiftung, 2008). There is a lesson to be learned from this empirical finding: in a market economy, it is better not to rely on moral saints. Although it is in line with the individualist paradigm of liberal economics, relying on benevolent consumers is bound to fail.

The empirical data are also unfavourable to the preferred solution of business ethics, namely relying on corporate social responsibility. If consumers do not care, this hampers substantive efforts of corporate social responsibility. Avoiding harmful externalisation and exploitation simply does not pay. This is why we are still waiting for fairly produced consumer electronics and why early industrial working conditions are still the norm, and not the exception, in developing countries.

In order to avoid misunderstandings, let me state clearly that this refutation of the moral saint approach is not intended as a criticism of fair trade organisations. They are thoroughly admirable organisations which secure decent standards of work and remuneration for millions of workers in the developing world. I just doubt whether one should rely on benevolent consumers as a general strategy for realising fair terms of global economic cooperation. There are simply too few of them. So the question is: how to block harmful externalisation and unfair shares? I want to sketch briefly an intermediate and a long-term strategy.

a. The Intermediate Strategy: Fair Import Policies of Developed Countries

Developing countries would be ill advised to establish externality-blocking institutions and substantive minimum wage legislation unilaterally, because they would thereby merely price themselves out of the market. They are in competition with too many other countries which are ready to exploit their own desperate workforces. This explains why minimum wage legislation, if it exists at all, is generally not very ambitious, often requiring wages even below the level of domestic living wages, and why there is a considerable lack of enthusiasm for enforcing minimum wages and other legal standards. It furthermore explains the popularity of special export zones which undercut even the low domestic environmental, labour and remuneration standards.

Fortunately, another strategy is available. Developed countries, on their part, should waive the gains they derive from exploitative labour and environmental destruction in developing countries. Instead, they should turn to fair import policies by insisting on minimal standards of remuneration, labour law, collective bargaining rights, and environmental protection. A promising example links import quotas with compliance with labour standards (Sibbel & Borrmann, 2007).

Needless to say, there is a danger that fair import policies will be perverted into new forms of protectionism. Thus the policies should be set up in cooperation with NGOs, domestic unions, and the ILO.

b. The Long-Term Strategy: Fair and Effective Global Institutions

There exists one suitable remedy for dealing with the shortcomings of free trade. They should be dealt with in the same way in which the shortcomings of free markets have been dealt with from the very beginning, namely by designing appropriate political-economic institutions which block externalities effectively, which restrict competition to the field of innovation, which guarantee fair shares and protect infant industries in developing countries, and so on. In pursuit of these goals we have to ramp up national institutions or to set up entirely new institutions. Taking a closer look at the political-economic institutions developed by the European Union and their potential for being extended to the global level might prove to be particularly rewarding in this regard.

Conclusion

This paper has been dedicated to a systematic analysis of the weaknesses of the doctrine of free trade. There is no need to emphasise that the critique of free trade is not a criticism of trade or markets as such. Markets are efficient instruments for coordinating economic activity, also on a global scale. The paper has aimed to provide systematic arguments for establishing appropriate economic institutions, for blocking unwelcome consequences of economic activity and for securing fair terms of global economic cooperation. Against the background of a deepened financial and economic crisis, fair and effective institutions of trade appear to acquire particular importance and urgency.

References

Aristotle (1984). "Nicomachean Ethics". J. Barnes (ed.). *The Complete Works of Aristotle.* Princeton. Princeton University Press. Pp. 1729-1867.

Feinberg, J. (1973). *Social Philosophy.* Englewood Cliffs. Prentice Hall.

Keynes, J. M. ([1936] 1953). *The General Theory of Employment, Interest, and Money.* San Diego. Harvest Book.

Krugman, P. & Wells, R. (2006). *Macroeconomics.* New York. Worth Publishers.

Max Havelaar-Stiftung (Schweiz) (ed.). (2008). *Jahresbericht 2007.* [Electronic Version.]. Zürich. Ropresa.

Miller, D. (1999). "Two Cheers for Meritocracy". D. Miller (ed.). *Principles of Social Justice* Cambridge. Mass. Harvard University Press. Pp. 177-202.

Pfeffer, C.P. (2007). *Plutopia. Policies for Globally Sustainable Common Wealth.* Retrieved February 15. 2009. From http://www.scribd.com/doc/27972/Plutopia

Pojman, L. P. & MacLeod, O. (1999). *What Do We Deserve? A Reader on Justice and Desert.* New York. Oxford University Press.

Ricardo, D. ([1817] 1973). *The Principels of Political Economy and Taxation*. London. Everyman.

Schmoller, G. v. (1923). *Grundriß der Allgemeinen Volkswirtschaftslehre*. Berlin. Duncker & Humblot.

Sibbel, L. & Borrmann, P. (2007). "Linking Trade With Labor Rights: The ILO Better Factories Cambodia Project". *Arizona Journal of International and Comparative Law*. Vol. 24. No.1. Pp. 235-249. Electronic Version

Shaw, B. ([1937]1982). *The Intelligent Woman's Guide to Socialism, Capitalism, Sovietism and Fascism*. London. Penguin Books.

Smith, A. ([1776] 1991). *An Inquiry into the Nature and Causes of the Wealth of Nations*. New York. Prometheus Books.

Stigler, G. (1946). "The Economics of Minimum Wage Legislation". *American Economic Review*. Vol. 36. No. 3. Pp.154-156.

Stiglitz, J. (2006). "Social Justice and Global Trade". *Far Eastern Economic Review* 169(2) 18-22.

Stiglitz, J. & Charlton, A. (2005). *Fair Trade For All: How Trade Can Promote Development*. New York. Oxford University Press.

Thomas Aquinas ([1265-1273] 1948). *Summa Theologica*. New York. Benziger Brothers.

United Nations Development Programme (ed.). (2005). *Human Development Report 2005. International cooperation at a crossroads* [Electronic Version]. New York.

Van Parijs, Ph. (1995). *Real Freedom for All: What (if Anything) Can Justify Capitalism?* New York. Oxford University Press.

Van Parijs, Ph. (2007). "Global Distributive Justice". R. Goodin, P. Pettit & T. Pogge. (ed.) *Blackwell's Companion to Political Philosophy*. Oxford. Blackwell. Pp. 638-652.

Walzer, M. (1983). *Spheres of Justice: A Defense of Pluralism and Equality*.New York. Basic Books.

Whip Cosmopolitanism into Shape: Assessing Thomas Pogge's Global Resources Dividend as an Instrument of Global Justice

Paulo Barcelos

And who is my neighbor?
Luke, 10:29

Ah! if we would talk less of being humane and calculated more, reasoned, and took a conscientious attitude to our duties!
Anton Chekhov, "The Wife"

I

I will address Thomas Pogge's *Global Resources Dividend* (GRD) in a twofold way: as an illustration and as a pretext. On the one hand, as way of defending a distributive conception of global justice from two major criticisms: that which cast doubt upon the practical feasibility of such a scheme, and that which contests its moral reasonableness. I will try to ascertain both the moral justification and the viability of the GRD, even in the Westphalian state system.

On the other hand, I will employ the GRD as a pretext for advancing a principle of global distribution that synthesizes and the global egalitarian position and the statist scepticism towards such a stance – that is, to sustain that within a cosmopolitan perspective there is room for the existence of special distributive duties among co-citizens. Using as a conceptual framework some terms of Herbert Hart's taxonomy of rights I shall seek to propose, contra Pogge, the eminently dual character of the individual's duties facing others, comprising an universal duty towards humanity at large and an equally valid set of specific duties towards those with whom he has some sort of special relationship.*

I shall start by following Thomas Nagel in his statement that a distributive conception of global justice is usually faced with two common

* I am indebted to Gabriele De Angelis for his helpful comments on my paper and overall extremely careful editing of the volume.

objections (Nagel, 2005). These call into question the very possibility of existence of such a criterion of evaluation and reformulation of global socio-economic systems and institutions as a way of reacting against world poverty and inequality.

The first argument opposed to global justice casts doubt on its practical feasibility. It derives from the understanding of every consideration of justice as being congenitally bound to the existence of a sovereign state. Moral rules can, certainly, be achieved by intellection alone, but their coming into being as political norms that regulate social institutions and practices depends on its insertion on a juridical system backed by an authority which, disposing of the monopoly on the legitimate use of physical force (Weber, 2002), might compel obedience to the laws. In short, the effectuation of justice in a social context depends on the existence of a state. Given the fact that the global order does not constitute such a political body nor any other where there is an ultimate sovereign that might put laws to practice, adherents of the global justice thesis disregard one of the basic dictates of modern politics, decreed by Hobbes in the chapter 26 of his "Leviathan": *Auctoritas, non veritas, facit legem.*

Along with this argument, that devaluates a fairness-based global justice as an impracticable utopian chimera, there is a second challenge, which questions its philosophical justification. A distributive conception of global justice, deriving as it does from the principles of moral cosmopolitanism, must start from the premise of the universal status of every human being as the ultimate unit of moral concern and, therefore, of the equal right of every person, irrespective of their national origin, to have a stake in the allocation of social goods. The critics of this approach claim that such distributive design of basic institutions may only legitimately be brought into play where there is a strong political bond among individuals. One may establish a duty of charity or humanitarian assistance towards peoples outside our society, but if we are to think of distributive principles there is no point in extending its scope beyond the group of people with whom we share a scheme of cooperation comprised of legal and economic rules and political institutions. Justice is, thus, an associative obligation, and it is morally unjustified to extend it beyond the borders of the State, which constitutes a scheme of cooperation that deeply shapes the citizens' lives and upon which the collective well being is dependent on.

This said, my aim in this paper will be twofold. Firstly, I'll briefly expose Thomas Pogge's *Global Resources Dividend* (GRD) and try to prove that it constitutes an instrument of a cosmopolitan economic justice that succeeds in overcoming the above mentioned criticisms, that is both morally justified and viable in the Westphalian state system. Secondly, I shall apply the GRD as an illustration, as a pretext for developing a proposition for a principle of global distribution that seeks to synthesize the statist and the global egalitarian claims, that is, to sustain that within a cosmopolitan perspective there is room for the existence of special distributive duties among co-citizens.

II

Pogge advances the moral justification of the GRD through the enunciation of three basic and interwoven assumptions about poverty and inequality. First of all, he introduces a shift in the way the moral obligation of the well-off towards the poor is usually conceived. It has traditionally been assumed that, if such an obligation was to be conceived, it should rest upon a positive duty on the side of the well-off to assist those in acute distress. This duty to help when faced with suffering is what underlies charity and humanitarian aid, but it leaves room for individuals to ignore harms they feel have not been brought about by their direct action, especially if such harms happen to distant others in the opposite part of the world. To Pogge, anchoring the obligation towards distant others merely on a positive duty to help would, therefore, not be enough. What he endeavours is, instead, to shift the attitude towards poverty from the field of charity to the sphere of justice, and thus he advances the plea for "radical inequality as an injustice that involves violation of a negative duty by the better-off" (Pogge, 2002). This negative duty requires us "not to uphold injustice, not to contribute to or profit from the unjust impoverishment of others" (Pogge, 2008, p. 440). What he sustains when he enunciates this duty as being violated by the well-off is that the status of the impoverished is dependent on the action of the former, whose wealth is correlated with the poverty of the latter, since they both share an order of institutional practices that place individuals in a scheme of deep economic interdependence. They share, in brief, what Rawls has termed the "basic structure of society", or more exactly, "the way in which the major social institutions distribute fundamental rights and duties and determine the division of advantages from social cooperation" (Rawls, 1971, p.7). In conclusion, anyone who passively contributes to the maintaining of an unfair social structure is violating a negative duty and therefore harming the poor.

This claim opens the way to the second assumption, pertaining to the scope of the basic structure. Pogge sustains that this scheme of interdependence that constrains individual choices and possibilities – the first and foremost field of application of the principles of justice, according to Rawls – is not merely present at the level of the domestic society embodied by the Nation-state, but has an international equivalent. Societies, in fact, are not closed self-sufficient entities, and the reasons for their poverty (and consequently for the poverty of their citizens) are not merely endogenous. As Pogge convincingly demonstrates, states are interconnected through a global network of market trade and diplomacy that subjects poor societies to the rules of the world economy designed by the affluent countries in virtue of their vastly superior military and economic strength. These rules and practices constitute a global basic structure analogous to the domestic one, which is naturally implicated in the reproduction of the existing radical inequality between peoples and individuals. This is further reinforced by the fact that in international economic competition the states do not share the same starting positions, since some peoples – usually those which remain poor – were subjected to a history of colonization pervaded by grievous wrongs that severely traumatized their cultures and institutions and consequently prevented them from accomplishing welfare.

These sources of global injustice attest Pogge's third assumption, which is the corollary of the two that preceded it. State boundaries, he sustains, are morally irrelevant in a distributive justice reasoning. In the words of Charles Beitz, who shares this assumption with Pogge, "since boundaries are not coextensive with the scope of social cooperation, they do not mark the limits of social obligations" (Beitz, 1979, p. 151). It is, thus, through such argumentation that both Pogge and Beitz respond to and surmount the second basic criticism of egalitarian global justice conceptions I alluded to in the beginning of the text. Even if we conceive the principles of justice as being strictly associative obligations, designed to regulate the societies' basic structure, then, for the same reasons, they will also have to be applied internationally, since there is a second-level basic structure at the global level.

Surmounted that second instance of criticism of cosmopolitan theories, Pogge's conception still has to face the first one, which doubts of their practical feasibility. This shall be done by advancing the terms of the distributive mechanism Pogge proposes for the redesign of the world economic ground rules: the *Global Resources Dividend*.

Its purpose and method follow from a not yet mentioned source of global injustice that Pogge additionally considers: the uncompensated exclusion of the world poor from the use of natural resources. He claims that there is an inherent unevenness in the current appropriation of goods from the world's reserves. They are, in the vast majority, consumed by the populations from the affluent states without giving an equitable compensation to the globally least well-off for their disproportionate consumption, since what those wealthy states pay for the importation of resources like oil goes to the producing countries' national elites and not to the people at the bottom of the economic chain. Those people are, nevertheless, entitled to a fair share of the limited natural supplies. It is to advance a fairer re-equilibrium of the distribution of the world's resources that Pogge proposes a dividend that "modifies conventional property rights so as to give legal effect to an inalienable moral right of the poor" (Pogge, 2005, p. 52).

The GRD takes the form of a tax on consumption, to be applied on the extraction of any kind of resources on the territory of every state. To guarantee the reasonableness of the levy, not every resource would be taxed and there would be a differentiation on the standards of taxation according to each good: the GRD, for instance, should not be imposed on the land used for cultivation of basic agricultural commodities (Pogge, 1994, p. 203). It will, conversely, be based on resources and pollutants with high resource content and whose discouragement of use seems especially desirable for the sake of future generations, crude oil extraction being the classic example. Pogge estimates that a modest taxation – correspondent to 1% of gross world product, for instance – would be sufficient to prevent the development of excessive inequalities and hence to guarantee the preservation of global background justice.

One of the strengths of this model is the compatibility with the modern state system: it does not need to postulate a profound erosion of sovereignty or a latent development of a cosmopolitan global democracy to be operative. This adequacy to the world current institutional order can be ascertained by taking two facts into consideration. On the one hand, the GRD does not interfere with each state's sovereign control over the resources within its national territory. Every individual has a stake in all limited natural resources, but that right does not allow them to participate in decisions about whether or how those resources are to be used if they are part of the territory of a foreign state, as that is a prerogative belonging to the autochthonous people (Pogge, 2008, p. 439). The people might therefore decide whether or not to extract what their territory has conceded them; the condition is that if they do so they will have to pay a proportional tax on what was extracted. This tax, Pogge claims, is enacted on behalf of humanity, as an actualization of the Lockean proviso, developed in the chapter 27 of the *Second Treatise of Government*, stating that an individual might only exclude the common right of all men from the goods he collects as long as he leaves "enough, and as good left in common for others".

On the other hand, and more importantly, the functioning of the GRD does not demand the establishment of anything like a world government. A decentralized structure relying on an institution analogous to the United Nations or the World Bank would be enough to assure the application of rules and sanctions. National governments would be responsible for the transfer of the GRD amounts through this facilitating organization (Pogge, 1994, p. 202), which would also supervise the measurement of the amount of funds each state had to allocate. In case of non-compliance Pogge proposes economic sanctions to be imposed against the defector: levies on imports from and exports to that country until the sum it owes to the GRD is attained. The funds collected will be disbursed to impoverished countries' governments. If the funds are misused there are other ways of canalizing funds to the improvement of the condition of the domestic poor: by making cash payments directly to them or by administering development programmes through existing United Nations agencies or through suitable Non-Governmental Organizations (Pogge, *Ibid.*; 2008, p. 446).

III

Considering these main outlines of Thomas Pogge's GRD, one can perhaps conclude that Pogge, in his proposal, has not carried cosmopolitanism departure assumptions to their ultimate consequence. If, indeed, one is to conceive individuals as the ultimate unit of moral concern and, faced with global radical inequality, to believe the international realm to constitute a global basic structure fully analogous to the domestic one, then the logical corollary of these premises would be that the same principles of justice enforced domestically must be integrally transferred to the global sphere. That would mean, to an egalitarian thinker, to defend the universalization of Rawls's difference principle. Pogge's GRD stands however to a much more, in his words, "modest" proposal. He does so deliberately, since what he is trying to achieve is a conception of global justice which is workable, which might gain the support necessary to be implemented and to sustain itself in the world as we know it (*Ibid.*). A conception that, in short, may convincingly overcome the stated criticisms cosmopolitanism is usually faced with.

Along with feasibility, what this modest proposition operates by advancing a mitigated way of working with cosmopolitan assumptions is also the opening of a possibility for a conciliation of that normative general edifice with something which only apparently may arise as antithetic. We may directly reefer to Pogge's words to clarify this issue. In his article "An Egalitarian Law of Peoples" he sustains that:

> It is perfectly permissible for us and our government, in a spirit of patriotic fellow-feeling, to concentrate on promoting the interests of our own society and compatriots, even if foreigners are much worse off, I need not deny this

> claim, only to qualify it: Partiality is legitimate only in the context of a *fair* competition (Pogge, 1994, p. 221).

Assuming that preserving the fairness of international competition might be assured by the adoption of a corrective mechanism like the GRD, I shall try to radicalise Pogge's assertion and suggest something which he perhaps would not accept: the eminently dual character of the individual's duties facing others, comprising an universal duty towards humanity at large and an equally valid set of specific duties towards those with whom he has some sort of special relationship. Pogge does not share this claim. He, as a strong egalitarian, faced with the existence of what he alleges to be a global scheme of social cooperation that mirrors the basic structure of a domestic society, claims for the adoption of the same egalitarian distributive principles that are often considered for the domestic sphere, in particular the Rawlsian principles of "justice as fairness" (the GRD device would not be sufficient in an ideally fair world, but it is proposed as an instrument, immediately operative in the nowadays international sphere, to guarantee a minimal standard of equality among peoples). I, on the contrary, will try to defend that, if it is true that there is a universal distributive obligation (different, as he have seen, from mere charity or humanitarian assistance) that comprises all men as individuals, there might also be a second-level obligation specifically binding the members of each social body. This dualism, I sustain, stems from a fundamental disanalogy between the domestic and the global sphere, and I will seek to justify it – and therefore contest the validity of the alleged moral irrelevance of state borders – without abdicating the cosmopolitan basic assumption of the individual as the ultimate unit of moral concern.

For that I shall use as a conceptual framework some terms of Herbert Hart's taxonomy of rights. In his "Are there any Natural Rights?" Hart starts by answering affirmatively to the titled question asserting that there is one absolute natural right, which is not created by men's voluntary action, like other moral rights are, but derives its source from the ontological constitution of men *qua* men – it is the equal right of all men to be free. What this right prescribes, in his words, is that

> in the absence of certain special conditions which are consistent with the right being an equal right, any adult human being capable of choice (1) has the right to forbearance on the part of all others from the use of coercion or restraint against him save to hinder coercion or restraint and (2) is at liberty to (...) any action which is not one coercing or restraining or designed to injure other persons (Hart, 1984, p.75).

As we can see from the initial part of the quoted sentence, this natural right, being universal in its scope, is also conditional. In the presence of certain special circumstances the enforcement of a second class of rights, *special rights*, is allowed, which permits a coercive interference with the autonomous sphere of individual freedom. What rights are these, and in which conditions do they emerge? Hart postulates that these rights arise out of "special transactions" between individuals or out of some "special relationship" in which they stand to each other (Hart, 1984, p. 84). One of the instances that typify this special relation among individuals is political obligation. In a common social environment, the specific political condition shared by individuals that allows for the mutual constraining of each others' liberty is what Hart terms the "mutuality of restrictions". This, in his words, designates the fact that "when a number of people conduct any joint enterprise according to rules and thus restrict their liberty, those who have submitted to these restrictions when required have a right to a similar submission from those who have benefited by their submission" (Hart, 1984, p. 85).

This indicates that individuals are placed with their compatriots in a particular arrangement of obligations and benefits which is not shared with humanity at large but is specific to their social condition. In this way, compatriots take priority over foreigners in a number of cases, including some where the natural right of all men to be free is deactivated, something which can only exist among those whose special relations of co-citizenship might permit exceptions to the general morality. Examples of these situations are supplied by Robert Goodin. Only in a domestic society, for instance, can we take the property of our fellow citizens for public purposes, and only then can we submit them to pay taxes or conscript them for service in our armed forces (Goodin, 1988, p. 668).

What we can discern from this perspective is that, while the negative duties (that is, the duties not to harm others) are constant and unchangeable towards foreigners, they are substantially lowered in the domestic dimension: we may legitimately impose burdens upon compatriots that may not be imposed upon outsiders. This is compensated by a substantial increase in the duties to provide positive assistance towards one another. Examples of what is rendered to constituents of a political body such as the state (ore, more exactly, what the constituents provide each other) include protection against attacks to their physical integrity, access to a legally regulated market, establishment of a system of property rights and entitlements (Sangiovanni, 2007, p. 20), or the setting of political participation rights and opportunities. This is because the social institutions that compose a state are maintained by the ensemble of its citizens in that they surrender on an equal basis a certain amount of moral autonomy, equally submitting to the same set of civil obligations and practices, and thus being entitled to a commensurate share of rights.

My endeavour here is to suggest that if egalitarian principles are to be established as a demand of justice, it is not reasonable to sustain the radical cosmopolitan assumption that they should be extended globally, in an integral and univocal way. What justice requires cannot be the same for both the domestic and the global spheres since they are not morally overlapping; there is a differentiated impact of each one on the life of individuals. It is undeniable that the global realm has a deep repercussion on people's life conditions and opportunities. That circumstance, as we have seen, is what justifies the plea for international principles of distributive justice. The supranational sphere, however, does not synthesize the social and institutional conditions of a polity: there is not a world demos, there are not mechanisms of participatory global democracy, and the instance that provides each individual the basic conditions and guarantees to act on a plan of life continues to be the domestic one.

Justice is not a strictly associative imperative. Distributive equality, on the contrary, if it is to be declared as an obligation derivative of justice, might only be regarded, as Andrea Sangiovanni sustains (2007), as a requirement of reciprocity, binding exclusively those who share the alluded class of special political rights and obligations. This does not mean that the international standard of justice should be a marginal one. It should, on the contrary, be sufficiently robust to guarantee the integral fulfilment of what Hart stated to be the natural right of every man: that no economic condition should be so severe as to deprive the individual of his equal liberty to be free, or, as Rousseau famously stated in the second book (chapter eleven) of the "Social Contract", that no citizen shall ever be so poor "that he is compelled to sell himself".

The Global Resources Dividend seems to be the distributive mechanism that could fulfil this requirement. What it would achieve in terms of wealth distribution is perfectly consonant with the application of Hart's basic right. In Pogge's terms, the GRD seeks to ensure "that all human beings can meet their own basic needs with dignity", which could as well be seen as a abbreviated formulation of the Article 25(1) of the Universal Declaration of Human Rights.

In fact, and in conclusion, if the GRD proves to be a philosophically sound argument, it would importantly advance the scope of what, in John Rawls terms, might constitute an achievable *realistic utopia*.

References

Beitz, C. (1979). *Political Theory and International Relations*. Princeton. Princeton University Press.

Beitz, C. (1983). "Cosmopolitan Ideals and National Sentiment". *The Journal of Philosophy*. Vol. 80. No. 19. Pp. 591-600.

Beitz, C. (1999). "Social And Cosmopolitan Liberalism". *International Affairs*. Vol. 75. No. 3. Pp. 512-99.

Caney, S. (2008)). "Global Distributive Justice and the State". *Political Studies*. Vol. 56. No. 3. Pp.487-518.

Caney, S. (2001). "Review Article: International Distributive Justice". *Political Studies*. Vol. 49. No. 5. Pp. 974-997.

Goodin, R. (1988). "What's so Special about our Fellow Countrymen?" *Ethics*. Vol. 98. No. 4. Pp. 663-686.

Hayward, T. (2005). "Thomas Pogge's Global Resources Dividend: A Critique and an Alternative". *Journal of Moral Philosophy*. Vol. 2. No. 3. Pp. 317-332.

Hart, H. L. A. ([1955] 1984). "Are There Any Natural Rights?". J. Waldron (ed.). *Theories of Rights*. Oxford. Oxford University Press. Pp. 77-90.

Held, D. (1991). "Democracy, the Nation-State and the Global System". D. Held (ed.) *Political Theory Today*. Cambridge. Polity Press. Pp. 197-235.

Hobbes, T. ([1660] 1968). *Leviathan*. Harmondsworth. Penguin.

Locke, J. ([1690] 1980). *The Second Treatise on Civil Government*. Indianapolis and Cambridge. Hackett Publishing Company.

Miller D. (1995). *On Nationality*. Oxford. Clarendon Press.

Nagel. T. (2005). "The Problem of Global Justice". *Philosophy & Public Affairs*. Vol. 33. No. 2. Pp. 113-147.

Nussbaum, M. (1996). *For love of country: Debating the limits of patriotism*. Boston. Beacon Press.

Pogge, T. (1992). "Cosmopolitanism and Sovereignty". *Ethics*. Vol. 103. No. 1. Pp. 48-75.

Pogge,. T. (1994). "An Egalitarian Law of Peoples". *Philosophy & Public Affairs*. Vol. 23. No. 3. Pp. 195-224.

Pogge, T. (2002). *World Poverty and Human Rights: Cosmopolitan Responsibilities and Reforms*. Cambridge. Polity Press.

Pogge, T. (2005). "Real World Justice". *The Journal of Ethics*. Vol. 9. No. 1-2. Pp. 29-53.

Pogge, T. (2008). "Eradicating Systemic Poverty. Brief for a Global Resources Dividend". T. Brooks (Ed.) *The Global Justice Reader*. Malden. Blackwell.

Rawls, J. (1971). *A Theory of Justice*. Cambridge. Harvard University Press

Rawls, J. (1999). *The Law of Peoples*. Cambridge. Harvard University Press.

Rousseau, J. J. (1978). *On the Social Contract*. New York. St. Martin's.

Sangiovanni, A. (2007). "Global Justice, Reciprocity, and the State". *Philosophy & Public Affairs*,. Vol. 35. No. 1. Pp. 3-39.

Weber, M. (1958). "Politics as a Vocation". H. H. Gerth & C. W. Mills (eds.). *From Max Weber. Essays in Sociology*. New York. Oxford University Press.

About the Contributors

Diogo P. Aurélio, IFL/FCSH, Universidade Nova, Lisbon.

Paulo Barcelos, IFL/FCSH, Universidade Nova, Lisbon.

Gabriele De Angelis, IFL/FCSH, Universidade Nova, Lisbon.

Adam D. Etinson, New College, University of Oxford.

Daniel Kofman, Department of Philosophy University of Ottawa

James Garrison, University of Hawai'i, at Mānoa.

Sylvie Loriaux, Department of Legal Philosophy, Radboud University Nijmegen (NL) and Centre for Law and Cosmopolitan Values, University of Antwerp (Belgium).

Heiner Michel, Center for Teacher Education and School and Classroom Research, Goethe-University, Frankfurt am Main.

Rekha Nath, Department of Philosophy, University of Alabama.

Gianfranco Pellegrino, LUISS, Rome.

Regina Queiroz, IFL/FCSH, Universidade Nova, Lisbon.

Kok-Chor Tan, Department of Philosophy, University of Pennsylvania.

Milica Trifunovic, University of Aachen.

Paulo Tunhas, University of Porto.

Subject Index

Index of Names

Bei Fragen zur Produktsicherheit wenden Sie sich bitte an:
If you have any questions regarding product safety,
please contact:

Walter de Gruyter GmbH
Genthiner Straße 13
10785 Berlin
productsafety@degruyterbrill.com